Lecture Notes in Computer Science 15977

Founding Editors

Gerhard Goos
Juris Hartmanis

Editorial Board Members

Elisa Bertino, *Purdue University, West Lafayette, IN, USA*
Wen Gao, *Peking University, Beijing, China*
Bernhard Steffen, *TU Dortmund University, Dortmund, Germany*
Moti Yung, *Columbia University, New York, NY, USA*

The series Lecture Notes in Computer Science (LNCS), including its subseries Lecture Notes in Artificial Intelligence (LNAI) and Lecture Notes in Bioinformatics (LNBI), has established itself as a medium for the publication of new developments in computer science and information technology research, teaching, and education.

LNCS enjoys close cooperation with the computer science R & D community, the series counts many renowned academics among its volume editors and paper authors, and collaborates with prestigious societies. Its mission is to serve this international community by providing an invaluable service, mainly focused on the publication of conference and workshop proceedings and postproceedings. LNCS commenced publication in 1973.

Joseph Schuchart · Aurelien Bouteiller ·
Sascha Hunold · Julien Jaeger ·
Christoph Niethammer · Brian Smith
Editors

Recent Advances in the Message Passing Interface

32nd European MPI Users' Group Meeting, EuroMPI 2025
Charlotte, NC, USA, October 1–3, 2025
Proceedings

Editors
Joseph Schuchart ⓘ
Stony Brook University
Bay Shore, NY, USA

Aurelien Bouteiller ⓘ
AMD
Austin, TX, USA

Sascha Hunold ⓘ
TU Wien
Vienna, Austria

Julien Jaeger ⓘ
CEA
Arpajon, France

Christoph Niethammer ⓘ
High Performance Computing Center
Stuttgart (HLRS)
Stuttgart, Baden-Württemberg, Germany

Brian Smith ⓘ
Oak Ridge National Laboratory
Oak Ridge, TN, USA

ISSN 0302-9743   ISSN 1611-3349 (electronic)
Lecture Notes in Computer Science
ISBN 978-3-032-07193-4   ISBN 978-3-032-07194-1 (eBook)
https://doi.org/10.1007/978-3-032-07194-1

© The Editor(s) (if applicable) and The Author(s), under exclusive license
to Springer Nature Switzerland AG 2026
Chapter "Concepts for Designing Modern C++ Interfaces for MPI" is licensed under the terms of the Creative Commons Attribution 4.0 International License (http://creativecommons.org/licenses/by/4.0/). For further details see license information in the chapter.

This work is subject to copyright. All rights are solely and exclusively licensed by the Publisher, whether the whole or part of the material is concerned, specifically the rights of translation, reprinting, reuse of illustrations, recitation, broadcasting, reproduction on microfilms or in any other physical way, and transmission or information storage and retrieval, electronic adaptation, computer software, or by similar or dissimilar methodology now known or hereafter developed.
The use of general descriptive names, registered names, trademarks, service marks, etc. in this publication does not imply, even in the absence of a specific statement, that such names are exempt from the relevant protective laws and regulations and therefore free for general use.
The publisher, the authors and the editors are safe to assume that the advice and information in this book are believed to be true and accurate at the date of publication. Neither the publisher nor the authors or the editors give a warranty, expressed or implied, with respect to the material contained herein or for any errors or omissions that may have been made. The publisher remains neutral with regard to jurisdictional claims in published maps and institutional affiliations.

This Springer imprint is published by the registered company Springer Nature Switzerland AG
The registered company address is: Gewerbestrasse 11, 6330 Cham, Switzerland

If disposing of this product, please recycle the paper.

Preface

The Message Passing Interface (MPI) remains a foundational standard for scalable parallel computing across distributed-memory systems. EuroMPI is the premier forum for users, developers, and researchers to exchange ideas on MPI and its applications. Topics include proposed MPI extensions, MPI-based libraries and languages, interoperability with other parallel programming models, applications on emerging architectures, and novel algorithms and tools—with emphasis on quality, portability, performance, and scalability. Held annually since 1994, EuroMPI has a long and rich tradition.

The 32nd edition, EuroMPI/USA 2025, was hosted at UNC Charlotte from October 1–3, 2025, and co-located with IWOMP 2025, the 21st International Workshop on OpenMP. The joint organization of these events fosters cross-community interaction and facilitates the exchange of ideas and experiences, advancing message-passing, shared-memory parallelism, and their combined use in parallel programming paradigms.

EuroMPI/USA 2025 invited full-paper submissions on all aspects of message-passing parallel programming with MPI and related or competing models, including, but not limited to, the following topics:

- Efficient and scalable implementations of message-passing constructs
- Architectures and systems: exascale computing, accelerator utilization, and hardware–software interaction
- Message passing for accelerator-based systems, including multi-GPU, TPU, and AI accelerators
- Programming models and paradigms related to MPI for large-scale, distributed-memory systems, including hierarchical, hybrid, and PGAS models
- Extensions to and limitations of MPI, including alternative interfaces and approaches
- Optimizations for parallel (MPI-)I/O mechanisms
- Hybrid and heterogeneous programming with MPI and other interfaces
- Support for data-intensive applications using message passing
- Fault tolerance in message-passing systems and libraries
- MPI-based programming in cloud and non-dedicated environments
- Performance evaluation of MPI and MPI-based applications
- Automatic tuning of application and library performance
- Verification of message-passing protocols and applications
- Applications leveraging advanced message passing, particularly in scientific computing
- Parallel algorithms within the message-passing paradigm
- Interactions between message-passing libraries and runtime systems
- Use of MPI in Artificial Intelligence (AI) and Large Language Models (LLMs), and associated challenges
- Integration with and comparison to competing industry standards (e.g., NCCL, RCCL)

EuroMPI/USA 2025 received a number of high-quality submissions prior to the conference. Each of the 16 submissions underwent at least three reviews (most received four, some five), evaluated for originality, technical quality, clarity, and relevance. Conflict-of-interest rules excluded committee members from reviewing or accessing reviewer information for their own submissions. Reviews followed a single-anonymous model. If needed, the program committee discussed submissions to reach consensus. Ultimately, 10 papers were accepted for presentation and publication, with final decisions made by the program committee chairs. This year featured contributions highlighting the integration of MPI with C++, the behavior of MPI in multi-threaded contexts, correctness verification, as well as performance and scalability of implementations.

Poster and short-paper submissions were also possible. They received at least two single-anonymous reviews each and were not included in the proceedings. Four posters were presented at the conference.

We thank all authors for their valuable contributions, the reviewers for their careful and constructive evaluations, and the local organizing committee for their dedication in making the conference possible.

August 2025

Joseph Schuchart
Aurelien Bouteiller
Sascha Hunold
Julien Jaeger
Christoph Niethammer
Brian Smith

Organization

General Chair

Joseph Schuchart   Stony Brook University, USA

Local Chair

Yonghong Yan   University of North Carolina, Charlotte, USA

Program Chairs

Christoph Niethammer   HLRS, Germany
Julien Jaeger   CEA, France

Publication Chairs

Sascha Hunold   TU Wien, Austria
Joseph Schuchart   Stony Brook University, USA

Poster Chair

Aurelien Bouteiller   AMD, USA

Finance and Registration Chair

Brian Smith   Oak Ridge National Laboratory, USA

Program Committee

C. Nicole Avans   Tennessee Technological University, USA
Amanda Bienz   University of New Mexico, USA

Claudia Blaas-Schenner	VSC Research Center, TU Wien, Austria
Wesley Bland	Intel, USA
George Bosilca	NVIDIA, USA
Matthew Dosanjh	Sandia National Laboratories, USA
Edgar Gabriel	AMD, USA
Al Geist	Oak Ridge National Laboratory, USA
Sayan Ghosh	Pacific Northwest National Laboratory, USA
Ryan E. Grant	Queen's University, Canada
William Gropp	University of Illinois at Urbana-Champaign, USA
Tobias Haas	University of Stuttgart, Germany
Jeff Hammond	NVIDIA, Finland
Marc-André Hermanns	RWTH Aachen University, Germany
Quincey Koziol	NVIDIA, USA
Stefano Markidis	KTH Royal Institute of Technology, Sweden
Guillaume Mercier	ENSEIRB/Inria, France
Howard Pritchard	Los Alamos National Laboratory, USA
Kento Sato	RIKEN R-CCS, Japan
Martin Schreiber	Université Grenoble Alpes/Inria/Laboratoire Jean Kuntzmann, France
Martin Schulz	Technical University of Munich, Germany
Jeff Squyres	Cisco, USA
Hari Subramoni	The Ohio State University, USA
Shinji Sumimoto	University of Tokyo, Japan
Ahmad Tarraf	TU Darmstadt, Germany
Rajeev Thakur	Argonne National Laboratory, USA
Jesper Larsson Träff	TU Wien, Austria
Chen Wang	Lawrence Livermore National Laboratory, USA
Aaron Welch	Oak Ridge National Laboratory, USA
Hui Zhou	Argonne National Laboratory, USA

Contents

On the Potential of Compression Hiding in MPI Applications   1
   Yicheng Li and Michael Jantz

Implementing True MPI Sessions and Evaluating MPI Initialization
Scalability 18
   *Hui Zhou, Kenneth Raffenetti, Yanfei Guo, Michael Wilkins,
and Rajeev Thakur*

Layout-Agnostic MPI Abstraction for Distributed Computing in Modern
C++ 36
   Jiří Klepl, Martin Kruliš, and Matyáš Brabec

Verifying MPI API Usage Requirements with Contracts 54
   *Yussur Mustafa Oraji, Simon Schwitanski, Alexander Hück,
Joachim Jenke, Sebastian Kreutzer, and Christian Bischof*

Review of MPI Continuations and Their Integration into PMPI Tools 73
   *Alexander Optenhöfel, Joachim Jenke, Ben Thärigen,
and Joseph Schuchart*

MPI Finally Needs to Deal with Threads 89
   Joseph Schuchart, Joachim Jenke, and Simon Schwitanski

Performance Analysis of Open MPI on AMR Applications
over Slingshot-11 106
   *Maxim Moraru, Howard Pritchard, Derek Schafer, Galen Shipman,
and Patrick Bridges*

Examining MPI and its Extensions for Asynchronous Multithreaded
Communication 122
   Jiakun Yan, Marc Snir, and Yanfei Guo

Extending the SPMD IR for RMA Models and Static Data Race Detection 143
   *Semih Burak, Simon Schwitanski, Felix Tomski, Jens Domke,
and Matthias Müller*

Concepts for Designing Modern C++ Interfaces for MPI 165
C. Nicole Avans, Alfredo A. Correa, Sayan Ghosh, Matthias Schimek, Joseph Schuchart, Anthony Skjellum, Evan D. Suggs, and Tim Niklas Uhl

Author Index 185

On the Potential of Compression Hiding in MPI Applications

Yicheng Li[✉] and Michael Jantz

University of Tennessee, Knoxville, Knoxville, TN 37996, USA
yli137@vols.utk.edu, mrjantz@utk.edu

Abstract. The increasing disparity between computing capabilities and communication bandwidth has become a major bottleneck in High Performance Computing (HPC) applications. To address this challenge, we introduce a framework that leverages early data compression for communication data within the Open MPI library with the use of userfaultfd (uffd) for efficient write detection. By integrating the high-speed LZ4 compression algorithm, the proposed framework minimizes communication overhead by reducing the size of data transmitted among processes while hiding compression overhead behind either pack or communication overhead. Applying our uffd framework onto Livermore Unstructured Lagrangian Explicit Shock Hydrodynamics (LULESH) highlights the potential of the framework in reducing data communication volumes and overall communication latency, paving the way for improved performance in HPC environments.

Keywords: HPC · MPI · Open MPI · Userfaultfd

1 Introduction

The rapid advancement of computational capabilities has significantly outpaced the improvements in communication speed, creating a notable imbalance that often hinders the performance of many scientific applications. This growing disparity between computing power and the ability to swiftly transfer data across systems poses a considerable bottleneck, affecting not only the efficiency but also the scalability of complex computations. In the realm of HPC, where vast amounts of data are processed and exchanged, the impact of this imbalance is especially pronounced.

To combat this challenge, the strategy of minimizing the volume of data that needs to be exchanged emerges as a particularly effective solution. By reducing the amount of data transmitted, it is possible to alleviate the pressure on communication channels, thus enhancing the overall performance of the application.

In this context, the implementation of data compression techniques within MPI communication protocols offers a promising avenue for mitigating the disparities between computational speed and communication efficiency. By compressing data before transmission and decompressing it upon receipt, it is possible to significantly decrease the size of the data being exchanged. This reduction in data volume directly translates to reduced communication time, effectively narrowing the gap between computing and communication speeds.

Many prior works have employed compression to reduce MPI communication costs. However, these works are mainly focused on how to compress application data, but do not consider the question of when and where to compress data. Existing approaches always compress MPI buffers immediately before sending the data to the Network Interface Card (NIC). Thus, they can miss opportunities to overlap compression with other useful application activity.

In this work, we investigate the potential of compressing application data early so that it can be overlapped with other application activity as it is being compressed within Open MPI [9] framework. First, we investigate the potential of hiding compression overhead by surveying several mini-applications/benchmarks in Sect. 4. Then we introduce the proposed framework with uffd in Sect. 5 and summarize the performance and future improvements in Sect. 6.

This work makes the following important contributions:

1. A survey of existing and state-of-the-art techniques for incorporating compression into MPI communication, highlighting their benefits and limitations.
2. The design and implementation of a novel framework that offloads compression tasks to idle compute resources and strategically overlaps compression with communication by exploiting the gap between the last memory write and data transmission.
3. An in-depth investigation and practical application of the Linux's uffd mechanism for efficient write-fault detection and handling in support of compression-aware communication strategies.
4. A detailed analysis of the trade-offs among compression ratio, compression overhead, and communication performance, providing clear guidance on scenarios where compression delivers net benefits.

In summary, the application of compression in MPI communication represents a strategic response to the growing divide between the capabilities of modern computing hardware and the limitations of data transfer speeds. By intelligently managing the volume of data that must be communicated, it is possible to significantly improve the performance and efficiency of scientific applications, paving the way for the next generation of HPC breakthroughs.

2 Related Work and Motivation

Reducing the volume of communicated data is a well-established strategy to mitigate the communication bottleneck in HPC applications, particularly in MPI-based parallel programs. Data compression has emerged as a promising solution to this challenge by reducing the amount of data transmitted over the network, potentially leading to improved overall performance. However, to realize the benefits of compression, it is crucial to carefully manage the trade-offs among three key factors: the compression ratio, the overhead associated with compression and decompression, and the resulting impact on communication latency. Several studies have explored integrating compression into MPI communication. Early efforts by Filgueira et al. [2–4] proposed adaptive compression strategies in collective MPI operations. These work dynamically select compression techniques based on runtime characteristics such as data size and system load. Shan et al. [12] investigated how lightweight compression algorithms could be leveraged to reduce message size in MPI_Alltoall operations, reporting measurable performance gains on large-scale systems.

A particularly promising direction involves integrating the compression and decompression processes into existing MPI communication or pack operations. By integrating compression seamlessly into MPI_Pack, prior work has demonstrated that it is possible to maintain portability while improving communication efficiency. For example, Zhou et al. [13] explored modifying the MPI datatype engine to insert compression at pack time, allowing compression to be performed just before the data are transferred, thus minimizing its perceived overhead. Similarly, Ramesh et al. [11] introduced a modular framework that allows transparent compression insertion within MPI libraries, focusing on preserving MPI semantics while optimizing runtime behavior.

Despite these advancements, challenges remain in selecting appropriate compression schemes for various data characteristics, and in managing the overheads associated with compression algorithms. Our work builds upon these previous studies by further hiding and offloading compression in between writes and communication. We focus specifically on offloading compression and utilize Linux's uffd interface for write-detect functionality to attemptively delay compression until the last memory modification before communication, thereby hiding compression latency within naturally occurring communication gaps.

The Linux uffd interface was originally introduced to enable user-space handling of page faults, offering mechanisms to trap and respond to page accesses, including reads, writes, and missing pages. This feature has since attracted attention in a variety of system-level research efforts due to its flexibility in controlling memory access behavior and enabling novel memory management policies. Gidra et al. [5] were among the first to demonstrate the utility of uffd in distributed shared memory systems, where they used it to implement fine-grained page migration and consistency management in the user space. Similarly, Peng et al. [10] and McFadden et al. [8] utilized uffd in the context of UMap, a user-space page-fault handling system designed to virtualize and remap large memory regions in HPC environments. Their work showcased the potential of uffd to abstract remote or slow memory devices behind traditional memory interfaces.

Despite these advances, the application of uffd to performance-critical workflows, especially in HPC applications, is still immature. Zussman et al. [14] investigated using custom page access monitoring via uffd to optimize data movement, but their work stopped short of tightly coupling such mechanisms with communication layers such as MPI. The integration of uffd into core application logic, particularly for latency-sensitive use cases such as dynamically compressing data between the last memory write and an MPI communication, remains an underexplored area.

In this paper, we aim to bridge this gap by proposing a novel use of uffd to attemptively detect the last write to a memory region before communication. By leveraging write-detection semantics, we are inserting compression into the gap between the final write and subsequent data transfer, enabling compression to be performed asynchronously and hidden behind other computation or communication. To the best of our knowledge, this work represents a new and practical use of uffd for overlapping computation and communication with compression in MPI-based applications.

3 Experiment Setup

3.1 Platform

We conducted our experiments on a system equipped with an Intel Xeon Gold 6246R CPU featuring 16 physical cores and 32 hyper-threading cores with Debian GNu/Linux 11 (bullseye). Our framework, integrated with LULESH, was executed using 8 processes, supplemented by an additional 16 processes dedicated to handling write-faults and performing compression. The supplementary processes were assigned to separate physical cores, distinct from those assigned to the primary 8 processes. Since LULESH requires a cubic number of processes for execution, this configuration represents the maximal deployment feasible on the current system. All our tests are conducted using Open MPI version 4.1.7.

3.2 LZ4 Compression Ratio and Speed Performance

LZ4 [1] is a lossless compression algorithm known for its exceptionally fast compression and decompression speeds, making it highly suitable for performance-critical scenarios. We selected LZ4 for our compression/decompression algorithm because our uffd framework has the potential to effectively mask the compression overhead, while decompression overhead remains serialized with the main execution thread. Figure 1, in log scale for y axis, illustrates the compression and decompression speeds along with the compression ratios. In this test, we varied the percentage that represents the likelihood that the data sequences are identical. LZ4 excels specifically in compressing identical data sequences, thus, longer sequences of identical data lead to higher compression ratios and faster compression/decompression speeds.

To complement our evaluation among benchmark performances, we also examined the high-compression variant of LZ4, known as LZ4 HC. LZ4 HC trades off compression speed for improved compression ratios by employing a more exhaustive search algorithm to find longer and more optimal matches. Although this increases compression overhead, the decompression performance remains as fast as standard LZ4, preserving its suitability for our proposed framework.

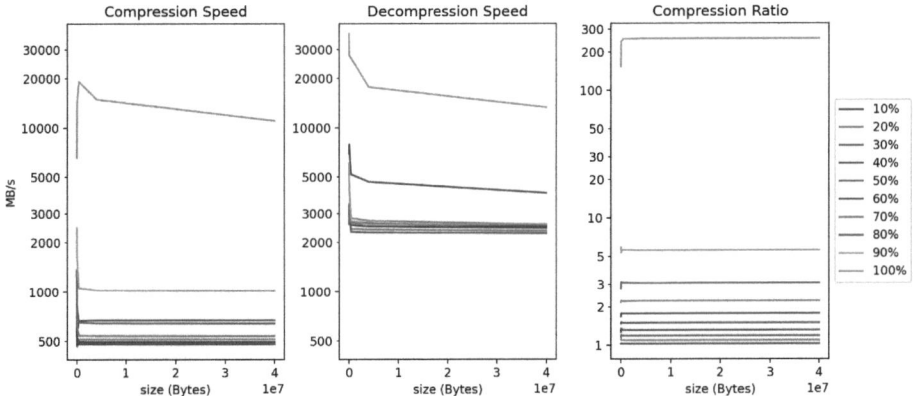

Fig. 1. LZ4 compression algorithm speed and compression ratio by percentage of the same consecutive data

3.3 Benchmarks

We selected four benchmarks from the CORAL-2 [6] benchmarks and the SPEChpc [7] benchmarks, together with LULESH, whose communication patterns closely resemble the use case for our framework. Table 1a presents the descriptions of the benchmarks, while Table 1b gives the full input command that we used for each benchmark. We then applied LZ4 and LZ4 HC compression algorithms to perform on-the-fly compression/decompression into specific parts of the point-to-point communication and extract measurements to see if our uffd framework would theoretically improve benchmark's runtime.

We then applied our framework onto LULESH for evaluation. LULESH is a highly simplified application developed by Lawrence Livermore National Laboratory. Through continuous development, LULESH has evolved into a widely analyzed proxy application in the DOE co-design efforts for Exascale computing. This application represents a step towards addressing the complex requirements of hydrodynamics modeling in computational simulations.

Running LULESH with Open MPI enables the application to leverage distributed computing environments effectively. To do this, LULESH requires the number of processes initiated by MPI to be a cube of any number, such as 1, 8, 27, 64, 216, and so forth. This constraint ensures that the spatial problem domain is partitioned into a collection of volumetric elements that can be distributed and processed efficiently across the computing nodes in a structured manner.

The default LULESH is computation bound. It separates computation from communication as there is no overlap to make computation more efficient since communication is only a negligible portion of the entire application runtime. We chose LULESH because of its communication pattern, where each iteration is using the same buffer with the same size. Because of LULESH's relatively small code base, it stands out as one of the easiest applications to integrate and to test our framework.

Table 1. HPC benchmarks and corresponding test commands

Benchmark	Description
PENNANT	A mini-app from CORAL-2 modeling unstructured mesh physics, focusing on Lagrangian and radiation hydrodynamics. It serves as a compact proxy for large-scale multi-physics codes.
LBM	Simulates fluid dynamics using the Lattice Boltzmann Method. It models mesoscopic flow behavior and emphasizes parallel scalability and memory bandwidth.
SPH-EXA	Implements the Smoothed Particle Hydrodynamics method for fluid and solid dynamics. Designed to explore portability and scalability across HPC platforms.
Minisweep	Models sweep-based transport used in neutron and radiative transfer simulations. Captures communication-heavy patterns with directional dependencies.
LULESH	A proxy for shock hydrodynamics on unstructured meshes, modeling core compute patterns of typical hydrodynamics codes for performance benchmarking.

(a) Descriptions of Selected Mini-Apps

Benchmark	Test Command
PENNANT leblanc	mpirun -np 32 –bind-to hwthread –map-by hwthread ./build/pennant ./test/leblanc/leblanc.pnt
PENNANT leblancbig	mpirun -np 32 –bind-to hwthread –map-by hwthread ./build/pennant ./test/leblancbig/leblancbig.pnt
LBM	runhpc –config=config.cfg –action=ref 505.lbm_t
SPH-EXA	runhpc –config=config.cfg –action=ref 532.sph_exa_t
Minisweep	runhpc –config=config.cfg –action=ref 521.miniswp_t
LULESH	mpirun -np 8 –bind-to hwthread –map-by hwthread ./lulesh2.0 -s ${Problem Size} -i 50

(b) Test Commands for Selected Mini-Apps

4 Potential Compression Hiding for Applications

We ran most of the benchmarks from Table 1a with 32 ranks, bound, and mapped to hardware thread. Since each benchmark has a large code base, we tried our best to insert on-the-fly compression into the communication. As MPI benchmarks, it is common to pack and unpack data before communication. However, for some benchmark, we are unable to identify the pack or the unpack. For benchmarks that uses non-blocking communication, we timed the entire communication from the first invoked communication function to the MPI_Wait or MPI_Waitall, thus individual overhead for send or receive is not timed. We represent the time of data-over-the-wire as "Total_Communication." We collect the entire duration of the communication, then subtract the serialized component (other attributes in Fig. 2) to calculate the supposedly data-over-the-wire duration.

Most of the benchmarks in Fig. 2 contain one non-blocking MPI communication from the sender and the receiver or both the sender and the receiver are using blocking MPI communication. We ignored communication that is completely non-blocking for easier compression insertion, thus the number we present in Fig. 2 only reflects a portion of the total communication for some benchmarks.

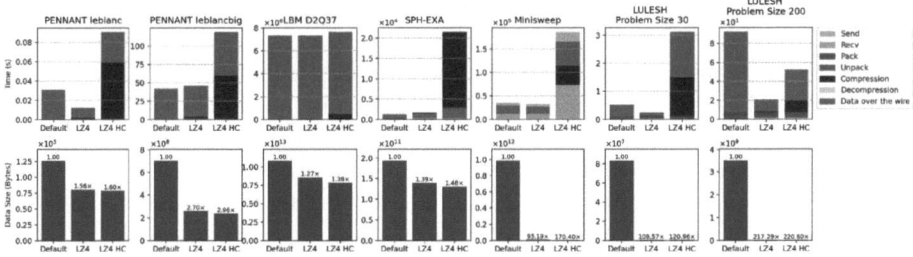

Fig. 2. Aggregate time comparison, data size comparison and compression Ratio for different benchmarks, LZ4 and LZ4 HC on-the-fly compression applied

The benchmarks shown in Fig. 2 achieve moderate compression ratios on communication data, except for Minisweep and LULESH, however, the effectiveness varies significantly. Although some benchmarks achieve reasonable compression ratios, their overall performance remains suboptimal. As demonstrated by our tests with LZ4 compression in Sect. 3.2, the data from these benchmarks may not be ideally suited for LZ4 compression, as it typically achieves high compression ratios only when the data contain extensive sequences of identical values.

In case of suitable data for LZ4, data in Minisweep give a 93 compression ratio. However, the improved runtime is only 1.091x compared to the default run as Minisweep stresses more on network latency instead of total throughput. For each send in Minisweep, the size of the data per communication only goes up to 8MB. In comparison, each MPI_Send in LBM can put 1 GB over the wire.

In addition to the compression ratio, excessive compression overhead would also result in significant performance degradation. Using the higher-overhead compression algorithm, LZ4 HC, results in compression overhead dominating the communication process, causing the receiver to stall and significantly increasing the overall communication time for on-the-fly approach. However, some benchmarks are more tolerable for higher compression overhead, as their communication overhead is much higher, which gives an opportunity to hide compression overhead behind communication.

Our objective in this paper is to introduce an efficient approach to both benefit from reduced-size communication and hide the potentially high compression overhead.

5 Approach for Automated Compression Hiding

In the realm of high-performance computing, the Open MPI represents a cornerstone for the implementation of the MPI standard. This standard facilitates communication among processes that perform a parallel task, typically across a variety of hardware and network configurations. One of the most common approaches in HPC applications to exchange data is to use MPI point-to-point communication. MPI point-to-point communication refers to the direct exchange of messages between two specific processes in a parallel computing environment. It involves a sender and a receiver, where the sender uses functions like MPI_Send to transmit data, and the receiver uses functions like MPI_Recv to accept it. This form of communication is fundamental in MPI as it provides precise control over how data is exchanged, making it suitable for fine-grained synchronization and data exchange. MPI point-to-point operations can be either blocking or non-blocking, allowing flexibility depending on the communication and computation overlap requirements. These operations are essential for building more complex communication patterns in HPC applications.

In a typical MPI point-to-point communication, developers can either let MPI datatype engine handle non-contiguous data transfer or they can pack data explicitly into contiguous form by hand. Some applications would choose to use non-blocking communication to hide pack overhead behind network latency. In this workflow, the common way to apply compression is to compress data right before the communication and send the compressed counterpart, and on the receiver side, decompress the received buffer and copy it into the user buffer. Such approach does not take into the account of compression overhead, as in Sect. 4, the results show that the benefit from exchanging reduced-size data could be offset by the compression and decompression overhead. In our uffd framework, we aim to hide compression overhead by offloading compression onto idle computing resources while trying to compress data early by detecting the last write-fault before communication.

Figure 3 presents a sophisticated design tailored for augmenting the Open MPI framework with a compression-offloading mechanism that operates via a dedicated worker thread and another dedicated thread for detecting writes via uffd. It also presents the data structures employed behind the scenes.

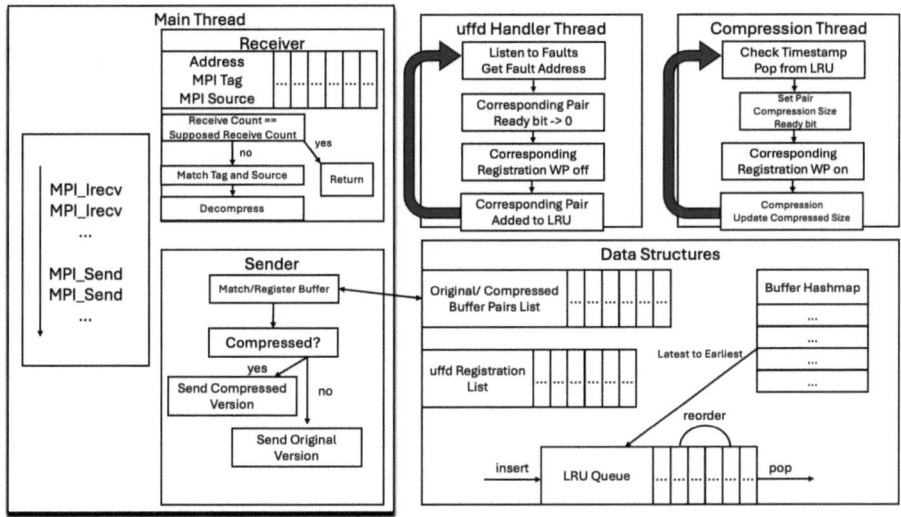

Fig. 3. Thread compression design for the Open MPI

5.1 Data Structures

The designed system incorporates tracking pairs of the original send buffers and their compressed counterparts, maintaining a Least Recently Used (LRU) queue to identify the earliest writes. It also includes a list of registered memory regions and a structure that stores receiving addresses, matching MPI tags and source ranks.

An array is used to store pairs of send buffers and their compressed counterparts. Initially, the array is allocated to hold 30 pairs, doubling in size whenever it reaches capacity. For applications like LULESH, 30 pairs are sufficient. Each pair contains additional tracking data, including the buffer's aligned page address, its aligned page size, and synchronization flags used for coordination among the main thread, the uffd handler thread, and the compression thread. When an send buffer is first encountered, a compressed buffer is allocated with a size equal to the original buffer plus an extra 100 bytes, ensuring compression always succeeds. The final compressed size is then recorded after a successful compression.

The LRU mechanism ensures efficient tracking of buffer usage while minimizing overhead. It includes a hashmap for fast buffer lookup and a double-linked list for finding the earliest write buffer. Given LULESH's communication pattern, the total number of possible inserted buffers is considerably low (9 entries per rank). When a buffer is being compressed, its entry is removed from the LRU. This removal involves deleting the corresponding node from the double-linked list and deleting its reference from the hashmap.

Each insertion or lookup operation begins by hashing the send buffer's address using the predefined hash function (buffer address mod its size mod

1024). If the buffer is found in the hashmap, its corresponding node is moved to the front of the double-linked list, ensuring that it remains the most recently modified entry. Otherwise, a new node is created and inserted in the front.

Our first implementation of the LRU naively pops an item from the LRU queue and lets the compression thread perform compression on the buffer. However, if there are excessive writes going into one uffd registration, the back-and-forth write-protect on and off will limit LULESH's ability to advance main thread. Thus, our first implementation let the compression thread sleep for certain (1000) microseconds, before putting write-protect back onto the registration region. However, this approach is not as efficient as the node popped from the LRU queue could be written during the sleep. Our second approach adds a timestamp onto each of the nodes when queueing the send buffers into the LRU queue. It will check the current timestamp against the first node in the queue, if there is enough time (1000 microseconds) passed, then it will pop off the node and ask compression thread to perform compression.

The delay before popping a node from the LRU can vary across buffers, as some receive more frequent writes than others. In our experiments, we observed that if this delay is too short, the write instruction will not have enough time to be processed, thus it can prevent the main thread from advancing, ultimately causing the application to stall.

To optimize synchronization among the main thread, the uffd handler thread, and the compression thread, several mutex locks are utilized, preventing race conditions when updating the LRU structure. Additionally, since the number of tracked buffers is small, traversal and updates in the double-linked list remain computationally inexpensive. The combination of a hashmap and a double-linked list provides efficient $O(1)$ lookup, insertion, and deletion, making the LRU implementation well-suited for handling the buffer management needs.

When MPI send function is called, uffd registrations are recorded to track buffer usage. The recorded information includes the buffer's original address and size, along with its aligned page address and aligned size, which ensure coverage from the buffer's start to its end. Since uffd operates at the page level, all registered addresses and sizes must be aligned with the page boundaries of the system.

The aligned page address is particularly important because fault addresses resulting from write protection are also aligned at the page level. If the buffer's starting address is unaligned, uffd registration will fail.

Furthermore, it is possible for data writes to occur outside the designated buffer but still within the aligned buffer region. While this does not impact correctness, it may result in additional buffers being queued for handling, particularly those that begin within the first page of the aligned buffer region. However, this behavior does not compromise data integrity, as only the relevant pages will be treated as dirty pages and queued in LRU for compression.

Since overlapping registrations are not allowed, every new buffer registration is checked against all existing registered entries to detect potential overlaps within the aligned buffer region. If an overlap is found, the system first removes the write-protect from the affected region and unregisters the previous entry. The overlapping buffers are then merged into a single contiguous region, which is subsequently re-registered with uffd.

Merging ensures efficient management of the uffd mechanism. Additionally, merging minimizes the number of registered memory regions, reducing the overhead associated with tracking and handling multiple disjoint registrations. To maintain consistency, a mutex lock is used to prevent any uffd operations on the memory region in between registration and unregistration.

5.2 At Uffd Registration

When send is called, the framework anticipates that the buffers passed to it will be reused frequently, though the actual data may change. After registration, it is important to clear the write-protect mode first, since the memory could have been used and written already, otherwise, the uffd registration will not work even though there is no error from setting write-protect. This step is unnecessary if, for certain, the to-be registered memory region has not been touched.

5.3 Uffd Handler Thread

During MPI initialization, a dedicated uffd handler thread is spawned from the main process to manage write faults on registered buffers. Its primary role is to clear the write-protect on memory regions when writes occur.

When an incoming write triggers a page fault, the fault address is aligned to the system's page size. The handler thread checks this aligned fault address against the recorded page-aligned addresses to determine which registered buffer has been modified. Once identified, the handler proceeds to remove the write-protect from the corresponding memory region.

The main thread halts execution until the write-protect is cleared. Once the protection is removed, the handler thread queues the corresponding send buffer into the LRU queue, updating its access history with a timestamp in the double-linked list.

To minimize performance overhead, the uffd handler thread is designed to perform only essential operations, avoiding unnecessary operations, as its priority is to clear write-protect as quickly as possible, preventing delays in the main thread's execution.

5.4 Compression Thread

At MPI initialization, a dedicated compression thread is spawned alongside the main thread to handle data compression and reapply write-protect on registered memory regions. This thread operates asynchronously to ensure efficient memory management and apply early compression without blocking MPI communications.

The compression thread continuously monitors the LRU queue for available send buffers. When a buffer is detected, the compression thread will compare the current timestamp to the timestamp attached to the first node in LRU, if enough time has passed, the first node is popped from the queue and processed for compression. Then, the compression algorithm is applied to the buffer, aiming to reduce its size while preserving data integrity.

If compression is successful and the resulting compressed buffer is smaller than the original, the compression thread sets the compressed size for the buffer, signaling that it is available for transmission in its compressed form. At this stage, the write-protect has already been re-applied before the start of compression to the registered memory region to ensure that subsequent writes will trigger the uffd mechanism again.

The compression thread operates in an endless loop, following these steps:

1. Check the LRU queue for an entry to compress.
2. Pop the entry from LRU (if enough time has passed) and locate its corresponding buffer pair.
3. Pre-set compression ready bit to be true and pre-set compressed size to be larger than the original buffer.
4. Apply write-protect to the corresponding uffd registration.
5. Perform compression on the buffer. The compressed size is recorded if compression is successful and the resulting data size is smaller than the original buffer size.

If a write occurs during compression, the ready bit is set to false. The compression thread, unaware of this change, still proceeds with compression. But since ready bit is first set to be true before the compression, the final check on the ready bit ensures that the send function will be notified if additional writes occurred even if there is a compressed buffer available.

5.5 Synchronization

Each registered memory region is associated with a unique uffd ID, which is created at the initialization of each MPI rank (MPI_Init or MPI_Init_thread). This unique ID establishes a strict one-to-one correspondence among the main thread, uffd handler thread, and compression thread, ensuring proper coordination. Multiple mutex locks are employed to maintain synchronization across different operations:

1. Buffer Pairs Array Lock – Ensures orderly operations upon creating, resizing, and accessing the buffer pairs array.
2. uffd Registration Lock – Protects against race conditions when unregistering, registering, or merging registered memory regions.
3. LRU Lock – Maintains orderly insertion, popping, and rearrangement of entries in the LRU queue.
4. Per-Buffer Pair Lock – Protects against race conditions when the compression thread modifies the compressed buffer size upon successful compression.

Mutex locks alone are insufficient to verify a valid compressed counterpart. Hence, a combination of a ready bit and compressed size ensures that send function always accesses an up-to-date compressed buffer.

6 Performance

In most scientific applications, non-contiguous data is packed into a contiguous buffer before communication to ensure efficiency, since sending the entire data is unnecessary and costly. LULESH is one of the applications that packs data before sending the packed buffer. In our framework, the buffer addresses are registered and recorded at communication, i.e. MPI_Send, MPI_Isend, while compression thread is running in the background compressing invalidated buffers. Thus, as LULESH packs buffer, the registered memory region will receive a write-fault, and then the uffd handler thread will proceed to invalidate all the recorded buffer pairs that reside within the same uffd registration region.

In our current implementation, the registration regions are merged if they are contiguous in memory. In LULESH, it allocates several packed buffers for communication, and these packed buffers are contiguous in memory, thus, in our current implementation applied onto LULESH, all the packed buffers belong to one uffd registration. As a result, one write-fault will invalidate all buffer pairs, and insert all pairs into LRU, and compression thread will have to compress these buffers even some of them do not get written.

Due to LULESH's communication pattern, packing before communication, all buffers will be invalidated and will be asked to be compressed. For that reason, no buffer will be compressed and ready for communication. Thus, we implemented a wait loop before each MPI send call to wait for all items in the LRU to be popped off. Such strategy will create additional overhead to the main thread when the overhead of compression cannot be overshadowed by the reduced communication. This additional overhead is shown in Fig. 5 where there is a gap in aggregate compression duration between the default LULESH and the uffd version at small problem sizes.

6.1 Exchanged Data Size

Figure 4 shows the difference in exchanged sizes for all three versions. LZ4 works exceptionally well on the benchmark's data and the compression ratio could reach 217. This difference in exchanged data sizes reflects in the total aggregate communication duration in Fig. 5. The uffd uses the same compression algorithm, but the exchanged data size exceeds the plain version. This difference is caused by the implementation of the uffd framework. We used a naive hash for a quick address and size pair lookup, and there is collision in the hash. These collisions cause addresses not added to the LRU queue and thus not compressed.

The collision effect also reflects in the aggregate decompression overhead. Since the uffd version compresses less data, the time it takes to decompress is less than the plain version.

6.2 Uffd Framework Performance on LULESH

Figure 5 presents the performance comparison among the default LULESH, the plain compression version, and the uffd version. We ran LULESH using 8 ranks,

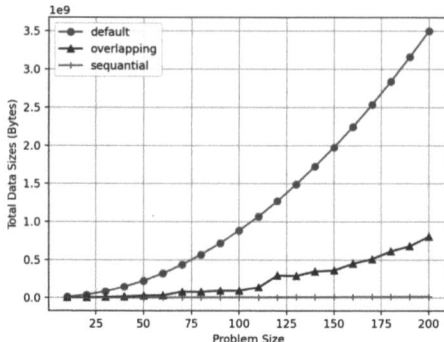

Fig. 4. Communication data size comparison between the default LULESH, the uffd version and the plain compression version

bound and mapped them to hardware thread #1 to #8. Due to the limitation of our machine (32 hardware thread), 8 ranks is the maximum number of processes we can deploy with uffd and compression threads running without interfering the main thread.

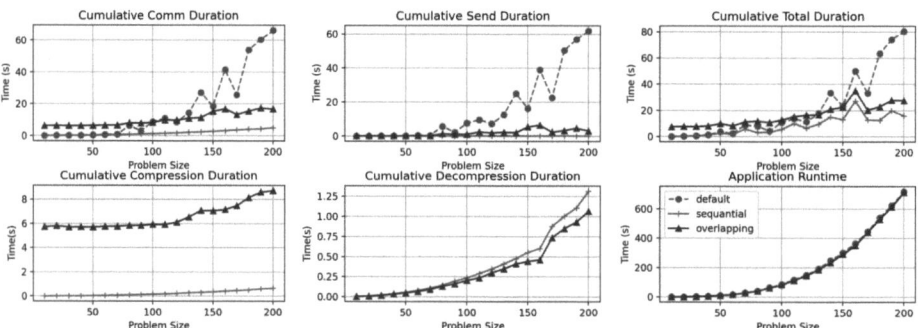

Fig. 5. Performance comparison for the default version, the sequential compression version and the overlapping compression version on LULESH

In default LULESH, it issues non-blocking sends all at once, followed by an MPI_Waitall to ensure the completion. On receive side, it issued non-blocking receives, each followed by an MPI_Wait and then unpack the received buffer into the user buffer.

In order to correctly timed the sends separately, we modified the non-blocking sends to blocking sends. Although blocking send in MPI does not guarantee the completion on the receiver side, it gives a better sense on how fast data is transmitted into the NIC. We timed each operation (compression, send, wait, decompression) separately so that we are able to compare the uffd version to plain version and understand what situation it would be useful.

Table 2 shows the aggregate communication time for LULESH with 50 cycles for problem size 200. The aggregate send duration is proportional to the data size.

Table 2. Aggregate time comparison for LULESH with problem size 200 at 50 iterations

	Cumulative Total Duration (s)	Send Duration (s)	Compression Duration (s)
Default LULESH	80.52964	62.01993	N/A
Sequential Compression LULESH	15.99959	0.10532	0.66322
Overlapping Compression LULESH	27.60461	3.11604	8.71220

Because communication in LULESH only takes an insignificant amount of the total runtime, any reduction in communication can hardly be reflected. However, combining the results of Fig. 5 and Table 4, most of the improvement in communication comes from how well the compression algorithm is able to compress the data. As the compression ratio increases while the compression overhead stays relatively low, there will be an improvement in the communication.

6.3 Uffd Framework Evaluation and Future Improvements

Applying our current uffd framework onto LULESH improves LULESH's communication on large problem sizes, but still comes short compared to the plain compression version. We conclude that there are several key factors and propose some future improvements to our uffd framework:

1. uffd's hash collisions are causing some send buffers not to be compressed for each iteration in LULESH. Since each iteration sends exactly the same buffers, the collided buffers will never be compressed.
2. Due to the merging of registration, and all send buffers in LULESH are either overlapped or contiguous in memory, one write-fault will invalidate all previously compressed buffers. With that, our current strategy of waiting for all items to be compressed adds additional overhead to each communication. It might be beneficial to change uffd registration from per memory region to per page basis, thus, one write-fault will only invalidate buffers that resides within the same page.
3. LULESH's pack then send communication pattern will cause the send buffer to be invalidated, thus, the compressed counterpart will never be ready at the send call. Ideally, if LULESH is able to perform all pack operations then invoke communication on all pack buffers, uffd will have a much better chance finishing all the compression depending on how heavy the pack or the communication is. Depending on how heavy the pack is and the latency from the intra- or inter-communication, the compressions from uffd could be completely hidden.

While our current uffd framework demonstrates potential for improving communication performance in LULESH, several inherent issues still hinge, such as persistent hash collisions, coarse-grained registrations, and communication patterns that conflict with compression overhead compared to plain compression version. Addressing these identified challenges will present promising pathways for hiding compression overhead while gaining the benefit of exchanged compressed counterpart.

7 Conclusion

In conclusion, we introduced an innovative framework for early compression in the Open MPI, utilizing the uffd mechanism for efficient write detection combined with the high-performance LZ4 compression algorithm. Our approach effectively reduces communication overhead by compressing data prior to transmission, significantly improving performance. Through detailed experimentation using the LULESH, we demonstrated that the proposed framework has the potential to hide compression overhead while decreasing communication overhead with reduced volume of data exchanged. Additionally, we explored the framework's applicability to other HPC benchmarks, revealing potential benefits across various applications. Our work in uffd shows promising results for its application in real-world scenarios, even though uffd research itself remains relatively immature. Future enhancements, including collision-resistant hashing, finer-grained uffd registrations, adjustments to application communication patterns, and selecting alternative compression algorithms to achieve higher compression ratios, offer promising avenues to further optimize this framework. Ultimately, our work contributes valuable insight toward application of the uffd and addressing communication bottlenecks in high-performance computing environments, laying a foundation for more efficient parallel computing solutions.

References

1. Collet, Y.: LZ4 - Extremely fast compression (2024). https://lz4.org. Accessed 27 Mar 2024
2. Filgueira, R., Carretero, J., Singh, D.E., Calderon, A., Núñez, A.: Dynamic-compi: dynamic optimization techniques for mpi parallel applications. J. Supercomput. **59**, 361–391 (2012)
3. Filgueira, R., Singh, D.E., Calderón, A., Carretero, J.: Compi: enhancing mpi based applications performance and scalability using run-time compression. In: Recent Advances in Parallel Virtual Machine and Message Passing Interface: 16th European PVM/MPI Users' Group Meeting, Espoo, Finland, September 7-10, 2009. Proceedings 16, pp. 207–218. Springer (2009)
4. Filgueira, R., Singh, D.E., Carretero, J., Calderón, A., García, F.: Adaptive-compi: enhancing mpi-based applications' performance and scalability by using adaptive compression. Int. J. High Perform. Comput. Appl. **25**(1), 93–114 (2011)
5. Gidra, L., Boehm, H.J., Fernandes, J.: Utilizing the linux userfaultfd system call in a compaction phase of a garbage collection process (2020)

6. Laboratory, L.L.N.: Coral-2 benchmarks. https://asc.llnl.gov/coral-2-benchmarks. Accessed 11 Mar 2025
7. Li, J., et al.: Spechpc 2021 benchmark suites for modern hpc systems. In: Companion of the 2022 ACM/SPEC International Conference on Performance Engineering, pp. 15–16 (2022)
8. McFadden, M., et al.: Umap: a user level memory mapping library
9. Message Passing Interface Forum: MPI: A Message-Passing Interface Standard Version 4.0, June 2021. https://www.mpi-forum.org/docs/mpi-4.0/mpi40-report.pdf
10. Peng, I., McFadden, M., Green, E., Iwabuchi, K., Wu, K., Li, D., Pearce, R., Gokhale, M.: Umap: enabling application-driven optimizations for page management. In: 2019 IEEE/ACM Workshop on Memory Centric High Performance Computing (MCHPC), pp. 71–78. IEEE (2019)
11. Ramesh, B., Zhou, Q., Shafi, A., Abduljabbar, M., Subramoni, H., Panda, D.K.: Designing efficient pipelined communication schemes using compression in mpi libraries. In: 2022 IEEE 29th International Conference on High Performance Computing, Data, and Analytics (HiPC), pp. 95–99. IEEE (2022)
12. Shan, H., Williams, S., Johnson, C.W.: Improving mpi reduction performance for manycore architectures with openmp and data compression. In: 2018 IEEE/ACM Performance Modeling, Benchmarking and Simulation of High Performance Computer Systems (PMBS), pp. 1–11. IEEE (2018)
13. Zhou, Q., et al.: Designing high-performance mpi libraries with on-the-fly compression for modern gpu clusters. In: 2021 IEEE International Parallel and Distributed Processing Symposium (IPDPS), pp. 444–453. IEEE (2021)
14. Zussman, T., Jiang, T., Cidon, A.: Custom page fault handling with ebpf. In: Proceedings of the ACM SIGCOMM 2024 Workshop on eBPF and Kernel Extensions, pp. 71–73 (2024)

Implementing True MPI Sessions and Evaluating MPI Initialization Scalability

Hui Zhou[✉], Kenneth Raffenetti, Yanfei Guo, Michael Wilkins, and Rajeev Thakur

Argonne National Laboratory, Lemont, IL 60439, USA
{hzhou321,raffenet,yguo,wilkins,thakur}@anl.gov

Abstract. Sessions is one of the major features introduced in the MPI-4 standard. It offers an alternative to the traditional world communicator model by allowing applications to construct communicators from process sets, thereby eliminating the dependency on MPI_COMM_WORLD. The Sessions model was proposed as a more scalable solution for exascale systems, where MPI_COMM_WORLD was viewed as a potential scalability bottleneck. However, supporting Sessions is a significant challenge for established codebases like MPICH due to the deep integration of the world model in traditional MPI implementations. Although MPICH added support for the MPI-4 standard upon its release, it still internally relied on a global world communicator. This approach enabled applications written using the Sessions model to function, but it did not fulfill the full design intent of Sessions, which meant to decouple MPI from MPI_COMM_WORLD. We describe MPICH's effort to support "true" MPI Sessions, including a major internal refactoring. We describe the architectural changes required to support true Sessions and evaluate the resulting implementation's scalability. Our results demonstrate that true Sessions can offer significant scalability benefits by adopting explicit hierarchical designs.

1 Introduction

The MPI Forum released Version 4 of the Message Passing Interface (MPI) Standard in 2021 [15], introducing several major features, most notably MPI Sessions [13]. The MPI Sessions model offers an alternative to the traditional MPI paradigm by enabling applications to construct communicators from locally defined process sets, rather than relying on the default global communicator, MPI_COMM_WORLD, and deriving all others from it.

The primary motivation behind MPI Sessions was to remove the dependency on MPI_COMM_WORLD, which was anticipated to be a major scalability barrier to exascale computing. However, concerns over the scalability of MPI_COMM_WORLD appear to have been overstated. Since the petascale era, MPI has proven its ability to scale to over a million processes [5], while the anticipated billion-process scale has yet to materialize. In practice, exascale computing has been successfully achieved, largely due to advancements like massively parallel accelerators (e.g., GPUs), without the need to eliminate MPI_COMM_WORLD. In fact, a primary objective for exascale facilities has been to achieve a 50× performance improvement over previous systems without necessitating substantial code modifications in existing applications [3]. Empirical evidence suggests that MPI_COMM_WORLD has not posed a fundamental limitation to scalability.

Another motivation for introducing MPI Sessions was to address MPI's limited support for dynamic behavior. Various software components can initialize separate MPI Sessions independently without coordination. This includes non-overlapping Sessions, effectively enabling MPI to be initialized and finalized multiple times within a single application. Such capability is particularly beneficial for workflow-oriented applications that orchestrate multiple independent tasks, each potentially using MPI [22]. Second, the MPI Sessions functionality includes an info argument in MPI_Session_init, allowing customization of each session with parameters that are typically global, such as MPI thread levels. Third, the dynamic nature of MPI Sessions enables innovative solutions for fault tolerance and resource management, including the ability to shrink or grow the number of participating processes during an application's execution.

The inclusion of MPI Sessions in MPI 4.0 has reignited interest and spurred research into addressing some long-standing challenges. Active areas of exploration include resource management [8,9], fault tolerance [18], and job malleability [19]. However, to date, there have been limited evaluations of the scalability of MPI Sessions.

MPICH [10] has played a critical role in MPI's evolution. It was the first widely adopted implementation and served as a prototyping platform during the development of MPI-1. During MPI-2, MPICH supported the standardization process through early implementations of features like ROMIO for MPI-IO [20]. Although this implementation-driven standardization model weakened during MPI-3, MPICH still became the first full implementation of the MPI-3 standard. Continuing this tradition, MPICH released full support for MPI-4—including MPI Sessions—in the same month the standard was published.

However, MPICH's initial MPI Sessions implementation relies on an internal world communicator behind the scenes. Therefore, while MPICH provides the MPI Sessions interface, it is limited to standard-defined process sets, namely, mpi://WORLD and mpi://SELF. Such limited support is permitted by the MPI specification but is not in line with the "true" spirit of the MPI Sessions proposal that saw a world communicator as optional. Developers who wished to explore the possibilities of MPI Sessions either had to build their own solution or look to other MPI libraries with more full-featured support.

Implementing a true MPI Sessions model in MPICH presents significant challenges for two main reasons. First, MPI was originally designed around MPI_COMM_WORLD, which abstracted away the need for applications to manage process identities beyond simple integer ranks. This design choice simplified the application interface and allowed implementations internal flexibility. MPICH, in particular, uses a device-dependent model with internal, implementation-specific process-addressing schemes. However, a true Sessions model demands a device-independent, standardized process-addressing mechanism, which requires major architectural changes in MPICH.

Second, MPICH's design philosophy clearly separates performance-critical runtime paths from less performance-critical initialization stages. It avoids dynamic mechanisms in favor of a structured, two-phase model consisting of an initialization phase followed by a runtime phase. The true MPI Sessions model breaks the long standing assumption that a single, global initialization phase always occurs—an assumption that MPICH relies on for efficient global setup. This shift necessitates a significant redesign of MPICH's initialization and resource-management infrastructure.

However, there are also strong motivations for MPICH to support true MPI Sessions. Beyond enabling ongoing research efforts and accommodating next-generation HPC applications that embrace more dynamic designs, implementing a device-independent infrastructure for process sets and MPI groups has the potential to simplify MPICH's device layer and promote more sustainable development and maintenance. Furthermore, the effort to support true MPI Sessions aligns with MPICH's broader goal of strengthening support for dynamic processes, which already serve a sizable user base.

To this end, we recently performed a substantial code restructuring in MPICH to enable support for true MPI Sessions. Following this work, we evaluated the scalability of initialization across three MPI implementations: (1) the newly refactored MPICH with true MPI Sessions support, (2) MPICH version 4.3.0, which still relies on an internal world communicator, and (3) Open MPI version 5.0.7, which also includes support for true MPI Sessions. These evaluations were conducted on Aurora, the new exascale system at the Argonne Leadership Computing Facility (ALCF). Our findings indicate that MPI Sessions provide comparable initialization scalability across all three implementations on this system. Notably, true MPI Sessions enable the construction of a sparsely connected world communication pattern, which may reduce resource usage during initialization, albeit modestly.

2 Background

We begin with some essential background, including an overview of MPICH's architecture, the Process Management Interface (PMI), and key considerations for efficient MPI startup.

2.1 MPICH Architecture

MPICH adopts an architectural design that facilitates vendor adoption, as illustrated in Fig. 1. The key abstraction is the ADI (Abstract Device Interface), which separates the codebase into two primary layers: the MPIR (MPI Runtime) layer and the MPID (MPI Device) layer. An additional binding layer sits above the MPIR layer, handling parameter validation and conversions [24].

The architectural design allows the MPICH project to focus on MPI semantics, implementation strategies, and high-level algorithms, while enabling MPI vendors to concentrate on hardware-specific performance optimizations. Broadly, the MPIR layer is responsible for hardware-independent functionality, while the MPID layer handles hardware-specific implementations. However, this separation is not absolute. In most communication routines, after the binding layer completes parameter checks and conversions, control is passed quickly to the corresponding ADI routine in the device layer. This design allows the device layer to take the full control of performance-critical code paths, ensuring no optimization opportunities are lost [11].

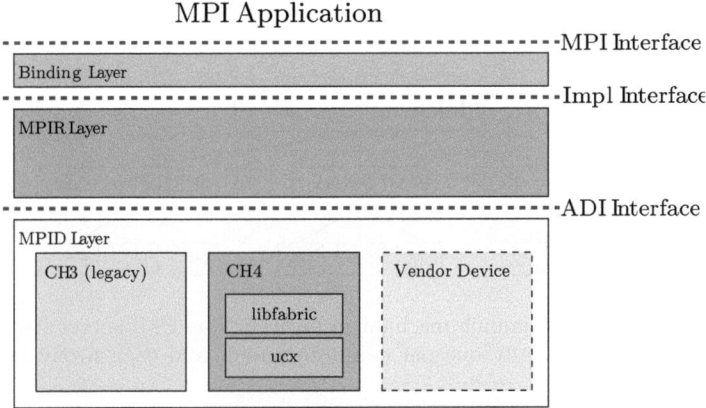

Fig. 1. MPICH architecture. The binding layer handles parameter checking and converts MPI object handles to internal structure pointers. The MPIR layer provides device-independent utilities, while the device layer implements hardware-specific functionality. MPICH maintains CH3 and CH4 as reference device implementations. Vendors may adopt CH3/CH4 or implement their own devices that conform to the ADI interface.

The ADI design introduces some complexity, particularly during the initialization stage. Subcomponents within both the MPIR and device layers require initialization and may depend on one another, requiring a carefully coordinated initialization order. As a result, MPICH adopts a roughly three-stage initialization process, illustrated in the following pseudocode:

```
void MPIR_Init() {
    MPIR_Pre_Init();   /* dev-independent init */
    MPID_Init();       /* dev-dependent init */
    MPIR_Post_Init();  /* dev-dependent MPIR-layer init */
}
```

However, this initialization process mixes local and collective steps. A local initialization step does not involve communication or synchronization with other processes. In contrast, a collective initialization step involves coordination across processes, often requiring data exchange and execution barriers. In the pseudocode above, MPIR_Pre_Init is entirely local, but both MPID_Init and MPIR_Post_Init may contain a mix of local and collective components. This interleaving poses a major challenge in the context of MPI Sessions, because MPI_Session_Init is defined by the MPI standard as a strictly local-only routine. Isolating local-only initialization from this tightly coupled structure requires significant restructuring across layers (vertically) and components (horizontally). Furthermore, MPI Sessions do not assume the presence of a global, world-level collective initialization stage. As a result, any initialization logic that previously relied on this assumption must be redesigned. Collective components must now operate under weaker assumptions, increasing complexity and implementation effort.

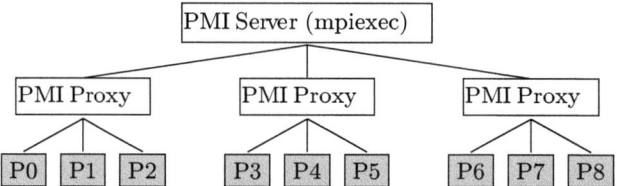

Fig. 2. A common process launch mechanism in MPI. The PMI server (e.g., *mpiexec*) launches PMI proxies (usually one per compute node), and each proxy launches the MPI processes for its node.

2.2 Process Management Interface (PMI)

The MPI specification omits an important detail: how processes are launched and how they exchange wire-up information to bootstrap a communicator. To fill this gap, MPICH introduced the Process Management Interface (PMI) [4]. The original version, known as PMI-1, is distributed with MPICH as a header file, *pmi.h*, and is widely adopted by most MPI implementations and process managers, including Slurm [23] and Flux [1]. MPICH also provides its own PMI implementation in its upstream releases, including a job launcher, hydra [4].

PMI does not define the process launch mechanism itself. For illustrative purposes, we refer to a common setup shown in Fig. 2. In this example, mpiexec is used to launch 9 MPI processes across 3 nodes. mpiexec acts as the PMI server, launching one PMI proxy per node, which in turn launches the MPI processes on that node. The PMI server maintains connections with the PMI proxies, typically using TCP, while each PMI proxy communicates with its local MPI processes using Unix pipes. Together, the PMI server, proxies, and MPI processes form a spanning tree that enables data exchange among all MPI processes.

Figure 3 illustrates a typical implementation of data exchange between two MPI processes using PMI_Put, PMI_Barrier, and PMI_Get. In this design, each

PMI proxy maintains its own key/value store (KVS), and synchronization is achieved during the collective PMI_Barrier. Both PMI_Put and PMI_Get are local operations that communicate only with the PMI proxy on the same node. PMI_Barrier is a global collective that requires participation from all MPI processes. This approach is efficient in scenarios where all processes are collectively exchanging data–only a single PMI_Barrier is needed to propagate all key/value pairs across the system.

An alternative design may keep a single copy of KVS in the PMI server, requiring each PMI_Put and PMI_Get to traverse to the server. While this eliminates the need for a global barrier, it introduces a scalability issue: completing an all-to-all exchange would require $O(P^2)$ point-to-point traversals, where P is the number of processes. Furthermore, a PMI_Get call may block if the corresponding PMI_Put has not yet been completed by the sender.

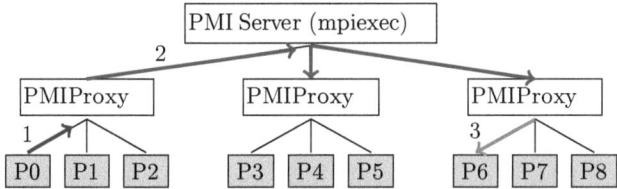

Fig. 3. An example of data exchange using PMI. (1) P0 use PMI_Put to send data to its PMI proxy. (2) All MPI processes call PMI_Barrier, during which proxies synchronize local data to the PMI server, and the PMI server propagates the data to other proxies. (3) P6 calls PMI_Get to retrieve the data from its local proxy.

The PMI-1 interface is relatively simple. In 2010, PMI-2 was proposed to improve scalability. It introduced two key features. First, PMI-2 supports an optional node scope for its key-value store, allowing intra-node Put and Get operations to bypass global synchronization and avoid the use of barriers. This made intra-node data exchange significantly more efficient by avoiding the need for inter-proxy synchronization. Second, PMI-2 allows concurrent PMI operations from multiple threads, potentially improving performance for MPI+threads applications. However, PMI-2 redefined the PMI interface rather than evolving it incrementally from PMI-1, creating adoption challenges. While MPICH supports both PMI-1 and PMI-2, PMI-1 remains the default. Interestingly, the scalability concerns that motivated PMI-2 never fully materialized. Intra-node communication can be efficiently handled via shared memory, bypassing PMI, and multithreaded access to PMI is avoided by restricting its use to the initialization stage, where concurrency is usually not required. Interestingly, MPI Sessions allows the possibility of calling MPI_Session_init or the communicator creation routines from concurrent threads, thus requiring multithread support in PMI. MPICH's support for multithreaded usage of MPI Sessions requires an extension to PMI-1 that allows concurrent barrier operations distinguished using string tags.

During the early push toward exascale computing, PMI's scalability limitations again came under scrutiny. It was anticipated that exascale systems might involve 50,000 to 100,000 nodes [7], where PMI-1's barrier-based data exchange could significantly delay job startup. In response, PMIx was introduced in 2017 [7]. Although it is presented as an extension of PMI, PMIx has a much broader scope, addressing tasks from efficient executable loading to supporting multiple programming models beyond MPI. Comparing PMIx directly to PMI-1 or PMI-2 is not straightforward. As noted in its original proposal, PMIx's data exchange interfaces were designed primarily for compatibility with legacy systems. While its scope may have since evolved, it remains unclear whether PMIx fundamentally addresses the core limitations of PMI-1.

Currently, only a subset of the PMIx specification, primarily those features that parallel PMI-1, is required to support MPI implementations. However, as future versions of MPI introduce capabilities such as fault tolerance and system malleability, broader PMIx functionality may become increasingly important. While MPICH will continue to support the PMI-1 interface, extensions may be necessary to acquire certain advanced PMIx features.

2.3 Efficient MPI Startup

The efficiency of launching large-scale MPI jobs is influenced by several factors, including the workload manager, resource manager, shared file system, network infrastructure, and the MPI initialization process itself. In this paper, we focus specifically on the MPI layer. Once the MPI processes are instantiated, each process must gather local information and exchange it with its peers–typically via PMI. A straightforward implementation of this process might look as follows:

```
PMI_Put(rank, myaddr);
PMI_Barrier();
for (int i = 0; i < size; i++) {
    PMI_Get(i, &addrs[i]);
}
```

The PMI interface is designed for simplicity, but its implementations are often not optimized for large-scale environments. For instance, MPICH uses ASCII-based wire protocols, and communication between PMI proxies and the PMI server frequently occurs over TCP connections using the SSH protocol. While this approach is sufficient for medium-scale jobs (e.g., a few thousand processes), it becomes a bottleneck at higher scales. In scenarios with high process-per-node (PPN) counts and thousands of nodes, the address exchange phase can take tens of minutes, significantly impacting total job runtime.

A key insight is that on modern exascale systems, a significant amount of parallelism resides within nodes. In large jobs, the total number of processes is often driven more by high PPN than by the number of nodes. Consequently, intra-node address exchanges can be efficiently handled via shared memory rather than PMI. By limiting PMI communication to one "node root" per node and performing the rest of the exchange via shared memory, the overall time spent in `MPI_Init` can be drastically reduced to negligible levels [17].

2.4 The MPI Sessions API

The MPI Sessions API, introduced in the MPI-4 standard, provides a more flexible approach to initializing and managing MPI environments. Unlike traditional initialization via `MPI_Init` or `MPI_Init_thread`, which implicitly sets up `MPI_COMM_WORLD`, the Sessions model replaces it with the following pseudo code:

```
MPI_Session_init(info, errhan, &session);
MPI_Group_from_session_pset(session, "mpi://WORLD", &group);
MPI_Comm_create_from_group(group, "stringtag", info, errhan,
    &comm);
```

Both `MPI_Session_init` and group preparations are local calls, while `MPI_Comm_create_from_group` is collective over the participating process group. In the rest of the paper, we refer to `MPI_Session_init` as local initialization and `MPI_Comm_create_from_group` as communicator bootstrapping.

3 Implementation

MPICH is a mature project with many downstream vendor implementations, including Cray MPICH [12], Intel MPI [14], ParaStation MPI [16], and MVAPICH [21]. When introducing major features such as MPI Sessions, it can be tempting to start with a clean-slate design and backport functionality as needed. This strategy was previously used in the development of shared-memory communication in the CH3 device [6] and lightweight communication in the CH4 device [11], helping to minimize disruption to production environments and downstream vendors. However, starting from scratch often results in long transition periods, during which prior features must be re-implemented, past mistakes may be repeated, and hard-earned lessons must be re-learned. To avoid this, we adopted a strategy of gradual refactoring. Ultimately, we achieved a new design that enabled the implementation of MPI Sessions within the existing codebase. This incremental approach is validated through comprehensive continuous integration (CI) testing and iterative feedback from downstream users and vendors, ensuring both stability and forward progress.

The remainder of this section outlines the key stages involved in preparing for and ultimately implementing full MPI Sessions support in MPICH.

3.1 Separating Local and Collective Initialization

The functions `MPI_Init` and `MPI_Init_thread` are collective and must be called by all processes, whereas `MPI_Session_init` is a local operation. Therefore, the first step in implementing MPI Sessions is to disentangle local-only initializations–suitable for `MPI_Session_init`–from those that require synchronization across processes. To do this, we split each component's initialization into two distinct phases: a local phase and a collective phase. While conceptually simple, this separation introduces implementation complexities and can be tedious to apply uniformly across all components. There is some discretion in deciding which operations belong to the local phase. For instance, initializing self-communication could, in principle, be handled locally, since it does not depend on other processes. However, from a semantic standpoint, it may be more appropriate to delay this step until the creation of the first communicator, as establishing self-communication parallels connecting with a peer. In our implementation, we chose to move as much logic as possible into the local phase to ease the later task of eliminating the dependency on MPI_COMM_WORLD.

This separation of local and collective initialization enabled us to implement the complete MPI Sessions API in MPICH 4.0. However, because the collective phase still involves constructing a default global context, every process must participate in the first non-self call to MPI_Comm_create_from_group, during which an internal world communicator is established. While it supports the majority of applications using MPI Sessions, it retains a hidden dependency on the world communicator. The remaining subsections describe recent work that eliminates this dependency and realizes true MPI Sessions support. This improved implementation is expected to be included in the next MPICH release.

3.2 Communicator-Independent Process IDs

In traditional MPICH implementations, each device defines its own process ID mechanism, typically derived from internal communication data structures. These IDs are used to access communication metadata, such as remote addresses and connection states, resulting in tight coupling between process identity and device internals. To enable true support for MPI Sessions–without relying on comm_world–a process ID scheme must be available before device-layer data structures are initialized.

To this end, MPICH introduces a communicator-independent process ID scheme defined at the MPIR layer. Each process is uniquely identified by a pair: a world ID and a world rank. World Rank corresponds to the process's PMI ID, which, in a traditional world model, is the same as its rank in MPI_COMM_WORLD. World ID is a sequential integer assigned locally by each process. World ID 0 always refers to the process's original world, where the process is created in. New worlds encountered via dynamic process creation or internal mechanisms are assigned incrementally higher world IDs. A world is defined as a group of processes sharing a PMI namespace—a logical unit of coordination that shares a key-value store. In the world model, a world consists of processes that make up MPI_COMM_WORLD.

A key step in constructing communicators is exchanging process metadata, either via PMI or through a direct connection established via the dynamic process interface. When all process IDs originate from the same PMI interface, they can be directly mapped to PMI identifiers (e.g., PMI namespace and PMI IDs) for metadata exchange. However, dynamic processes may not share a common PMI context. Therefore, MPICH must explicitly exchange world information during dynamic process operations (e.g., MPI_Accept and MPI_Connect). This ensures proper mapping between remote and local world IDs and allows processes to populate their local world tables with the appropriate metadata. This design enables MPICH to support a wide range of PMI implementations and dynamic process scenarios, providing flexibility while maintaining consistency.

MPICH's device layers have been modified to adopt this MPIR-defined process ID scheme. While this change reduces the device layer's flexibility in designing its own communication databases, it eliminates redundant implementations and promotes consistency across devices by offloading ID management to a centralized, device-independent layer.

3.3 Group-Collective Address Exchange Over PMI

A key step in bootstrapping communicators is the exchange of network addresses using PMI. In the traditional MPI_COMM_WORLD model, all processes collectively exchange addresses, as described in Sect. 2.2. However, in the MPI Sessions model, a global initialization stage may not exist. Instead, users may choose to bootstrap a communicator over a subset of processes rather than the entire process set.

MPICH can be configured to work with different PMI interfaces including PMI-1, PMI-2, and PMIx. Group-level data exchange in PMIx is supported via PMIx_Put, PMIx_Get, and PMIx_Fence. In particular, PMIx_Fence accepts a process array as an argument, allowing it to execute a blocking barrier across a specified group while collecting data posted via PMIx_Put. However, support for performing PMIx_Fence over subsets of MPI_COMM_WORLD remains inconsistent across implementations. In testing our implementation on the Cray Programming Environment using the Parallel Application Launch Service (PALS), we observed that jobs could hang or crash. As a workaround until the PMIx implementation issues are fixed, we introduce a fallback environment variable, which when set, all processes must call MPI_Comm_create_from_group collectively, allowing PMIx_Fence to be executed over MPI_COMM_WORLD. Processes not part of the target group participate only in the PMIx_Fence call to ensure progress and consistency.

To support group-level data exchange in PMI-1 or PMI-2, extensions are required. We propose a new collective operation, PMI_Barrier_group:

```
int PMI_Barrier_group(const int *group, int count);
```

This extension achieves the same semantics as PMIx_Fence over a group of processes. When using a PMI server that supports this extension, such as MPICH's bundled process launcher, Hydra, there won't be restrictions. Otherwise, the same fallback environment variable must be set and all processes are required to call MPI_Comm_create_from_group collectively.

An additional PMI extension is required to support multithreaded usage. However, since most applications do not require concurrent access to communicator bootstrapping, we defer this work to future development.

3.4 Atomic Shared Memory Initialization

Unlike network communications, where remote connections can be established on demand, shared memory communication requires all participating processes to share a common memory segment. The segment must be large enough to accommodate all local processes on the node even if some are not present during the initial communicator bootstrapping phase. Additionally, each process must ensure that its peers are ready before using the shared memory for communication. In previous versions of MPICH, which includes an explicit global initialization stage, shared memory initialization is accomplished via collectives in which all local processes participate. To support the true Sessions model, however, we cannot rely on collectives since not all local processes may be present during the communicator bootstrapping. Therefore, we redesigned shared memory initialization based on atomic operations.

Atomic shared memory creation is performed using the POSIX API shm_open. Each process initially calls shm_open with the flag O_CREAT | O_EXCL. The first process to succeed in this call becomes the "root" and is responsible for creating and initializing the shared memory segment. All other processes, upon failing the initial call, subsequently invoke shm_open again–this time to open the segment created by the root. Other processes must wait for the root to complete initializing the memory. This is coordinated in two steps. First, processes call fstat on the file descriptor returned by shm_open to ensure that the root process has set the size of the region before mapping it. Second, processes read an atomic variable named root_ready from a fixed location in the shared memory region until the value indicates the root process has completed setup. In addition, each process maintains its own atomic ready flag. During a communicator bootstrapping call, each process waits for the ready flags of all other local processes in the group before completing the call, ensuring the communicator is fully initialized and safe to use upon return.

3.5 Bootstrapping Communicators from Sparse Connections

PMI is designed primarily for bootstrapping MPI and emphasizes simplicity over communication efficiency. While this approach is adequate for small to medium-sized jobs involving thousands of processes, it becomes unsuitable for large-scale all-to-all address exchanges. In jobs with hundreds of thousands of processes—often with high process-per-node (PPN) counts—using PMI for such exchanges can make MPI initialization prohibitively slow. To improve scalability and efficiency, we use PMI only to exchange addresses between node roots within the target communicator. Once this exchange is complete and connections are established, a sub-communicator consisting of the node roots—referred to as node_roots_comm—becomes operational. Within each node, after local processes initialize shared memory, another sub-communicator composed of all local processes—referred to as node_comm—is also brought online. With both node_roots_comm and node_comm active, communication paths are established between any pair of processes. At this point, the communicator forms a sparsely connected graph rather than a fully connected (logical all-to-all) topology. In the final phase, we perform an MPI_Allgather across all processes to exchange address information and establish a logical all-to-all connection. This step is executed using MPI collectives instead of PMI, as MPI can take advantage of high-bandwidth interconnects such as InfiniBand and shared memory, providing significantly better performance. Because the communicator begins in a sparsely connected state, we employ a specialized hierarchical collective algorithm to efficiently perform the `MPI_Allgather`. After this stage, the communicator is fully bootstrapped and ready for use.

While previous versions of MPICH included a similar algorithm that used node roots to bootstrap all-to-all address exchange, it assumed a world initialization context. In this work, we redesigned the algorithm to support arbitrary communicator bootstrapping.

4 Experimental Evaluation

MPICH's implementation of MPI Sessions modifies only the MPI initialization process and the bootstrapping of initial communicators. Runtime communication behavior remains unchanged between the world and Session models. Therefore, our evaluation focuses on the scalability of initialization, specifically comparing the world model against the Session model. All experiments were conducted on the Aurora system at the Argonne Leadership Computing Facility [2], using between 1 and 2048 nodes, with 96 processes per node (PPN). Each node is equipped with two Intel Xeon CPU Max Series processors, 512 GB of DDR5 RAM, six Intel Data Center GPUs, and eight Slingshot 11 network endpoints. To ensure a clear measurement of MPI initialization scalability, MPICH's GPU support was disabled, as GPU initialization introduces significant time and memory overhead that can obscure the interesting part of the measurements. A high PPN configuration was chosen to emphasize scalability challenges. Although additional experiments were performed with 12 PPN, those results are omitted due to space constraints.

4.1 Comparing World Initialization

Traditional MPI applications can be adapted to use MPI Sessions by replacing calls to `MPI_Init` or `MPI_Init_thread` with an initial call to `MPI_Session_init`, followed by `MPI_Comm_create_from_group` using groups derived from the process sets "mpi://SELF" and "mpi://WORLD". These steps create communicators functionally equivalent to `MPI_COMM_SELF` and `MPI_COMM_WORLD`, respectively. In MPICH, communicators created via MPI Sessions behave identically to those created under the traditional world model.

Figure 4 presents the initialization time and memory usage for the development version of MPICH (MPICH-dev). Initialization time is calculated as the average, across all processes, of the duration taken to execute `MPI_Init`, `MPI_Session_init`, and `MPI_Comm_create_from_group`, respectively. Memory usage is estimated based on the `MemFree` field from `/proc/meminfo`, capturing the total memory consumed by all processes on a node. To minimize interference from phase misalignment among processes on the same node, deliberate pauses are inserted between measurement phases.

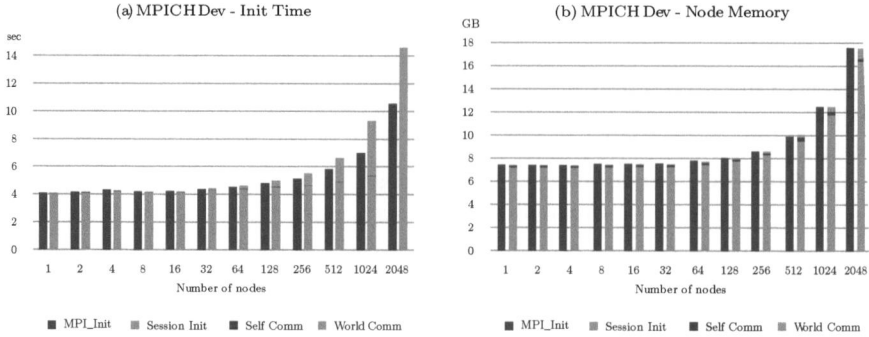

Fig. 4. Comparing MPI Initialization between the world model and the session model using mpich-dev. The session model measurements are split into session init and bootstrapping the self and the world communicators. (a) Initialization times in seconds. (b) Node memory usage in GB.

The results reveal several key observations. Local initialization, represented by `MPI_Session_init`, accounts for the majority of both initialization time and memory usage. Only a small fraction of this cost is due to MPICH itself. The bulk originates from lower-level components such as libfabric and hardware supporting libraries. The overhead is likely due to slow hardware initialization on hybrid-node architectures with multiple GPUs and NICs, with performance further degraded under high PPN as processes compete for resources. Additional overhead may come from dynamic loading of supporting libraries, which stresses shared file systems at scale. The memory allocations may include buffers anticipating a full world communication, which may explain why the local initialization also increases in both the initialization time and memory consumption as the total number of nodes increase.

As an anecdote, MPICH defaults to using the `tcp;rxm` libfabric provider instead of the `cxi` provider when a job runs on a single node. This choice avoids the resource limitations associated with the `cxi` provider for single-node jobs. Our initial experiments showed a memory usage outlier at the 1-node scale, caused by `tcp;rxm` allocating significantly more memory (17GB) than `cxi`. By explicitly selecting the `cxi` provider, we obtained the consistent measurements shown in Fig. 4.

Creating the self communicator incurs a negligible, constant cost. In contrast, constructing the world communicator, the only collective step during initialization, scales with node count in both time and memory, though it only becomes a significant factor at scales above 1024 nodes.

Overall, session-based initialization takes slightly longer than the world model, while both models exhibit comparable memory usage. The reason for the longer initialization time in the sessions model is not entirely clear. One contributing factor may be the additional context ID allocation required during communicator bootstrapping in the sessions model. However, we suspect the more significant factor is overhead caused by process imbalance. In the world model, local initialization and world communicator construction are combined, which may help mask some of the load imbalance.

4.2 Comparing Implementations

To provide a broader comparison, we conducted the same set of experiments using MPICH 4.3.0 and Open MPI 5.0.7.

Figure 5 shows the results for MPICH 4.3.0, the current stable release, which implements MPI Sessions using an internal world communicator. As a result, it only supports bootstrapping either the self or world communicator. The comparison between the world and session models in MPICH 4.3.0 is similar to that observed with MPICH-dev. Comparing Fig. 5 and Fig. 4, MPICH 4.3.0 demonstrates faster initialization times but significantly higher memory usage, especially at larger node counts. The initialization time difference is mainly attributed to the redesign of the address exchange algorithm. MPICH 4.3.0 assumes world initialization, whereas the new address exchange algorithm in MPICH-dev supports arbitrary communicator bootstrapping. This flexibility introduces additional steps for collecting and parsing process compositions, which increases the overall initialization time. The memory consumption difference, on the other hand, is due to an unrelated optimizations in the MPICH development branch. MPICH 4.3.0 statically allocates address tables for all potential internal communication endpoints. These tables are replicated for each network interface card (NIC) on the node and for every process. In contrast, MPICH-dev employs a more dynamic approach to address table allocation, significantly reducing memory usage at the cost of a negligible increase in runtime latency when additional address vector (AV) entries are required for new contexts.

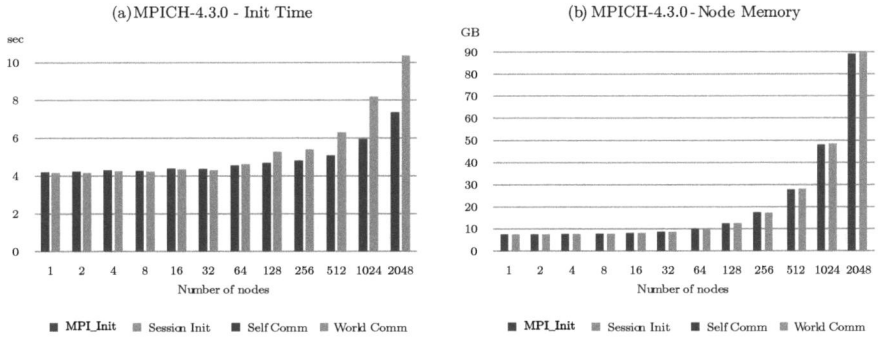

Fig. 5. Comparing MPI Initialization between the world model and the session model using MPICH 4.3.0. (a) Initialization times in seconds. (b) Node memory usage in GB.

Running Open MPI on Aurora, especially with the session model, presents several challenges. We experienced crashes or hangs using system job launcher

(PALS from the Cray Programming Environment), in particular when performing group-level communication bootstrap. Thus, we ran experiments using Open MPI's `mpiexec` instead. Even so, we encountered instability at high node counts, and were unable to obtain results at 1024 and 2048 nodes due to frequent job failures.

As shown in Fig. 6, Open MPI uses less memory overall but exhibits longer initialization time compared to MPICH. Notably, the time for both `MPI_Session_init` and self communicator bootstrapping increases super-linearly with the number of nodes. Although neither step is collective, we suspect that some components of the software stack may still introduce implicit synchronization overhead, contributing to the observed scaling inefficiencies. Using Open MPI's bundled `mpiexec` on Aurora is likely to have integration issues with the system resource manager. Thus, further insights are needed to interpret this experiment.

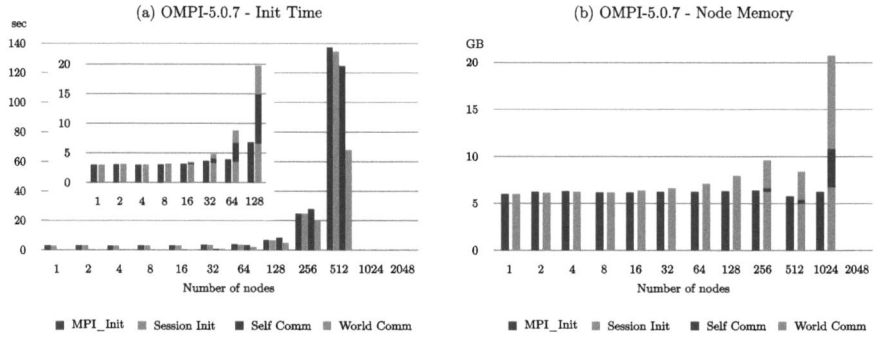

Fig. 6. Comparing MPI Initialization between the world model and the session model using Open MPI 5.0.7. (a) Initialization times in seconds. A zoomed section show the same data from 1 to 128 nodes. (b) Node memory usage in GB.

4.3 Sparse World Initialization

By supporting true MPI Sessions, applications can bypass the creation of a global world communicator altogether. One compelling use case is a sparsely connected hierarchical topology, in which all processes on a node form a node communicator, and a designated node root from each node joins a second communicator, the node roots communicator. This hierarchical structure still enables global collective operations through explicitly programmed algorithms. For example, an `MPI_Allreduce` can be implemented as follows:

```
MPI_Reduce(buf, recvbuf, count, datatype, MPI_SUM, 0,
    node_comm);
if (node_comm->rank == 0) {
```

```
    MPI_Allreduce(MPI_IN_PLACE, recvbuf, count, datatype,
        MPI_SUM, node_roots_comm);
}
MPI_Bcast(recvbuf, count, datatype, 0, node_comm);
```

Let m represent the number of processes per node (PPN). Compared to a fully connected world communicator, this hierarchical setup reduces the number of internode connections by approximately a factor of m^2. The actual resource savings, however, depends on the overhead associated with establishing internode connections.

Figure 7 compares initialization time and memory usage between the traditional world model and the Sessions-based sparse model. The results confirm that constructing a sparse world using MPI Sessions reduces both initialization time and memory consumption relative to building a full world communicator in the Sessions model (Fig. 4). However, on Aurora, the traditional world model still initializes slightly faster. The sparse model does provide modest memory savings.

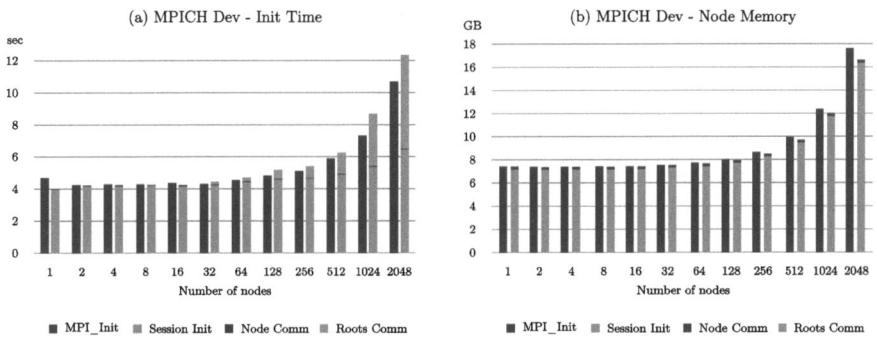

Fig. 7. Comparing MPI Initialization between the world model and the Sessions-based sparse model using mpich-dev. (a) Initialization times in seconds. (b) Node memory usage in GB.

A significant portion of both the initialization time and memory usage occurs during local initialization, incurred not by MPICH itself but by its lower-layer dependencies. We suspect that these costs are mostly implementation issues rather than the fundamental limit. Many dependency layers in an HPC system assume and optimize for a traditional world model.

5 Conclusions

MPI Sessions was introduced into MPI to address scalability challenges on exascale systems. We recently completed a significant code restructuring in MPICH to support MPI Sessions in alignment with its original design goal—eliminating dependence on MPI_COMM_WORLD. We evaluated MPI initialization scalability by comparing equivalent use cases between the traditional world model and the sessions model. As expected, when a fully connected world communicator is required, the sessions model does not provide a performance advantage over the world model. However, with our recent development, MPICH now supports the construction of sparsely connected communication structures without relying on a world communicator. Our experiments demonstrate that such sparse topologies can reduce memory usage and improve initialization time compared to the traditional all-to-all world communicator.

While MPI Sessions may not be essential for scalability alone, transitioning from the world model to the Sessions model introduces greater flexibility and dynamism at minimal cost and without significant performance penalties. This flexibility may become increasingly valuable for emerging and non-traditional application workflows.

MPI Sessions is a major addition in the MPI 4.0 standard, though it has yet to see widespread adoption. With robust support now available in MPICH, we aim to promote broader use and stimulate further research into the capabilities and practical use cases of MPI Sessions.

Acknowledgments. This research was supported by the U.S. Department of Energy, Office of Science, under Contract DE-AC02-06CH11357.

Disclosure of Interests. The authors have no competing interests to declare that are relevant to the content of this article.

References

1. Ahn, D.H., Garlick, J., Grondona, M., Lipari, D., Springmeyer, B., Schulz, M.: Flux: A next-generation resource management framework for large HPC centers. In: 2014 43rd International Conference on Parallel Processing Workshops, pp. 9–17. IEEE (2014)
2. Argonne Leadership Computing Facility: Aurora (2025). https://www.alcf.anl.gov/aurora
3. Atchley, S., et al.: Frontier: Exploring exascale. In: Proceedings of the International Conference for High Performance Computing, Networking, Storage and Analysis, pp. 1–16 (2023)
4. Balaji, P., et al.: PMI: A scalable parallel process-management interface for extreme-scale systems. In: European MPI Users' Group Meeting, pp. 31–41. Springer (2010)
5. Balaji, P., et al.: MPI on a million processors. In: Recent Advances in Parallel Virtual Machine and Message Passing Interface: 16th European PVM/MPI Users' Group Meeting, Espoo, Finland, September 7-10, 2009. Proceedings 16, pp. 20–30. Springer (2009)
6. Buntinas, D., Mercier, G., Gropp, W.: Implementation and evaluation of shared-memory communication and synchronization operations in MPICH2 using the Nemesis communication subsystem. Parallel Comput. **33**(9), 634–644 (2007)

7. Castain, R.H., Solt, D., Hursey, J., Bouteiller, A.: PMIx: process management for exascale environments. In: Proceedings of the 24th European MPI Users' Group Meeting, pp. 1–10 (2017)
8. Dosanjh, M.G., et al.: Implementation and evaluation of MPI 4.0 partitioned communication libraries. Parallel Comput. **108**, 102827 (2021)
9. Fecht, J., Schreiber, M., Schulz, M., Pritchard, H., Holmes, D.J.: An emulation layer for dynamic resources with MPI sessions. In: International Conference on High Performance Computing, pp. 147–161. Springer (2022)
10. Gropp, W., Lusk, E., Doss, N., Skjellum, A.: A high-performance, portable implementation of the MPI message passing interface standard. Parallel Comput. **22**(6), 789–828 (1996)
11. Guo, Y., et al.: Preparing MPICH for exascale. The International Journal of High Performance Computing Applications p. 10943420241311608 (2025)
12. Hewlett Packard Enterprise: Cray MPICH (2024). https://cpe.ext.hpe.com/docs/24.03/mpt/mpich/index.html
13. Holmes, D., et al.: MPI Sessions: leveraging runtime infrastructure to increase scalability of applications at exascale. In: Proceedings of the 23rd European MPI Users' Group Meeting, pp. 121–129 (2016)
14. Intel Corporation: Intel® MPI Library (2025). https://www.intel.com/content/www/us/en/developer/tools/oneapi/mpi-library.html
15. Message Passing Interface Forum: MPI: A Message-Passing Interface Standard Version 4.0, June 2021. https://www.mpi-forum.org/docs/mpi-4.0/mpi40-report.pdf
16. ParTec AG: ParaStation MPI (2025). https://github.com/ParaStation/psmpi
17. Raffenetti, K., Bayyapu, N., Durnov, D., Takagi, M., Balaji, P.: Locality-aware PMI usage for efficient MPI startup. In: 2018 IEEE 4th International Conference on Computer and Communications (ICCC), pp. 624–628. IEEE (2018)
18. Rocco, R., Palermo, G., Gregori, D.: Fault awareness in the MPI 4.0 session model. In: Proceedings of the 20th ACM International Conference on Computing Frontiers, pp. 189–192 (2023)
19. Suarez, E., Eicker, N., Hoppe, H.C.: The DEEP-SEA project: A software stack for heterogeneous and modular supercomputers. PARS-Mitteilungen, vol. 36 (2024)
20. Thakur, R., Gropp, W., Lusk, E.: Data sieving and collective I/O in ROMIO. In: Proceedings. Frontiers' 99. Seventh Symposium on the Frontiers of Massively Parallel Computation, pp. 182–189. IEEE (1999)
21. The Ohio State University: MVAPICH (2025). https://mvapich.cse.ohio-state.edu/
22. Wozniak, J.M., Dorier, M., Ross, R., Shu, T., Kurc, T., Tang, L., Podhorszki, N., Wolf, M.: MPI jobs within MPI jobs: a practical way of enabling task-level fault-tolerance in hpc workflows. Futur. Gener. Comput. Syst. **101**, 576–589 (2019)
23. Yoo, A.B., Jette, M.A., Grondona, M.: Slurm: Simple Linux utility for resource management. In: Workshop on job scheduling strategies for parallel processing, pp. 44–60. Springer (2003)
24. Zhou, H., Raffenetti, K., Bland, W., Guo, Y.: Generating bindings in MPICH. arXiv preprint arXiv:2401.16547 (2024)

Layout-Agnostic MPI Abstraction for Distributed Computing in Modern C++

Jiří Klepl[✉], Martin Kruliš, and Matyáš Brabec

Charles University, Malostranské náměstí 25, 118 00 Praha 1, Czech Republic
{klepl,krulis,brabec}@d3s.mff.cuni.cz

Abstract. Message Passing Interface (MPI) has been a well-established technology in the domain of distributed high-performance computing for several decades. However, one of its greatest drawbacks is a rather ancient pure-C interface. It lacks many useful features of modern languages (namely C++), like basic type-checking or support for generic code design. In this paper, we propose a novel abstraction for MPI, which we implemented as an extension of the C++ Noarr library. It follows Noarr paradigms (first-class layout and traversal abstraction) and offers layout-agnostic design of MPI applications. We also implemented a layout-agnostic distributed GEMM kernel as a case study to demonstrate the usability and syntax of the proposed abstraction. We show that the abstraction achieves performance comparable to the state-of-the-art MPI C++ bindings while allowing for a more flexible design of distributed applications.

Keywords: Distributed computing · Memory layout · Layout agnosticism · Noarr · C++ · Abstraction

1 Introduction

Distributed computing is one of the essential ingredients of high-performance parallel computing. MPI (Message Passing Interface) [8] represents one profound standard for this task, and it has many implementations, such as Open MPI [17] or MPICH [9]. Unfortunately, the MPI interface is rather old (considering the language development, especially in the past 25 years) and was designed on principles that are considered obsolete in modern C++, such as using void* pointers for generically typed buffers. Furthermore, optimizing HPC algorithms often requires the utilization of multiple fine-tuned memory layouts for the data structures, which is somewhat clumsy in MPI since it requires tedious manual construction of MPI datatypes for individual layouts. This makes any support for layout-agnostic data structures or traversal-agnostic index spaces challenging.

Layout agnosticism [16] separates the logical index space of a data structure (like an abstraction or an interface) from its physical memory organization (implementation). A layout-agnostic data structure (e.g., a matrix) defines only its logical index space (such as the indices for the column i and the row j) and provides an external mechanism (a layout definition) for mapping the logical indices to physical memory locations (offsets in a linear buffer). The programmer may choose different layout definitions to optimize the performance of the data structure for a given problem or specific hardware (memory) architecture while the algorithm that uses the data structure remains unchanged. A few examples of matrix memory layouts are depicted in Fig. 1.

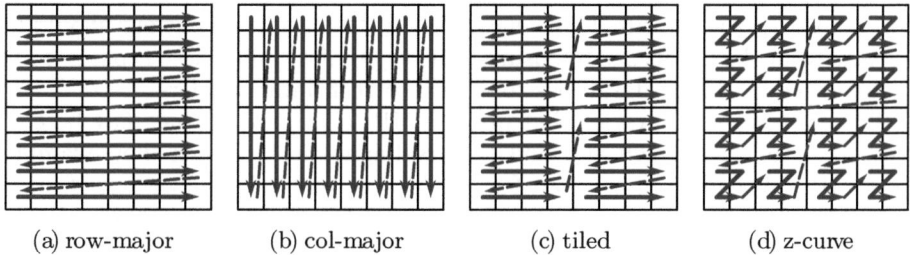

(a) row-major   (b) col-major   (c) tiled   (d) z-curve

Fig. 1. Examples of common matrix layouts

The selected physical layout may affect the performance significantly. For instance, when multiplying two matrices $A \times B$ using a naïve $\mathcal{O}(N^3)$ algorithm, the first matrix A is accessed in a row-wise pattern while the second B is read column by column. Therefore, matrix A could benefit from the row-major layout, while the column-major format would be better for B.

Unfortunately, selecting the best layout for a given problem/architecture is not always possible since a suboptimal data layout may be enforced by the API, and internal transformation of the data structure may be computationally demanding. However, a similar approach can be used to design traversal-agnostic algorithms [7] where iteration over an index space is abstracted, and the loops may be reordered, split into blocks, or even parallelized without changing the algorithm itself or the involved structures. Continuing with our matrix multiplication example, the three loops iterating over the i, j, k dimensions (where i, j represent an element in the output matrix and k iterates over its dot product elements) can be split into blocks (in six nested loops) so the matrices are processed in a tiled manner, which improves data locality for most matrix layouts.

In recent years, there has been a growing interest in zero-cost overhead layout-agnostic data structures such as `std::mdspan` [18] included in the C++23 standard [6] (designed by Kokkos), Kokkos views [19], CuTe layouts [11] by NVIDIA, or Noarr structures [7]. The traversal agnosticism has also been tackled from various standpoints. At the lowest level, the C++ compiler attempts to provide automated loop optimizations based on the polyhedral model [5,13]. However, the compiler sometimes has a limited perspective of the semantics of the algorithm, so various extensions (like Loopy [10]) were created that allowed the programmer to guide the compiler's loop transformations. An alternative approach is to use an abstraction layer for the data structure traversal. This may be achieved in a domain-specific language (DSL) such as Halide [15] or natively in C++ using meta-template programming (e.g., with Noarr traversers [7]).

When designing a fine-tuned HPC solution, a programmer must pay attention to all aspects affecting efficiency, which involves combining low-level code optimizations, memory layout optimizations, parallelization, and distributed computing. Particularly in the context of MPI applications, the data distribution handled by MPI communication primitives needs to work in synergy with layout-agnostic and traversal-agnostic program design and with (potential) layout transformations to ensure optimal efficiency. Finally, the layout definitions should be propagated in the datatypes to ensure basic type safety, and these types need to be translated into MPI datatypes to ensure correct data transfers.

There are several libraries that provide MPI abstractions that may be considered for the layout-agnostic and traversal-agnostic approach. For example, Boost.MPI can handle direct transfers of STL vectors and serialization of many other data structures. Some works, such as MPP or KaMPIng [12,20], achieve similar goals with even better performance. Although these libraries offer some level of type safety and convenience when transferring simple containers, they are not designed for uses where the data needs to be also transformed to a different layout. KokkosComm [1] allows the user to send or receive an arbitrary Kokkos view that represents an mdspan. However, its public interface assumes that the sender and receiver layouts are the same and unpredictably reorders the data for seemingly compatible Kokkos views, even with the same value type, rank, and dimension extents. This makes the library incompatible with the layout-agnostic approach without modifications to its interface.

We propose the Noarr-MPI library, a novel MPI abstraction that adopts principles and technologies from Noarr [7], a C++ library for managing data structure memory organization and traversal. We have implemented a prototype that handles basic wrapping and necessary interactions between Noarr and MPI libraries, automatic data transformations, initialization of MPI structures, and type checking. It also provides an MPI abstraction compatible with Noarr traversers. The main contributions of the paper are:

- We propose a novel layout-agnostic, type-checked abstraction for MPI, designed for modern C++ and compatible with paradigms presented in the Noarr library.
- We provide an open-source prototype as an extension of the Noarr library[1].
- We compare the features and performance of the Noarr-MPI library with state-of-the-art MPI abstractions, demonstrating the advantages of our approach.
- We demonstrate the proposed abstraction on a well-known matrix multiplication (GEMM) kernel, which serves as a practical example and provides a basis for comparison with other abstractions.

---

[1] The implementation is available at https://github.com/jiriklepl/noarr-mpi.

The paper is organized as follows. Section 2 introduces the Noarr library and related work. Section 3 discusses mapping Noarr structures to MPI datatypes and the type transformation process. The proposed implementation is detailed in Sect. 4. Section 5 evaluates the applicability of the proposed approach on a real-world example and presents the comparison with other abstractions. Section 6 concludes the paper.

2 Noarr Background

Our work is built on top of the Noarr library [7], so we start with a brief description of its main principles essential for our MPI abstraction.

Noarr structures are the core abstraction of the Noarr library. They represent a mapping from the index space with named dimensions to the linear memory space. Structures are assembled from *proto-structure* objects that represent specific transformations of the mapping. For example, vector<'i'>(N) introduces a dimension named 'i' with size N, and into_blocks<'i','b'>(Ns) splits dimension 'i' into two dimensions where 'b' is an index of a contiguous block of Ns elements and 'i' represents individual elements within a block.

Multiple proto-structure objects can be combined using the ^ operator—e.g., scalar<int>() ^ vector<'i'>(N) ^ vector<'j'>(M) defines a 2D structure with dimensions named 'i' and 'j' of sizes N and M, respectively, and a scalar type of int. This composition is hierarchical, meaning that the scalar<int>() is the base structure further transformed by vector<'i'>(N) and finally by vector<'j'>(M).

If 'i' represents the rows of a matrix and 'j' represents the columns, the scalar<int>() ^ vectors<'i', 'j'>(N, M) (a shorthand for the above) structure represents the column-major layout, while for the row-major we simply swap the dimension names: scalar<int>() ^ vectors<'j', 'i'>(M, N).

Each Noarr structure has a **signature** that specifies the order of the dimensions in the structure. For the scalar<int>() ^ vectors<'i', 'j'>(N, M) structure, the associated signature can be represented as $j \to i \to Int$. The signature becomes important when iterating over the structure, as it defines the default traversal order—in the example, dimension 'j' would be associated with the outermost loop.

The signature can be reordered using the hoist proto-structure that shifts a dimension to the front (outermost) position. For example, hoist<'i'> applied to the above structure would change the signature (and the default traversal order) to $i \to j \to Int$. The proto-structures change the signatures according to simple rewrite rules. For example, into_blocks<'i', 'b'>(Ns) replaces the appearance of i in the signature with $b \to i$, resulting in the signature $j \to b \to i \to Int$ if applied to the original structure. Besides the traversal order, the signatures also ensure the type safety of the transformations.

Noarr bags are smart pointers pairing Noarr structures with data buffers. They simplify the use of structures in code where the layout-agnostic data structure is usually materialized in memory. A bag[idx<'i', 'j'>(i, j)] expression accesses the element with index (i, j) regardless of the actual memory layout. Bags are designed to support both owning and observing semantics.

Noarr traversers are objects representing a traversal order over an index space of a Noarr structure or multiple structures. When constructed, they follow a combination of the default traversal orders of the given structures (prioritizing from the left). Traversers can be transformed by applying *proto-structures* to change the intended traversal order (similar to the construction of Noarr structures). For example, hoist changes the iteration order of the dimensions, and span restricts the iteration space along a given dimension. To ensure semantic correctness, proto-structures that change the physical layout (such as vector that expands the memory layout) are not allowed for traversers; however, some of them have corresponding counterparts for traversers. For example, vector can be replaced with bcast that introduces a new dimension to the traversal (a new loop) without implying a change in the physical layout.

Given a set of Noarr bags and a Noarr traverser, the user can define a lambda function representing a computation and combine it with the traverser via the | operator, as demonstrated in Listing 1. The traverser applies the lambda function to each element of the (possibly transformed) iteration space represented by a **Noarr state** object containing the indices of a given point in the iteration space (such as idx<'i', 'j'>(i, j)) that can be used to access the corresponding elements of the Noarr bags.

```
// Allocate bags for the matrices with the given layouts:
auto C = bag(scalar<int>() ^ vector<'i'>(M) ^ vector<'j'>(N));
auto A = bag(scalar<int>() ^ vector<'i'>(M) ^ vector<'k'>(K));
auto B = bag(scalar<int>() ^ vector<'k'>(K) ^ vector<'j'>(N));

traverser(C) | [&](auto state) {  // C provides iterations space over (i,j)
  C[state] = 0;
  traverser(A, B) ^ fix(state) | [&](auto state) {  // iterating over k (i,j were fix-ed)
    C[state] += A[state] * B[state];  // [] applies relevant index sub-set of state
  };
};
```

Listing 1. Naïve matrix multiplication kernel in Noarr

Noarr also provides constructs to parallelize the traversal of selected dimension(s) based on existing parallel libraries like OpenMP (CPU) or CUDA (GPU).

2.1 Related Work

Various libraries and tools have been developed to make the use of MPI more convenient and less error-prone in the context of C++ programming. We briefly discuss the most relevant libraries in the context of implementing layout-agnostic MPI abstractions. Most of these works have additional (orthogonal) goals, such as handling errors in MPI communication, or abstracting the non-blocking primitives to C++ promises and futures.

As the oldest, still relevant work, the Boost.MPI [4] library provides a higher-level interface for C++ STL containers and user-defined types in MPI communication by (de)serializing the data. It introduces a form of layout agnosticism to MPI via a *skeleton* object, which describes the layout of a particular data structure. Although the skeleton approach is quite generic (covering even linked lists or trees), its creation still involves costly (de)serialization. Furthermore, after creating the skeleton, the user has to ensure that the data structure is unchanged and that it is not paired with an incompatible skeleton (reducing the type safety of the communication).

The MPP library [12] improves on Boost.MPI by avoiding (de)serialization. It uses `MPI_Type_create_struct` to define the layout of general data structures. It can also efficiently transform layouts of arbitrary C++ containers by analyzing their type traits (querying the starting memory address of the elements, their size, and the number of elements).

Another improvement over Boost.MPI was introduced by the MPL header-only library [2], which enables MPI communication of data structures by defining their *layout*, which can be built (semi)automatically for trivial C++ types and standard containers. The layouts map well to MPI datatypes; however, their construction for non-trivial layouts is cumbersome.

More recently, Demiralp et al. [3] presented a modern C++ library for MPI that uses compile-time reflection on C++ types to generate appropriate MPI datatypes automatically. It introduced useful features such as exception-based error handling; however, its container support is limited to array-like contiguous containers (e.g., `std::span` or `std::vector`).

The KaMPIng library [20] is the most recent major work that aims to introduce some layout agnosticism and type safety to MPI. It maps C++ types to MPI datatypes at compile time via type introspection using template metaprogramming. It supports standard C++ containers and general trivially copyable types (which can be copied as contiguous sequences of bytes on homogeneous systems without needing to analyze their layout). However, it does not support non-contiguous containers, significantly limiting its usability in layout-agnostic applications.

The experimental KokkosComm library [1] is a recent addition to the Kokkos ecosystem that extends the Kokkos library [19] to support MPI communication. It is also the work that is closest to our Noarr-MPI abstraction in its general goal. Since Kokkos aims to maximize performance and portability, it offers some layout agnosticism via the `Kokkos::View` abstraction. It stands out as the only related library that supports sending and receiving non-contiguous multidimensional data automatically without requiring any data preprocessing (such as serialization or data packing). The authors show that using the automatically generated MPI Datatypes in communication performs on par with hand-written datatypes. However, the KokkosComm library is still in its early stages and does not sufficiently support the necessary primitives to implement a fully layout-agnostic MPI abstraction—most notably, it does not fully support scatter and gather operations.

None of the existing MPI-abstracting libraries provide a layout-agnostic abstraction that could automatically handle MPI communication involving multiple data layouts with different compatible physical layouts (e.g., row-major and column-major matrices of the same size). This is a significant limitation for use cases that call for a different layout of the data structures on the sending and receiving sides, which may easily happen if the layouts on the two sides are tuned independently to achieve the best performance. Using the existing libraries, the user has to manually define fitting MPI datatypes, which is tedious and error-prone, or resort to data packing and unpacking, which introduces additional overhead and is not transparent to the MPI backend. The Noarr-MPI library aims to eliminate this limitation by providing a layout-agnostic abstraction for MPI communication that can automatically handle the definition of the MPI datatypes based on the Noarr structures and traversers.

3   Noarr and MPI Layout Mapping

For successful Noarr-MPI binding, we need to define a mapping from Noarr structures to MPI datatypes. This mapping is non-trivial due to philosophical differences between the two libraries. On the other hand, datatypes both in MPI and in Noarr are constructed hierarchically from simple base types, giving us a common ground for the mapping.

```
auto row = scalar<int>() ^ vector<'n'>(n);
auto matrix = row ^ vector<'m'>(m);

/* MPI: */  MPI_Type_contiguous(n, MPI_INT, &row);
            MPI_Type_contiguous(m, row, &matrix);
```

Listing 2. Constructing an integer matrix in MPI and Noarr

Listing 2 illustrates two semantically identical definitions of a matrix layout in both libraries, showcasing their superficial similarities. The derived datatypes are strictly made of copies or sequences (so `MPI_Type_contiguous` can be used). However, more complex data layouts (with tiling or slicing) will require more complex transformation.

```
auto matrix_tiled = matrix ^ into_blocks<'m', 'M'>(M) ^ into_blocks<'n', 'N'>(N);

/* MPI: */  MPI_Type_contiguous(N, MPI_INT, &tileRow);
            MPI_Type_contiguous(n / N, tileRow, &row);
            MPI_Type_contiguous(M, row, &slice);
            MPI_Type_contiguous(m / M, slice, &matrix);
```

Listing 3. Tiling the matrix structure

Listing 3 shows a tiled transformation of the `matrix` type from the previous example that constructs a layout with the same underlying physical data but logically tiled into blocks of size $M \times N$ where each block is indexed by 'M' and 'N' (in Noarr). The contiguous blocks are specified separately to match the logical structure of the data. If a different logical ordering of the elements is required, the user has to use functions such as `MPI_Type_create_hvector` and then carefully arrange the order of MPI calls and their arguments.

3.1 Type Transformation

Here, we present a general approach for transforming Noarr structures into MPI datatypes via the `mpi_transform` function. It is used internally by the Noarr-MPI bindings, but can also be used directly by the user to create an RAII datatype handle that automatically releases the MPI datatype when it goes out of scope.

```
auto matrix_tiled = matrix ^ into_blocks<'m', 'M'>(M) ^ into_blocks<'n', 'N'>(N);

auto datatype_handle = mpi_transform(matrix_tiled);
datatype_handle.commit();

MPI_Bcast(data, (MPI_Datatype)datatype_handle, root, comm);
```

The type transformation is defined recursively according to the dimension hierarchy encoded in the signature of the structure. For `matrix_tiled`, the signature is $M \to m \to N \to n \to \text{Int}$ (resulting from the signature $m \to n \to \text{Int}$ of `matrix`). Generally, a signature is a tree with the outermost dimension in the root and the resulting scalar types in leaves. For each dimension, the process first constructs the MPI types of the nested dimensions and then uses them to construct the MPI type of the current dimension.

The datatype construction at each given dimension is usually equivalent to a single MPI call. The resulting MPI datatype has to match the traversal over the Noarr structure along the given dimension; namely, each (type_i, displacement_i) pair in the resulting MPI datatype has to match the types and relative offsets of all sub-items i. Based on the types and displacements, an appropriate MPI call is selected:

1. If the structure is stored contiguously and all types are the same (e.g., in the case of Noarr `vector`), the `MPI_Type_contiguous` can be used to construct the MPI datatype. This is the case for `matrix_tiled` in Listing 3.
2. If the structure is not stored contiguously but still follows constant strides, `MPI_Type_create_hvector` can be used.
3. If the offset of the first element is non-zero or the strides are not constant, we can use `MPI_Type_create_hindexed` to specify offsets for individual items.
4. If the structure is not uniform along the given dimension (i.e., $\text{type}_i \neq \text{type}_{i'}$ for some $i \neq i'$), the `MPI_Type_create_struct` can be used to create irregular MPI structures.

Noarr `get_length` and `get_size` functions are designed to determine the index ranges and the extents of the sub-structures. Additional trait-like functions, such as `is_uniform_along`, `stride_along`, and `lower_bound_along`, can be used to select the appropriate MPI call.

Figure 2 showcases the construction from Listing 2 disregarding the contiguity of the structure to illustrate the parametrization of the MPI calls. The block counts can be determined using `get_length`, and the stride parameters can be computed using `stride_along`.

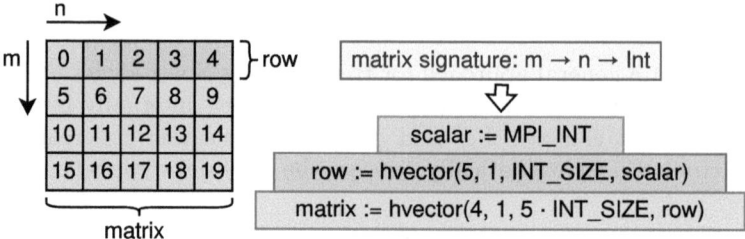

Fig. 2. Type transformation from Noarr structures to MPI datatypes

3.2 Layout-Agnostic Type Transformation

Our main objective is to enable the transfer of data structures with identical index spaces but different physical layouts. This will require data transformation during the transfer, which can be achieved seamlessly with the MPI communication primitives as long as the MPI datatypes are constructed properly.

To build on the matrix example, let us consider a broadcast operation where the source and destination structures are column-major and row-major matrices, respectively. Naïvely, we might construct a contiguous MPI datatype for each matrix, which would be efficient; however, it would also corrupt the data on transfer due to differing orderings of elements between the two structures, which is the case for frameworks like KokkosComm [1]. We need to ensure that the MPI datatypes are compatible and that they correctly represent the given data structures at the same time.

There are multiple ways to construct compatible MPI datatypes; perhaps the simplest one would be to reorder the signatures to a canonical form (e.g., lexicographically ordered dimensions). However, this can result in suboptimal transfers (the performance depends on how the layouts are described, not just on the layouts themselves), and it is impractical to affect efficiency by a mere choice of dimension names. To avoid this, a traverser can be provided to define the intended hierarchy of dimensions during the transformation via its signature. Since the traverser has the same index space as its Noarr structure parameters, we can construct it from the list of the structures involved in the communication to ensure correctness. Furthermore, the user may transform the traverser for the purpose of performance tuning (e.g., apply `noarr::hoist` to reorder the dimensions).

Constructing the MPI datatype for `matrix` according to the default traverser of the transposed matrix differs from the construction in Fig. 2 only in the dimension hierarchy (switching the order of `hvector` calls), which changes the order of the elements in the resulting MPI datatype. However, unlike in Listing 2, the `hvector` calls cannot be replaced with `contiguous`. The resulting MPI datatype is compatible with `MPI_Type_contiguous` over the memory space of the transposed matrix, enabling transfers between the two structures without data corruption.

4 MPI Interface Abstraction

Our MPI interface extends the Noarr traverser abstraction (for iterating over an index space) into an *MPI traverser* that combines a regular traverser with an MPI communicator, which enables a seamless extension of existing Noarr algorithms.

4.1 MPI Traverser

MPI traversers abstract iteration over an index space distributed over multiple ranks (MPI processes) in the same group (MPI communicator). They are inspired by Noarr CUDA traversers [7], which abstract work distribution over a CUDA thread grid (running on a GPU).

The construction of MPI traversers is shown in Listing 4. The constructor selects one dimension as the *ranking dimension* ('r'), and its index is bound to the MPI rank. The size of the ranking dimension must match the size of the communicator, and it is set automatically to this size if not specified explicitly. The resulting MPI traverser can be used as a regular Noarr traverser and in place of an MPI communicator in Noarr-MPI bindings (communication operations).

```
auto trav = traverser(matrix ^ into_blocks<'m', 'r', 's'>()); // naming the inner dim. 's'
auto MPITrav = mpi_traverser<'r'>(trav, MPI_COMM_WORLD);
auto slice = bag(scalar<float>() ^ vectors_like<'s', 'm'>(MPITrav)); // copy dims of MPITrav

if (mpi_get_comm_rank(MPITrav) == 0) {
  // Using `MPITrav` as a Noarr traverser (applying a lambda for execution)
  MPITrav | [&](auto state) { slice[state] = init(); };
}
// Using `MPITrav` as an MPI communicator for broadcast operation
broadcast(slice, MPITrav, 0);
```

Listing 4. Defining an MPI traverser over the dimension 'r'

In Listing 4, the matrix sized $m \times n$ is sliced along the 'm' dimension into r sub-matrices $s \times n$ where $s = m/r$ and r is determined automatically from the communicator size. The root node initializes the slice and then broadcasts it to all nodes in the communicator associated with the traverser.

4.2 Collective Communication

Simple type transformation from Noarr structures to MPI datatypes is sufficient for broadcasts and point-to-point communication that use the same logical layout for both the sending and the receiving processes. However, more complex operations like scatter and gather involve data structures with not only different physical layouts but also different logical layouts—the index space of one input structure being a subspace of the other input structure. The scatter and gather are representative collective operations for our transformations, and since they are symmetric, we discuss only the scatter operation in detail.

A naïve approach to scattering of general layouts would involve costly data (de)serialization; however, this can be avoided with the Noarr library and the type transformations described in Sect. 3.2, making the operation layout-agnostic thanks to constructing the MPI datatypes from the Noarr structures according to the logical ordering of elements dictated by the same traverser.

After constructing the MPI datatypes for the two input structures, the scatter operation uses the ranking dimension of the MPI traverser to determine the correct displacements of the sub-structures and scatters the data accordingly. Since the ranking dimension is bound to the MPI rank, it maps to the tiles of the source structure.

```
auto matrix = bag(matrix_tiled, buffer);

// We need to fix one block dimension (M=4) and associate r with blocking dimensions MxN
auto trav = traverser(matrix) ^ set_length<'M'>(4) ^ merge_blocks<'M', 'N', 'r'>();
auto MPITrav = mpi_traverser<'r'>(trav, MPI_COMM_WORLD);
// Specify the layout of the tile (with a matching index space)
auto tile = bag(scalar<float>() ^ vectors_like<'m', 'n'>(MPITrav));

if (mpi_get_comm_rank(MPITrav) == 0) {
  // Traverse `matrix` using the dimension lengths from `MPITrav`
  traverser(matrix) ^ set_length(MPITrav) | [&](auto state) { matrix[state] = init(); };
}
scatter(matrix, tile, MPITrav, 0);
MPITrav | [&](auto state) { modify(tile[state]); }; // Process the tile on each worker
```

Listing 5. Scatter operation using an MPI traverser

Listing 5 uses the tiled matrix from Listing 3 and scatters it across all processes where the tiles are processed by the `modify` function. The key aspect here is that we wish to divide the matrix into tiles so that each process handles one tile. However, dimensions 'M' and 'N' are both open, so we need to fix one of them to a specific value (in this case, 'M' is fixed to 4) so the remaining dimension can be set $N = r/M$ based on the number of processes (which is ensured by the `merge_blocks` association). The $M \times N$ grid of tiles is distributed so that MPI processes with ranks $0 \ldots N-1$ compute row of tiles with 'M' index 0, ranks $N \ldots 2N-1$ compute row where 'M' is 1, and so on. Currently, our implementation requires that M is selected as a divisor of r, and original matrix dimensions (m, n) must be divisible by M and N, respectively.

Perhaps the greatest benefit is that the layout of the tiles (`tile` structure) can be defined independently of the layout of the original matrix. The scatter operation performs the necessary transformation to convert the layouts, making the tile layouts and the computation performed on them independent of the original matrix layout. Thus, the layout-agnostic design can fully exploit the memory architecture and caches of the target node.

The proposed abstraction also ensures the type safety of the operation. The index space of the distributed structure has to be a subspace of the root structure index space, and the difference in the index spaces has to be covered by the dimension bound to the MPI communicator. This eliminates the possibility of a mismatch between the input structures and simplifies the API.

5 Evaluation

We evaluate the proposed Noarr-MPI library by comparing it with selected MPI abstractions in terms of the supported features, ease of use, and performance of the generated code. In the evaluation, we include the MPI libraries introduced in Sect. 2.1, which demonstrate at least some overlap with our main objectives (layout agnosticism and type safety): **MPI** (using standard MPI 4.0 interface) with C++ mdspans, **Boost.MPI** [4] with C++ mdspans, **MPP** [12], **MPL** [2], **KokkosComm** [1], and **KaMPIng** [20]. Our proposed solution is denoted **Noarr-MPI**.

For the approaches that support a sufficient level of layout agnosticism, we perform a case study of implementing a distributed general matrix multiplication (GEMM) kernel as defined in the Polybench/C benchmark suite [14], with each MPI process computing one sub-matrix of the output matrix by multiplying the corresponding sub-matrices of the input matrices. We discuss the necessary steps to implement the GEMM kernel in Sect. 5.2 and evaluate the performance of the implementations in Sect. 5.3.

5.1 Feature Comparison

The comparison of the individual libraries focuses mainly on the features related to the layout agnosticism.

Automatic transformations of layouts if the source and destination processes use a different layout datatype specification. This is a crucial feature for layout agnosticism as it allows for defining the layout of each data structure independently without specifying explicit data transformations.

Non-contiguous layouts—i.e., support for data structures that are not laid in one compact block of memory. This is especially essential for scatter and gather operations where many sub-structures will be non-contiguous.

Mdspan-like representation for the data structures involved in the communication. It allows the user to reason about layouts in terms of the logical order of the elements in the data structure while the library automatically handles the construction of the MPI datatypes.

Seamless libraries avoid unnecessary data packing or serialization when transferring the data structures. This is not a hard requisite, but it may improve efficiency.

Type safety of a library indicates that it should fail to compile the code if the source and destination data structures have incompatible index spaces.

Scatter/gather operations of multi-dimensional data structures are a crucial feature for layout agnosticism. Without this feature, the user has to specify a linearized view of the data, which intricately depends on the data layout and introduces unnecessary complexity and potential errors.

Table 1 summarizes the features of the evaluated libraries. The ✶ mark for the MPI support of auto-transformations denotes that these transformations are technically possible, but they require significant additional effort. The datatypes must be constructed imperatively, not automatically inferred, like in Noarr-MPI.

Table 1. Comparison of the MPI abstractions

	Noarr-MPI	native MPI	Boost.MPI	MPP	MPL	Kokkos	KaMPIng
Auto-transforms	✓	∗	✗	✗	✗	✗	✗
Non-contiguous	✓	✓	✓	✓	✓	✓	✗
Mdspan-like	✓	✗	✗	✗	✗	✓	✗
Seamless	✓	✓	✗	✓	✓	✓	✓
Type-safety	✓	✗	✓	✓	✓	✓	✓
Scatter/gather	✓	✓	✗	✗	✓	✗	✗

5.2 Programming Effort Discussion

Since conducting a comprehensive user study is beyond the scope of this paper, we provide a discussion of the necessary programming effort to implement the GEMM kernel using the libraries that support a sufficient level of layout agnosticism as described in Sect. 5.1 (supporting more than half of the discussed features). Using text-based or syntax-based metrics for this comparison would be misleading as the libraries differ significantly in their approach, and any practical layout-agnostic use of the libraries would be accompanied by support abstractions that would significantly reduce the amount of necessary boilerplate code. Instead, we focus on the necessary steps and required information that the user has to provide to implement the GEMM kernel using the evaluated libraries, disregarding the specific syntax or verbosity that could be hidden behind a shorthand abstraction.

An ideal tunable and generalizable implementation of the kernel would require only the *definition of the data layout* of each matrix and its privatized tile on a given worker process, the *scattering strategy*, the implementation of *the computation*, and some specification of *data dependencies* (in all the evaluated libraries, this is done via explicit calls representing MPI communication). For each of these general steps, we discuss the specific sub-steps that are needed to implement the GEMM kernel using the evaluated libraries.

Data Layout Definition. When using the Boost. MPI library or the standard MPI interface, we have used the `mdspan` abstraction designed by the Kokkos group and adopted in the C++23 standard [18] to define the data layout of each matrix and its privatized tiles. Using mdspans is sufficiently expressive and convenient for layout agnosticism. They are compatible with the libraries and do not introduce any unnecessary overhead. For the KokkosComm library, we use Kokkos views, which are very similar to the `mdspan` abstraction and the Kokkos library uses them natively.

Both of these approaches require the user to define the index ranges of each sub-matrix tile separately (and match them correctly), which creates an unnecessary source of potential errors. Noarr structures in the Noarr-MPI approach allow us to specify the index ranges collectively for all tiles. Additionally, the library can automatically deduce the ranges of the tiles (e.g., based on the number of MPI processes).

Scattering Strategy. Each library has its own way of defining how to scatter and gather the data. The Noarr-MPI library infers the correct MPI datatypes from the input and output data structures (Sect. 3.2). The inferred datatypes can be further tuned (for optimizing transformations) by reordering the logical order (hierarchy) of the dimensions of the given traverser (Sect. 4.1). Noarr-MPI also enables the user to easily specify the mapping of the tiles to the worker threads.

In the approach that uses just the standard MPI interface, we build the MPI datatypes by iteratively using the `MPI_Type_create_hvector` function with the extent and the stride of each dimension of the given mdspan from the rightmost to the leftmost (we have experimentally verified that this is the most efficient order for this use case; the supporting experiments follow the methodology described in Sect. 5.3 and are included in the replication package). This generalizes well to an arbitrary number of dimensions; however, this approach may be suboptimal for other use cases.

The KokkosComm library internally uses the same approach; however, its API does not support scattering and gathering. They offer non-blocking receive and send operations that can be used to emulate the scatter and gather operations with very little overhead but at much higher programming effort. Since the library does not consider layout agnosticism, its receive and send interface is unusable for our purposes (it works inconsistently for contiguous and non-contiguous data layouts). However, the library does publicly expose the necessary building blocks for layout-agnostic send and receive operations.

The Boost.MPI library does not support the scatter and gather operations natively for this use case, so we have opted to try two different approaches: the first one is to define wrappers that specify how the items of a mdspan should be serialized and deserialized via a simple iteration in the logical order of the elements and scatter this serialized data. The other approach is to use input and output archives in non-blocking send and receive operations; however, the second approach performed consistently worse, so it is not included in the evaluation. Using skeletons in the Boost.MPI is too cumbersome for this use case and is not included in the evaluation.

Computation Kernel Implementation. The computation kernel is implemented similarly across all libraries and is rather straightforward (almost verbatim copy of the GEMM loop nest from the PolyBench/C benchmark).

The only outlier is the Noarr-MPI library, which uses Noarr traversers. As analyzed in our previous work [7], the traverser abstraction significantly reduces the amount of explicit indexation, which can prevent potential errors and makes the code more flexible for possible tuning. In this aspect, the Noarr library is similar to `std::ranges` in C++20, which also allows for a more declarative design of algorithms. Even with a slight syntactical difference between the Noarr traversers and an explicit loop nest, all libraries follow the same conceptual pattern of the computation kernel and specifying it via a loop nest can be directly 1-to-1 mapped to Noarr traversers.

5.3 Performance Evaluation

In the performance evaluation, we measure only the code that would be executed repeatedly in a real-world application (i.e., the `scatter`, `compute`, and `gather` operations). We do not include the initialization of the MPI environment, allocation of the buffers, data validation, or cleanup operations. To ensure a fair comparison, all implementations allocate the data the same way, and all libraries use views with non-owning semantics and without any additional data movements except those necessary for scattering and gathering the data. Most importantly, all implementations perform the exactly same computation in the same order and on the same data layouts. We have also ensured that all implementations follow the same data distribution strategy (i.e., send/receive the same data on each given process). The details and all measured data can be found in our replication package[2].

The evaluation was performed on a Slurm-managed cluster with 8 nodes interconnected via InfiniBand FDR (56 Gb/s), each with two sockets equipped with Intel Xeon Gold 6130 processors, each comprising 2×16 hyper-threads. All GEMM implementations were compiled with GCC 14.2 and Open MPI 5.0.6 using the `Release` configuration as defined by CMake 3.27. The evaluation used the various datasets from the Polybench/C benchmark, which were modified to be divisible by the number of MPI processes; however, we visualize only the two opposite ends of the spectrum, MINI and EXTRALARGE (all dataset results are available in the replication package), which show interesting performance trends. For the MINI dataset, all dimensions are 64, and for the EXTRALARGE dataset, the dimensions are $n_i = 2048, n_j = 2560, n_k = 1408$. The performance is measured in seconds by a wall clock, and each visualized result is the average and standard deviation of 100 runs of the distributed GEMM kernel.

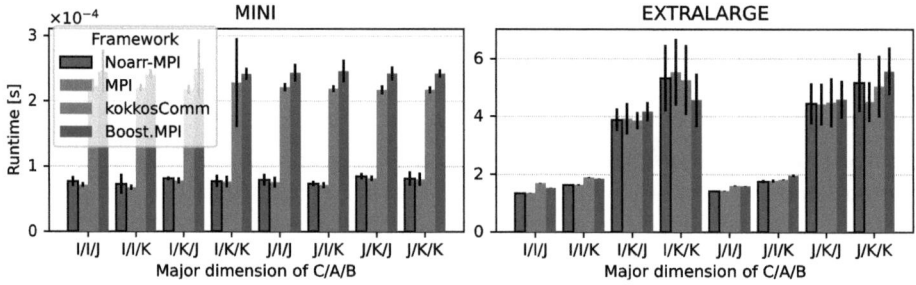

Fig. 3. Performance evaluation of the evaluated libraries (columns show mean runtime in seconds, error bars show standard deviation)

---

[2] The replication package is available at https://github.com/jiriklepl/noarr-mpi.

Figure 3 shows the results of the performance evaluation. The individual configurations (labeled on the x-axis) represent the major dimensions of the privatized tiles used in GEMM for the C, A, and B matrices written as `C/A/B` (using dimension names from Listing 1). For example, the I/I/J configuration denotes that the C and A matrix tiles are laid out in a row-major order and the B matrix tiles in a column-major order (C tiles are $I \times J$ matrices, A tiles are $I \times K$, and B tiles are $K \times J$). All implementations passed the validation checks.

The measurements performed on the MINI dataset show that the Noarr-MPI library performs on par with the standard MPI interface for C++, while the other approaches are significantly slower. The overheads on this dataset are dominated by the non-computational parts of the code (i.e., communication latency, datatype construction, and data movements during scattering). The SMALL and MEDIUM datasets show a similar trend as the MINI dataset, but the differences between the libraries are less pronounced.

In the case of the EXTRALARGE dataset, computational time significantly dominates the communication overhead. The less efficient configurations show a significant variation in performance due to inefficient memory accesses. For most configurations, the Noarr-MPI library performs on par or slightly better than the other libraries. The only significant outliers that show a performance drop when using the Noarr-MPI library are the I/K/K and J/K/K configurations, where the serialization strategy of the Boost.MPI implementation outperforms the other libraries, which defer the layout transformation to the MPI backend. However, for all four most efficient configurations, the Noarr-MPI library performs the best. The LARGE dataset shows a similar trend, but Noarr-MPI (and other libraries) do not experience the performance drop on the four less efficient configurations.

The comparison shows that the proposed Noarr-MPI library can achieve performance comparable to the state-of-the-art MPI C++ bindings while allowing for a more flexible design of distributed applications and thus improving the performance without expending the programming effort necessary to move the data correctly. Except for a few outliers, its performance is equivalent to hand-written MPI code using the C++ mdspan abstraction for computation.

6 Conclusion

Noarr-MPI is a novel C++ abstraction for MPI that introduces a layout-agnostic design to distributed computing. It builds on top of the Noarr library and closely follows its paradigms. We have used the abstraction to implement an MPI version of the GEMM kernel to demonstrate its applicability and performance compared to the state-of-the-art MPI C++ bindings and a hand-written implementation using the standard MPI interface. Our evaluation shows that the proposed abstraction achieves performance comparable to the state-of-the-art MPI C++ bindings while allowing for a more flexible design of distributed applications. Furthermore, it enables programmers to design distributed applications without expending effort on data layout transformations or complicated MPI datatype definitions. The abstraction is also compatible with Noarr traversers, allowing for seamless cooperation with CUDA and OpenMP traversers.

Acknowledgments. This paper was supported by the Johannes Amos Comenius Programme (P JAC, Natural and anthropogenic georisks) project CZ.02.01.01/00/22_008/0004605, by Charles University institutional funding SVV (grant 260821), and Charles University Grant Agency (grant 269723).

Disclosure of Interests. The authors have no competing interests to declare that are relevant to the content of this article.

References

1. Avans, C.N., Ciesko, J., Pearson, C., Suggs, E.D., Olivier, S.L., Skjellum, A.: Performance insights into supporting kokkos views in the kokkoscomm mpi library. In: 2024 IEEE International Conference on Cluster Computing Workshops (CLUSTER Workshops), pp. 186–187. IEEE (2024)
2. Bauke, H.: MPL - A message passing library (2014-2015). https://github.com/rabauke/mpl
3. Demiralp, A.C., Martin, P., Sakic, N., Krüger, M., Gerrits, T.: A C++ 20 interface for MPI 4.0. arXiv preprint arXiv:2306.11840 (2023)
4. Gregor, D., Troyer, M.: Boost. mpi. MPI, November (2006)
5. Grosser, T., Groesslinger, A., Lengauer, C.: Polly: performing polyhedral optimizations on a low-level intermediate representation. Parallel Processing Letters, p. 1250010 (2012)
6. ISO/IEC JTC1/SC22/WG21: working draft, standard for programming language c++. Tech. Rep. N4950 (2023). https://open-std.org/jtc1/sc22/wg21/docs/papers/2023/n4950.pdf, revises: N4944
7. Klepl, J., Šmelko, A., Rozsypal, L., Kruliš, M.: Abstractions for C++ code optimizations in parallel high-performance applications. Parallel Comput. p. 103096 (2024)
8. Message passing interface forum: MPI: a message-passing interface standard version 4.1 (2023). https://www.mpi-forum.org/docs/mpi-4.1/mpi41-report.pdf
9. MPICH Team: MPICH v4.3.0 Manpages (2025). https://www.mpich.org/static/docs/v4.3.0/
10. Namjoshi, K.S., Singhania, N.: Loopy: programmable and formally verified loop transformations. In: International Static Analysis Symposium, pp. 383–402. Springer (2016)
11. NVIDIA: CuTe layout documentation (2025). https://github.com/NVIDIA/cutlass/blob/main/media/docs/cpp/cute/01_layout.md, documentation on CuTe layout from the NVIDIA CUTLASS repository
12. Pellegrini, S., Prodan, R., Fahringer, T.: A lightweight C++ interface to MPI. In: 2012 20th Euromicro International Conference on Parallel, Distributed and Network-based Processing, pp. 3–10. IEEE (2012)
13. Pop, S., Cohen, A., Bastoul, C., Girbal, S., Silber, G.A., Vasilache, N.: GRAPHITE: Polyhedral analyses and optimizations for GCC. In: proceedings of the 2006 GCC developers summit, pp. 90–91. Citeseer (2006)
14. Pouchet, L.N., Yuki, T.: PolyBench/C 4.2.1 (2016). https://sourceforge.net/projects/polybench
15. Ragan-Kelley, J., Adams, A., Paris, S., Levoy, M., Amarasinghe, S., Durand, F.: Decoupling algorithms from schedules for easy optimization of image processing pipelines. ACM Trans. Graph. (TOG), pp. 1–12 (2012)

16. Šmelko, A., Kruliš, M., Kratochvíl, M., Klepl, J., Mayer, J., Šimůnek, P.: Astute approach to handling memory layouts of regular data structures. In: Algorithms and Architectures for Parallel Processing: 22nd International Conference, ICA3PP 2022, Copenhagen, Denmark, October 10–12, 2022, Proceedings, pp. 507–528. Springer (2023)
17. The open MPI community: open MPI v5.0.x — Open MPI 5.0.x documentation (2025). https://docs.open-mpi.org/en/v5.0.x/
18. Trott, C., et al.: MDSPAN. Tech. Rep. P0009r18, WG21 (2022). https://www.open-std.org/jtc1/sc22/wg21/docs/papers/2022/p0009r18.html
19. Trott, C.R., et al.: Kokkos 3: programming model extensions for the exascale era. IEEE Trans. Parallel Distrib. Syst. pp. 805–817 (2021)
20. Uhl, T.N., et al.: KaMPIng: flexible and (Near) Zero-Overhead C++ Bindings for MPI. In: SC24: International Conference for High Performance Computing, Networking, Storage and Analysis, pp. 1–21. IEEE (2024)

Verifying MPI API Usage Requirements with Contracts

Yussur Mustafa Oraji[1]($\boxtimes$), Simon Schwitanski[2], Alexander Hück[1], Joachim Jenke[2], Sebastian Kreutzer[1], and Christian Bischof[1]

[1] Scientific Computing, TU Darmstadt University, Darmstadt, Germany
yussur.oraji@tu-darmstadt.de
[2] High Performance Computing, RWTH Aachen University, Aachen, Germany

Abstract. Parallel programming models such as MPI and OpenSHMEM enable the use of large-scale distributed-memory computers in HPC. However, programmers often miss subtle rules regarding their APIs, such as properly synchronizing local memory accesses with communication and releasing acquired resources. Existing correctness tools aim to detect these issues automatically, but are typically model-specific. We propose the use of model-independent function annotations to avoid this dependency:Contracts allow the specification of generic pre- and postconditions at function declarations. We specify requirements that must be satisfied at each call site to avoid common MPI errors such as resource leaks and local data races. In contrast to traditional checkers, the transparent nature of contracts also allows for maintainability and extensibility of checks by the end user, as well as adapting the specific analyses to their use case. This paper presents a contract language and CoVer, an extensible static verifier to check the use of library-based parallel programming models. It applies data-flow analysis using the LLVM framework to verify these contract annotations. We compare detection accuracy against the static tools PARCOACH and MPI-Checker using RMARaceBench and MPI-BugBench, and compile-time overhead based on the mini-apps LULESH, miniVite, and the PRK Stencil Kernel. CoVer improved the detection accuracy by covering a wide variety of issues, while maintaining comparable overhead.

Keywords: MPI · Correctness · HPC · Parallel · Tools

1 Introduction

The prevalence of distributed-memory computers in HPC necessitates a wide variety of parallel programming models (PPMs). Most commonly used is the Message Passing Interface (MPI) [14], though others such as OpenSHMEM [16] and GASPI [6] exist and are actively used.

These models often share common requirements when interacting with their APIs. For example, MPI requires the library to be initialized before communication and finalized before the program terminates, the buffer of a non-blocking

```
1  MPI_Datatype type;
2  MPI_Type_contiguous(..., &type);
3  MPI_Type_commit(&type);
4  ... // Work
5  // Resource leak! (MPI data type not freed)
6  MPI_Finalize();
```

(a) Example of a resource leak.

```
1  int MPI_Type_commit(...)
2  CONTRACT(
3      POST { call!(MPI_Type_free) });
4
5  int shmem_ctx_create(...)
6  CONTRACT(
7      POST { call!(shmem_ctx_destroy) });
```

(b) Contracts forbidding resource leaks.

Fig. 1. Code containing an error, and a contract which prohibits that behavior

call may not be written to before the call completes, and acquired resources such as data types must be freed explicitly. Figure 1a is one example of a resource leak, caused by the custom MPI data type not being freed using MPI_Type_free. These issues are often not checked by the MPI library used, as they may be too expensive to check, or corrupt the state of the library [14, p. 26]

While tools such as MUST [8], PARCOACH [19] and MPI-Checker [5] perform error detection on these models, they do not exploit these similarities. Exceptions are RMASanitizer [23] and the SPMD IR [3], which provide this abstraction. However, support for the specific PPM must still be built into the respective tool, and extending them requires modification of the tool itself. This is because the API functions and requirements are hard-coded into each tool.

Using contracts, we may elevate these API-dependent definitions to API function declarations. Contracts allow imposing requirements, most often preconditions and postconditions, on the use of API functions. For example, both Kotlin [11] and C++ [1] do or will support contracts.

Consider the simple case of a resource leak: Traditionally, the information that a MPI_Type_free must occur after creating a data type, and any other requirement, is hard-coded into any tool checking for resource leaks. Alternatively, we may annotate these API calls with a contract, such as in Fig. 1b. This is sufficient to perform analysis, as now each function explicitly states the requirement. The required resource destruction call MPI_Type_free is mentioned in the contract. Multiple PPMs share a lot of these API requirements, and they can often be encoded in the same manner: The second contract analogously enforces that OpenSHMEM contexts do not leak.

Thus, contracts allow programmers to specify their own verification logic, which is transferrable to other PPMs, as well as niche code which otherwise would require fully custom tooling for verification. Contracts are additionally easier to maintain and understand than standard correctness checkers. They document the requirements of the API used in the code directly, while modification is easy should the API change in the future. This is in contrast to the current correctness checkers which, while reporting errors and debugging information, do not contain the actual analysis principles, which are a black box to the user, let alone permit modification thereof.

```
1  int value = 42;
2  if (rank == 0) {
3      value = 1;
4      MPI_Get(&value, ..., win);
5      printf("Value is: %d", value);
6  }
```

```
1  MPI_Win_fence(win);
2  MPI_Win_lock_all(win);
3  MPI_Get(&buf, ..., win);
4  // Follow-up error
5  MPI_Win_unlock_all(win);
6  MPI_Win_fence(win);
```

(a) Example of a local data race: Printed value undefined.

(b) Example of an RMA error: Mixed Synchronization paradigms

Fig. 2. Examples of common errors when utilizing MPI.

This paper presents CoVer, an extensible contract framework for PPMs. We define a contract language capable of covering a wide variety of different error classes. Contracts can be added to an API in the form of source-code annotations that express API usage requirements. Our tool scans the code for these contracts, and attempts to verify their fulfillment using efficient data-flow analysis. The analysis supports interprocedural contexts, including across translation units. Should these contracts be violated, an API usage error is detected and reported to the user. Our tool ships with premade contracts for common error classes, such as those described in Sect. 2, and extending it for both more PPMs and API functions is easy by simply adding more contract annotations. Thus, CoVer is fully independent of the programming model used. We present the following contributions:

– We present a generic contract language for use with PPMs.
– We implement suitable verification algorithms using data-flow analysis.
– We compare and evaluate our tool with others on both the detection accuracy and the compile-time overhead induced on MPI programs.

2 Error Classes

Due to the complexity of PPMs, a number of different error classes exist. This section presents a classification of errors that can be detected with static analysis, and our tool implementation supports. In our examples, we will be focusing on MPI as it is the most widely used.

Missing Initialization or Finalization. The simplest error class is not performing the required initialization or finalization of a programming model. As stated in the MPI Standard [14, p. 309] when using the world model, the use of an initialization function is required, a similar requirement exists for finalization. Similarly, for the session model, initialization using `MPI_Session_init` is required to create a valid communicator.

Local Data Race. A local data race occurs when a non-blocking communication and a local memory access, of which one is a writing access, target the same memory location without proper synchronization, as specified for MPI P2P communication in [14, p. 78], though it holds analogously for non-blocking collective and RMA communication. The value at that memory location then becomes nondeterministic depending on the scheduling of the MPI call. An example of this is given in Fig. 2a, where a non-blocking and writing `MPI_Get` is followed by a reading local memory access to the same variable without synchronization.

Handle Lifecycle. MPI defines resource handles such as data types, communicators, requests and more, which represent some allocated resource. A handle lifecycle error occurs when a resource is not freed (resource leak), when it is not initialized, or handled improperly: For example, even after initializing an MPI data type using a type constructor, it must be committed with `MPI_Type_commit` before being used. Figure 1a provides an example of a resource leak, a subtype of handle lifecycle issues, where an MPI data type is not destroyed after the program is finished using it.

Common Remote Memory Access Errors. When utilizing the Remote Memory Access (RMA) subset of MPI, additional restrictions must be followed. Before performing communication to a remote memory location, a corresponding MPI window [14, p. 548] must be created. Additionally, communication is only possible within an *epoch*, which must be started explicitly using an RMA synchronization call. There are multiple methods to do so, such as a locking mechanism, fences, and Post-Start-Complete-Wait. Notably, MPI does not allow mixing these synchronization methods, as done in the erroneous code in Fig. 2b.

3 Detection Methods

The error classes introduced are caused by violations of a corresponding requirement. This section introduces the contract language, which encodes these requirements, and then describes the specific data-flow analyses used.

3.1 Contract Language

Instances of the introduced error classes are caused by one of two possible scenarios:

1. A required call was not performed before or after another one
2. Some operation, forbidden until another call, was performed

For example, a call to `MPI_Type_free` *should occur after* the type was used in Fig. 1a. In the code containing a data race in Fig. 2a, after the `MPI_Get` a reading (or writing) memory access *should not occur until* the call is explicitly completed using another API call.

These criteria can be reworded into requirements which must hold before or after any function call of an API function f:

```
1  int MPI_Get(void* buf, ...) CONTRACT(
2  POST {
3    no! (write!(*0))
4    until! (call!(MPI_Win_fence,1:7))
5
6
7  });
8  int MPI_Win_fence(...);
9  int MPI_Win_unlock_all(...);
```

```
1  int MPI_Get(void* buf, ...) CONTRACT(
2  POST {
3    no! (write!(*0))
4    until! (call!(MPI_Win_fence)),
5    no! (read!(*0))
6    until! (call!(MPI_Win_fence))
7  });
8  int MPI_Win_fence(...);
9  int MPI_Win_unlock_all(...);
```

(a) Forbid local writes before fence completion.

(b) Forbid any buffer access before fence completion.

```
1  int MPI_Get(void* buf, ...) CONTRACT(
2  POST {
3    no! (write!(*0))
4    until! (call_tag!(rma_complete,$:7)),
5    no! (read!(*0))
6    until! (call_tag!(rma_complete,$:7))
7  });
8  int MPI_Win_fence(...) CONTRACT( TAGS rma_complete(1) );
9  int MPI_Win_unlock_all(...) CONTRACT( TAGS rma_complete(0) );
```

(c) Forbid any buffer access before any completion.

Fig. 3. Evolution of a contract forbidding local data races, changes bolded.

- Before (PRE):
  • PreCall(g): A call to g must occur before encountering f.
- After (POST):
  • PostCall(g): A call to g must occur after encountering f.
  • Release(g, op): When f is called, the operation op must not occur until g is called.

Thus, the requirement violated in Fig. 2a can be (roughly, without parameter info) described as Release(MPI_Win_fence, *read*), attached to the MPI_Get call. Additionally, op may also be a function call, for example to forbid communication calls until a type is committed.

Using these requirements, we can define our contract language. Any API function declaration may have a contract attached; we call the function that contains a contract definition the *contract supplier* of that definition. The contract may specify preconditions and postconditions describing requirements that must hold before or after any call of the contract supplier. These are described by the PRE and POST *scopes*. A scope contains *operations*, which, together with the scope, specify the requirement. Both PreCall and PostCall are represented by a function call operation, and they are differentiated by the scope in which the operation is used. For example, the contract in Fig. 1b describes a function call operation in the POST scope, which indicates the PostCall requirement.

Figure 3a is an example contract utilizing the release requirement, specifying a local memory write as the forbidden operation. The information in the parentheses around the write operation denote which memory location may not be written to; this is given as the parameter index of the contract supplier, which here is MPI_Get, as well as possible points-to relations using "&" and "*" in the conventional manner. However, these symbols only indicate a points-to relation in the memory, and not the literal operators as known from the C language. Thus, points-to relations can be described even for languages without these operators such as Fortran. For MPI_Get, this is the reception buffer, which is the first parameter. Thus, the index "0" is used in the write operation. The parameter contains a pointer to the actual memory location, which is why it is dereferenced with "*". Similarly, the call operation to MPI_Win_fence contains a variable mapping from the eighth parameter of the MPI_Get to the second of the fence call. These contain the window handles, which must match to ensure completion. Utilizing these indices instead of parameter names is required as the LLVM IR does not preserve parameter names, and thus our analyses cannot access them.

In the case of MPI_Get, the current contract is not sufficient. Currently, only writing operations are forbidden, though reading operations will also lead to a data race. To alleviate this, we allow the specification of formulae within a scope, provided as both conjunctions and disjunctions, i.e. requiring at least one or all to be satisfied. Additionally, they can be provided as an exclusive-or relation. This is required to detect mixed synchronization as shown in Fig. 2b.

The modified contract is given in Fig. 3b. It specifies two release requirements in conjunction, effectively requiring both to be fulfilled. However, using this definition, only an MPI_Win_fence is considered to complete the call. While all the other completion mechanisms may be added using disjunctions, the resulting contract would become very hard to read: This many disjunctions would bloat the size of the contract. As these are meant to be user serviceable, we instead implemented a tagging system. Using an additional TAGS scope, function properties can be added to API calls. These can then be referenced using a new CallTag operation, which can be used analogously to the Call operation.

The contract given in Fig. 3c utilizes this mechanism to support both fence and lock-all completion. As MPI_Win_fence and MPI_Win_unlock_all contain the window handle at different locations, we specify the parameter in the tag definition. Then, the contract can reference these using the marker "$".

To summarize, a contract is split into three scopes: The precondition, the postcondition, and the tags. The precondition may contain Call(Tag) operations, the postcondition both Call(Tag) and Release. These operations can be specified in formulae for more complex conditions.

3.2 Formal Data-Flow Analysis

Our analyses are built on the generic data-flow analysis framework presented by Nielson, Nielson, and Hankin [15]. The definitions introduced here will then be used to define the analyses in Sect. 3.3.

An analysis consists of its *transfer functions* and *analysis domain*. The transfer functions, given an input from the analysis domain and a code location, return an output from the analysis domain. These are used at each location in the code, where the transfer functions take as input the result of the predecessor transfer function. When no predecessor exists, i.e. the location is the initial location, it instead receives a designated *initial analysis value*.

To ensure correctness, we enforce restrictions on the possible definitions of the analysis domain; it must be a complete lattice satisfying the ascending chain condition.

Definition 1. *A complete lattice is a set* S *and ordering* $\sqsubseteq$ *where each subset* s *has a least upper bound* $\bigsqcup s$ *such that for any other upper bound* d *of* s: $\bigsqcup s \sqsubseteq d$.

Definition 2. *A chain is a set* $C = \{d_i \mid i \in \mathbb{N}, d_i \in S\}$ *where* $d_i \sqsubseteq d_{i+1}$ *and* S *is a complete lattice.* S *satisfies the ascending chain condition if for any chain as defined above,* C *is finite.*

This definition induces a special value: $\bigsqcup \emptyset$ is the unique least element in the set. Finally, we enforce monotonicity for the transfer functions.

The transfer functions are called on each code location with the information of the predecessor location of the last iteration. Should this be the first iteration, all but the initial location (which instead receives the initial analysis value) start with the least element $\bigsqcup S$. However, as the analysis information at one code location depends solely on the information of the predecessor (or the constant initial analysis value), if it does not change, there is no need to run the transfer function at that point again.

Instead, we keep a worklist: Initially, the worklist contains pairs with the initial code location and each successor. The transfer functions are applied for these pairs, and the least upper bound of old and new information is saved. Should the value at a location change, all pairs of that location and successor are added to the worklist. When the worklist is empty, the algorithm terminates.

This may cause locations to not be visited even if they are reachable. To avoid this, we extend the analysis domain by a unique new least element $\bot$ to indicate a location has not been visited. The transfer functions will never write back $\bot$, as it is not part of the original domain. This ensures that locations that are encountered during the worklist iteration are processed at least once.

Using these definitions, we make sure that in each iteration a code location may only save greater information (w.r.t $\sqsubseteq$), which makes the results in each iteration a chain. Therefore, due to the ascending chain condition, there may only be a finite number of iterations, ensuring termination. Once the last iteration is reached, the information does not change and therefore constitutes a fixed point, which is the end result of the analysis.

3.3 Verification Algorithms

To verify the contracts, we implement one analysis for each requirement (`PreCall`, `PostCall`, `Release`). Then, the formulae are resolved in a post-processing step, which is described in detail in Sect. 4.

```
1  MPI_Init(...);
2  ... // Work
3  if (...) ... // No finalize!
4  else MPI_Finalize();
5  exit(0);
```

Iter.	Worklist	Line 1	Line 2	Line 3	Line 4	Line 5
0	(1,2)	NCALL	⊥	⊥	⊥	⊥
1	(2,3), (2,4)	NCALL	NCALL	⊥	⊥	⊥
2	(3,5), (2,4)	NCALL	NCALL	NCALL	⊥	⊥
3	(2,4)	NCALL	NCALL	NCALL	⊥	NCALL
4	(4,5)	NCALL	NCALL	NCALL	CALL	NCALL
5	∅	NCALL	NCALL	NCALL	CALL	NCALL

(a) Example code where one branch does not call MPI_Finalize.

(b) Results of worklist iteration on code from Figure 4a.

Fig. 4. Verifying finalization using PostCall on code utilizing branching.

PostCall Analysis. To verify this requirement, an analysis needs to check whether a given target function (the function specified in the contract) is guaranteed to occur after any call site of the contract supplier. Thus, the analysis runs once for each call site, where the call site is the initial location. A simple analysis domain would therefore be the following:

Definition 3. *The* PostCall *analysis domain is defined as the set* PostCallD = {CALL, NCALL}, *where* CALL ⊑ NCALL *representing the target function being called and not called, respectively.*

As the state at the beginning of the analysis is unknown, the initial analysis value is defined as NCALL, and is written to the contract supplier call site at the beginning of the analysis. When iterating over the code, the only relevant instructions are those calling the target function. This leads to the following definition of the transfer functions:

Definition 4. *Let* d ∈ PostCallD, loc *a code location,* g *the target function. The* PostCall *transfer functions are defined as:*

- postcall$_{loc}$(d) = d *(Identity) if* loc *is not a call to* g.
- *Otherwise,* postcall$_{loc}$(d) = CALL.

Figure 4a is an example of missing finalization. However, the error is only present in one branch in the code. If the condition is never fulfilled, the code does not contain an error, otherwise it does.

The results of applying the worklist algorithm can be seen in Fig. 4. The analysis is initialized with the initial analysis information for the call site (line 1), and the unique least element ⊥ everywhere else. In each iteration applying the transformation function, the NCALL information from the initial location propagates further except for line 4, which does call the target function. In the last iteration, the result for line 5 is NCALL even though applying the transfer function with predecessor information CALL returns CALL. This is because the least upper bound ⊔{CALL, NCALL} is NCALL. Thus, the algorithm makes sure that if one branch fails verification, this information takes precedence over successful verification.

For the PostCall requirement, the end result is determined by whether at some point after each call site, the target function is guaranteed to be called.

```
1   ...
2   if (...) MPI_Win_create(..., &win)
3   else MPI_Win_create(..., win2)
4   MPI_Put(..., win);
```

(a) Example code where one branch performs window creation on an unrelated window.

Iter.	Worklist	Line 1	Line 2	Line 3	Line 4
0	(1,2), (1,3)	NCALL	⊥	⊥	⊥
1	(2,4), (1,3)	NCALL	PCHK({2})	⊥	⊥
2	(1,3)	NCALL	PCHK({2})	⊥	CALL
3	(3,4)	NCALL	PCHK({2})	PCHK({3})	CALL
4	∅	NCALL	PCHK({2})	PCHK({3})	ERR

(b) Results of worklist iteration on code from Figure 5a.

Fig. 5. Example of PreCall analysis with contract PRE {call!(MPI_Win_create,5:&7)} attached to MPI_Put

This is not the case here, as the information at the end of the code is NCALL. Thus, the analysis reports a violation.

PreCall Analysis. The PreCall analysis cannot start at the contract supplier: The relevant code is that *prior* to each call site. Instead, it starts at the program entry point. This presents another issue: When encountering the target function, the values of the parameters of the contract supplier are not yet known.

We mitigate this by saving the possible target functions (candidates) in additional analysis information representing *parameter check* (PCHK):

Definition 5. *The* PreCall *analysis domain is defined as the set* PreCallD = {CALL, PCHK(L), NCALL, ERR}, *where* ⊑ *is the order in the set definition and* L *is a set of code locations. The initial analysis value is* NCALL. *When comparing two instances of* PCHK, ⊑ *is equivalent to the reverse subset inclusion of the contained sets.*

Instead of setting the analysis information to CALL when encountering the target function as done in PostCall, it is instead set to PCHK if it was not already, and if it was the contained set L is expanded with the location of the new candidate. Then, once the contract supplier is found, and the current analysis information is PCHK, the analysis checks if the parameters specified in the contract match the parameters of any call site in L. Should that be the case, the analysis returns CALL. Otherwise, when no candidate locations exist or parameters do not match for any candidate, it returns ERR.

Definition 6. *Let* d ∈ PreCallD, loc *a code location,* f *the contract supplier and* g *the target function. The results of the* PreCall *transfer functions* precall$_{loc}$(d) *are defined as:*

- d, *if* d *is* ERR *or* CALL, *or* loc *is not a call to* f *or* g.
- PCHK(L ∪ {loc}), *if* loc *is a call to* g, d = PCHK(L)
- PCHK({loc}), *if* loc *is a call to* g, d ≠ PCHK
- CALL, *if* loc *is a call to* f, d = PCHK(L), ∃l ∈ L : *parameters of* l *match*.
- ERR, *otherwise*

Figure 5 provides an example code, contract and the resulting worklist iteration. The contract specifies that before calling `MPI_Put`, the window must be created using `MPI_Win_create`. This is facilitated using the parameter matching, which checks that the window pointer given in a previous `MPI_Win_create` must match the address of the window of the MPI_Put. The call at line 2 matches, which is why the first information saved to line 4 is CALL. However, the one at line 3 does not, and after the information propagates the correct result of ERR is returned instead. With `PreCall`, it is sufficient to simply check for the existence of the ERR analysis information to determine a contract violation, as it is at that point that the contract supplier was called without the target function prior. As that is the case for this example, an error is reported.

Release Analysis. The `Release` analysis, similarly to `PostCall`, starts iterating at each call site of the contract supplier and aggregates the result. The domain is defined as follows:

Definition 7. *The* `Release` *analysis domain is defined as the set* ReleaseD = {FULFILLED, FORBIDDEN, ERR}, *where* $\sqsubseteq$ *is the order in the set definition. The initial analysis value is* FORBIDDEN.

When starting the analysis, the releasing function cannot have been called yet, and as such the initial state is FORBIDDEN. Should the releasing function be encountered, the state changes to FULFILLED. If the forbidden operation is found beforehand, the state changes to ERR.

Definition 8. *Let* d $\in$ ReleaseD, *loc a code location*, g *the releasing function and* op *the forbidden operation. The results of the* Release *transfer functions* release$_{loc}$(d) *are defined as:*

- d *if* loc *is not a call to* g *or instance of* op, *or if* d *is* FULFILLED *or* ERR
- ERR *if* loc *is an instance of* op.
- FULFILLED *if* loc *is a call to* g.

The forbidden operation is a parameter to the contract, and thus not specified in the analysis itself. Per the definition of the contract language, it may be a memory access (reading or writing) or a function call.

4 Implementation

First, Sect. 4.1 introduces the LLVM framework, upon which our implementation is built. Then, Sect. 4.2 presents our tool architecture.

4.1 LLVM Analysis Framework

The LLVM analysis framework [12] can be roughly split into the frontends, such as the `clang(++)` frontends for C/C++ and `flang` for Fortran, which translate the source code to the LLVM Intermediate Representation (LLVM IR), and the

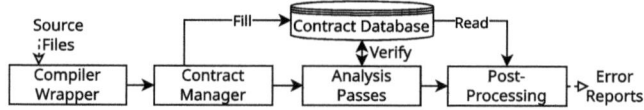

Fig. 6. Overview of the tool architecture.

backend, which runs compile-time passes on that IR to analyze and modify it after which code generation begins. One LLVM IR file is generated for each translation unit (TU), which then contain function definitions and declarations, and global variables.

Our analyses run on the level of the LLVM IR, for which the framework provides a plugin system to extend its functionality. A plugin may define additional functionality in the form of analyses and passes. LLVM allows analyses to return a result once finished. A pass may then retrieve the results of an analysis and perform work accordingly. The results of an analysis are cached. Should multiple passes request the results of the same analysis, LLVM only runs the analysis if the cache is not available, either because the analysis has not run yet or it has been invalidated.

4.2 Tool Architecture

The implementation is split into four parts, which can be seen in Fig. 6: the compiler wrapper, contract manager, the analyses, and post-processing.

The contracts are specified using annotations at function declarations, which can be added through additional headers, modification of the existing MPI header, or in user code. The compiler wrapper automatically includes a CONTRACT macro which hides the clang string annotation syntax for easier readability, as can be seen in Fig. 1b. It additionally defers object file generation to link time, which allows our analysis to run on the entire program, and thus for analysis across TUs. Once the program is supposed to be linked, the wrapper interjects and first executes each analysis and finally the post-processing pass.

Each check (PreCall, PostCall, Release) is implemented as a compiler pass, which first request the results of the contract manager. It is an LLVM analysis, which parses the contract string embedded into the code using an ANTLR [18] parser. The annotated strings from the macros are available on the level of the IR as an internal global variable @llvm.global.annotations, which is a list of all the annotations provided on source level, together with the location of the annotation. The parser generates the ContractTree, an internal representation of the contract. Each ContractTree consists of three parts, which correspond to the scopes defined in the contract; the list of tags, and a recursive data structure for the PRE and POST scope formulae including the connective used (conjunction, disjunction, or exclusive-or relation). The atomic formulae are expressions, which match the requirements defined in Sect. 3.1. Finally, the contract manager bundles the ContractTree representations of each contract, the function the contract was attached to, as well as a pointer to the status of the contract into a database. The contract status may be one of "unknown" (default), "fulfilled" or "violated", and is to be filled in by each analysis within the database.

The analyses are implemented as a direct translation of the formal definition given in Sect. 3.3. Each analysis checks if there are still contracts with unknown status. If there are, and the analysis is suitable for that type of contract, it attempts to verify the contract. We implement a generic worklist algorithm which is used by each analysis. The analyses simply implement the transfer functions, the least upper bound operator, and the analysis domain; the worklist algorithm calls into the analysis for the transfer functions and least upper bound operator, and saves the result.

The worklist algorithm is designed analogously to the theory presented in Sect. 3.2, but with a few extensions, namely support for interprocedural contexts as well as primitive support for OpenMP outlined sections [4]. When a function call is encountered and the definition is available, we push the next instruction to a stack, then jump to the function entry point. Once a function is finished, the stack is popped, and analysis resumes at the caller. Recursion does not cause issues, as due to the ascending chain condition, previously encountered functions can only be revisited finitely often. After the worklist algorithm is finished, it returns the map of each location to the analysis information. While support for OpenMP outlined sections is provided, allowing analysis on hybrid CPU/GPU code has not been tested. The worklist algorithm is called once on the program entry point in case of the `PreCall` analysis, and once for each call site of the contract supplier for the others.

Once the worklist is finished, the analyses write back the contract status depending on the result of the analysis. Using that information, the post-processing pass resolves the formulae iteratively by inspecting the type of the connective, then checking if the full formula is fulfilled. If it is, the information is written back and the parent formula is checked analogously. Finally, the post-processing pass performs error output for the user.

5 Evaluation

To evaluate the effectiveness of our tool, we compare against the static correctness checkers MPI-Checker [5] and PARCOACH-static [19] (referred to as PARCOACH from now on). We first assess the classification quality using the RMARaceBench [21] and MPI-BugBench [9] (Level 1) benchmarks, and then measure the compilation overhead of each tool on the proxy application miniVite [7], LULESH [10] and the PRK Stencil Kernel [24]. The raw data from our evaluation as well as the tool source is available at [17].

5.1 Classification Quality

We utilized the JUBE [13] benchmarking environment to run automated testing on the RMARaceBench [21] and MPI-BugBench [9] test suites. Each test is run by each tool, and classified as a true positive (TP), true negative (TN),

Table 1. Results of running each tool on the correctness benchmarks.

MPI-BugBench (Level 1)						RMARaceBench (MPI)					
Tool	TP	TN	FP	FN	Acc.	Tool	TP	TN	FP	FN	Acc.
CoVer	30	22	3	75	**0.40**	CoVer	20	43	19	43	**0.50**
PARCOACH	4	14	25	87	0.14	PARCOACH	19	34	34	**38**	0.42
MPI-Checker	15	**22**	**2**	91	0.28	MPI-Checker	0	**53**	**0**	72	0.42

TP: True Positive, TN: True Negative, FP: False Positive, FN: False Negative, Acc.: Accuracy

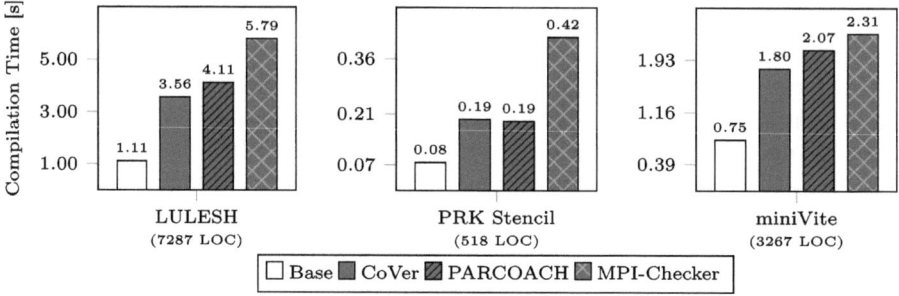

Fig. 7. Compilation time including analysis for each proxy application and tool.

false positive (FP), or false negative (FN). We then compute the accuracy as $\frac{TP+TN}{TP+TN+FP+FN}$.

The results can be seen in Table 1. Our tool has the highest accuracy across both benchmarks, with a consistently higher number of detected TPs. MPI-Checker had very few FPs, but still a lower accuracy due to the small number of reported issues in total. Finally, PARCOACH had the lowest accuracy, mostly due to the high number of FPs reported. However, the accuracy is still very low for all tools.

All tools missed a lot of errors, which can be seen by the high number of FNs. This is to be expected, as these benchmark suites contain tests which are unsupported by the tools considered. For example, though none of the tools support remote data races, both RMARaceBench and MPI-BugBench include them. However, by including these tests we can more accurately evaluate the quality of error reports; they are useful to check for possible FPs.

While our tool had the highest accuracy, mostly due to the various supported error classes, it also had a significant number of FPs on the RMARaceBench remote race test cases. These are caused by a limitation of the current data flow analysis that PARCOACH also suffers from. MPI-Checker uses symbolic execution, and is therefore not affected.

MPI-Checker had the least number of FPs. As it does not support data races, this is only relevant for the MPI-BugBench tests. However, the total accuracy remains low as a lot of errors were missed. The FPs that were present were due to the request-based RMA communication calls, which are unsupported, thus triggering the unmatched wait detection for the request handles therein.

PARCOACH reported a significant number of FPs in both the MPI-BugBench and RMARaceBench tests. It consistently reports impossible data races, where e.g. a communication is in conflict with a memory access that happens prior. This causes a high number of invalid reports. On the other hand, some communication calls are not supported, causing FNs due to unrecognized request-based RMA operations similarly to MPI-Checker. Further, as it performs only intraprocedural analysis, test cases utilizing function calls fail due to missing inspection thereof.

5.2 Overhead

We compiled the proxy applications LULESH [10], miniVite [7], and the PRK Stencil Kernel [24] serially 15 times each; the average compilation times are shown in Fig. 7. The low compilation time of the Stencil Kernel stems from its small size. Since the third-party tools lack support for multi-TU analysis, we chose the PRK Stencil Kernel as a single-TU representative. Nevertheless, the measurements are representative, and the minimum and maximum did not deviate for more than 10% in each run. Additionally, as PARCOACH only supports RMA communication, we chose the MPI RMA port of LULESH by Schwitanski et al. [23] for it. The PRK Stencil Kernel and miniVite already offer RMA variants, so no workarounds were needed.

While our tool and PARCOACH had similar overhead, MPI-Checker had the consistently highest overhead, up to 4.7x in LULESH and 5.9x when compiling Stencil. This is due to the symbolic execution engine used, which, while providing high accuracy, causes high overhead due to the state-space explosion problem.

All tools reported FPs across these tests. Real-world applications utilize complex code structures that are hard to analyze statically such as function pointers and pointer aliasing. None of the tools reported an error on miniVite, and most came from LULESH. This is mostly caused by the way LULESH structures its MPI calls, with requests being handled in big array structures. Both our tool and PARCOACH are unable to differentiate the array elements, leading to FPs. MPI-Checker reported the least number of FPs, and is the only tool not to report a FP on the PRK Stencil Kernel.

5.3 Discussion

While the correctness results for our tool are encouraging, the high number of FPs on the RMARaceBench tests is striking. These are due to a limitation in the current implementation of the worklist algorithm, which both PARCOACH and CoVer suffer from. As branch conditions are not inspected in any way, some invalid error reports are generated due to control flows that are impossible in practice. Figure 8a demonstrates this issue: While no error is present as the branch conditions are mutually exclusive, the invalid control flow entering both branches causes a false data race report. This would not occur if an `else if`

```
1   if (rank == 0) MPI_Irecv(buf, req)
2   if (rank == 1) MPI_Isend(buf, req)
3   MPI_Wait(req)
```

(a) Worklist inspects invalid path through both branches.

```
1   MPI_Rget(&buf,req)
2   buf++
3   MPI_Wait(req)
```

(b) Due to missing support for `MPI_Rget`, both third-party tools fail this test.

Fig. 8. Common issues during correctness evaluation.

is used instead, as then even for arbitrary branch conditions it is impossible to enter both branches. RMARaceBench only uses this problematic branching on the remote tests; the local data race tests were unaffected. This issue could be alleviated with a more precise analysis utilizing, for example, multi-value analysis as done by Burak *et al.* [3] or symbolic execution to prune impossible paths.

Our tool performed well in MPI-BugBench, with only three FPs but twice the number of TPs of MPI-Checker, the second place. This is mostly due to the improved error coverage: Our tool supports many of the error classes that MPI-Checker supports (unmatched or missing waits, double non-blocking), but also a lot more such as data races and RMA issues.

In contrast, MPI-Checker had the least number of FPs; due to the use of symbolic execution, more accurate analysis is possible in contrast to our data-flow approach. Additionally, some checks such as data type mismatches are significantly easier to perform on the level of the Clang AST: More source information is preserved compared to the LLVM IR, at which point pointer types are lost.

Both PARCOACH and MPI-Checker have issues with unsupported functions. One example that both share is request-based RMA operations. Consider the code given in Fig. 8b, which contains a data race. PARCOACH is unable to detect it as it is focused solely on "normal" RMA operations, and does not track requests. MPI-Checker reports a FP, as it considers the code to contain an unmatched wait. While it can track requests, it does not recognize the communication. The advantage of our tool is that it does not require built-in support for requests or specific functions, as the contracts provide that information; they specify both the functions and resources to track explicitly.

One of the main advantages of our approach is that these issues, i.e., API functions that were not considered during development of the tool, can be fixed by the user after shipping the tool by simply appending the corresponding contract. Should an API function f unknown to our tool start a communication request, it would also cause an unmatched wait report. The (simplified) contract for unmatched waits used in our premade header is `PRE { call_tag!(request_gen) }` attached to the `MPI_Wait`. Thus, simply adding the `request_gen` tag to that function is sufficient to correct the issue.

6 Related Work

Many tools detect MPI errors, such as MUST [8] and PARCOACH-dynamic [19]. RMASanitizer [23] additionally supports detecting GASPI [6] and OpenSHMEM [16] errors. These tools instrument the code, and then run the program while intercepting calls both from the instrumentation and the PPM. However, this causes high runtime overhead of up to 20x [23].

Static tools, such as PARCOACH-static [20] and MPI-Checker [5] trade runtime for compile-time overhead, which is often significantly smaller. PARCOACH-static works on the LLVM IR by generating a control-flow graph, and then iterating over it to detect local data races, but supports neither interprocedural analysis nor analysis across TUs. MPI-Checker, which runs on the Clang abstract syntax tree (AST), supports data type mismatches, unmatched or missing waits, double nonblocking calls without intermediate wait, and deadlock detection, with each check implemented by a corresponding analysis. Data type mismatches are checked by comparing the type of the variable used against the type specified in the MPI call, while unmatched waits are checked using symbolic execution. While interprocedural analysis is supported, analysis across TUs is not.

The SPMD IR [3] is a static tool on the LLVM Multi-Level Intermediate Representation (MLIR). It defines a mapping for the supported models to a special SPMD IR, where the analyses themselves work solely on the generated IR. Currently, there are checks for collective mismatches and ordering errors on collectives. The analysis iterates over the MLIR, ensuring that at each branching point the same collectives are used; if not, a collective mismatch is reported. While the analyses are independent of the model used, the tool itself is not, requiring the mapping of each model to the SPMD IR as part of the tool code.

VerCors [2] is a static contract framework for parallel programs. However, VerCors verifies communication algorithms, not the correct use of the API. Similarly to language-native contracts such as C++26 [1], specification of the relevant aspects for PPM API verification (calling behavior, memory accesses) is not possible. Thus, while our tools share the use of contracts, their use differs significantly.

7 Conclusion

Many correctness-checking tools for parallel programming models (PPMs) focus on a fixed number of supported models. This paper presents CoVer, an extensible contract framework to verify the correct use of PPMs.

We present a generic contract language, which can describe many of the most common API errors when utilizing PPMs. By utilizing contracts, the tool is not bound to a model, and may instead be utilized in any model where the contracts can be annotated. Our tool is implemented using the LLVM framework, and provides support for interprocedural and cross-translation-unit analysis.

We evaluated the tool using MPI-BugBench [9] and RMARaceBench [21], and compared against PARCOACH-static [19] and MPI-Checker [5]. Our tool has a high accuracy due to the wide variety of supported error classes. The overhead is comparable to PARCOACH-static in the region of a 2x–3x slowdown.

As other languages such as Fortran also compile down to LLVM IR, we plan to implement support for these languages by improving the tool frontend. Furthermore, we are evaluating the possibility of accelerating dynamic tools using the errors we detect at compile-time as done by Schwitanski *et al.* [22].

Acknowledgments. The authors would like to thank the Federal Ministry of Research, Technology and Space and the state governments (www.nhr-verein.de/unsere-partner) for supporting this work as part of the joint funding of National High Performance Computing (NHR).

Disclosure of Interests. The authors have no competing interests to declare that are relevant to the content of this article.

References

1. Berne, J., Doumler, T., Krzemieński, A.: Contracts for C++. https://www.openstd.org/jtc1/sc22/wg21/docs/papers/2025/p2900r14.pdf (visited on 05/13/2025)
2. Blom, S., Darabi, S., Huisman, M., Oortwijn, W.: The VerCors tool set: verification of parallel and concurrent software. In: Polikarpova, N., Schneider, S. (eds.) Integrated Formal Methods, pp. 102–110. Springer International Publishing, Cham (2017). https://doi.org/10.1007/978-3-319-66845-1_7
3. Burak, S., Ivanov, I.R., Domke, J., Müller, M.: SPMD IR: unifying SPMD and multivalue IR showcased for static verification of collectives. In: Blaas-Schenner, C., Niethammer, C., Haas, T. (eds.) Recent Advances in the Message Passing Interface, pp. 3–20. Springer Nature Switzerland, Cham (2025). https://doi.org/10.1007/978-3-031-73370-3_1
4. Dagum, L., Menon, R.: OpenMP: an industry standard API for shared-memory programming. IEEE Comput. Sci. Eng. **5**(1), 46–55 (1998). https://doi.org/10.1109/99.660313
5. Droste, A., Kuhn, M., Ludwig, T.: MPI-checker: static analysis for MPI. In: Proceedings of the Second Workshop on the LLVM Compiler Infrastructure in HPC. LLVM '15, pp. 1–10. Association for Computing Machinery, New York, NY, USA (2015). https://doi.org/10.1145/2833157.2833159
6. GASPI forum, GASPI: global address space programming interface 17.1, (2017). https://raw.githubusercontent.com/GASPI-Forum/GASPI-Forum.github.io/master/standards/GASPI-17.1.pdf on 30 Dec 2024
7. Ghosh, S., Halappanavar, M., Tumeo, A., Kalyanaraman, A., Gebremedhin, A.H.: MiniVite: a graph analytics benchmarking tool for massively parallel systems. In: 2018 IEEE/ACM Performance Modeling, Benchmarking and Simulation of High Performance Computer Systems (PMBS), pp. 51–56 (2018). https://doi.org/10.1109/PMBS.2018.8641631
8. Hilbrich, T., Schulz, M., de Supinski, B.R., Müller, M.S.: MUST: a scalable approach to runtime error detection in MPI programs. In: Müller, M.S., Resch, M.M., Schulz, A., Nagel, W.E. (eds.) Tools for High Performance Computing 2009, pp. 53–66. Springer, Berlin, Heidelberg (2010). https://doi.org/10.1007/978-3-642-11261-4_5

9. Jammer, T., et al.: MPI-BugBench: a framework for assessing MPI correctness tools. In: Blaas-Schenner, C., Niethammer, C., Haas, T. (eds.) Recent Advances in the Message Passing Interface, pp. 121–137. Springer Nature Switzerland, Cham (2025). https://doi.org/10.1007/978-3-031-73370-3_8
10. Karlin, I., Keasler, J., Neely, J.: LULESH 2.0 updates and changes. LLNL-TR-641973, 1090032, LLNL-TR–641973, 1090032 (2013). https://doi.org/10.2172/1090032
11. Kotlin contracts proposal, GitHub. (2019). https://github.com/Kotlin/KEEP/blob/master/proposals/kotlin-contracts.md. Accessed on 07 Feb 2025
12. Lattner, C., Adve, V.: LLVM: a compilation framework for lifelong program analysis and transformation. In: International Symposium on Code Generation and Optimization, 2004. CGO 2004, pp. 75–86 (2004). https://doi.org/10.1109/CGO.2004.1281665
13. Lührs, S.: Automated benchmarking with JUBE. FZJ-2020-02622, Jülich Supercomputing Center (2020). https://juser.fz-juelich.de/record/878080. Accessed on 28 Oct 2024
14. Message passing interface forum, MPI: a message-passing interface standard version 4.1, (2023). https://www.mpi-forum.org/docs/mpi-4.1/mpi41-report.pdf
15. Nielson, F., Nielson, H.R., Hankin, C.: Principles of program analysis. Springer, Berlin, Heidelberg (1999)
16. OpenSHMEM committee, OpenSHMEM: application programming interface version 1.5, (2020). http://openshmem.org/site/sites/default/site_files/OpenSHMEM-1.5.pdf. Accessed on 30 Dec 2024
17. Oraji, Y.M.: Artifact for 'verifying MPI API usage requirements with contracts'. https://doi.org/10.5281/zenodo.15574135
18. Parr, T.J., Quong, R.W.: ANTLR: A predicated-LL(k) parser generator. Software: Practice and Experience 25(7), 789–810 (1995). https://doi.org/10.1002/spe.4380250705
19. Saillard, E., Carribault, P., Barthou, D.: Parcoach: combining static and dynamic validation of MPI collective communications. Int. J. High Perform. Comput. Appl. **28**(4), 425–434 (2014). https://doi.org/10.1177/1094342014552204
20. Saillard, E., Sergent, M., Ait Kaci, C.T., Barthou, D.: Static local concurrency errors detection in MPI-RMA programs. In: 2022 IEEE/ACM Sixth International Workshop on Software Correctness for HPC Applications (Correctness), pp. 18–26 (2022). https://doi.org/10.1109/Correctness56720.2022.00008
21. Schwitanski, S., Jenke, J., Klotz, S., Müller, M.S.: RMARaceBench: a microbenchmark suite to evaluate race detection tools for rma programs. In: Proceedings of the SC '23 Workshops of The International Conference on High Performance Computing, Network, Storage, and Analysis. SC-W '23, pp. 205–214. Association for Computing Machinery, New York, NY, USA (2023). https://doi.org/10.1145/3624062.3624087
22. Schwitanski, S., Oraji, Y.M., Pätzold, C., Jenke, J., Müller, M.S.: Leveraging static analysis to accelerate dynamic race detection for remote memory access programs. In: Weiland, M., Neuwirth, S., Kruse, C., Weinzierl, T. (eds.) High Performance Computing. ISC High Performance 2024 International Workshops, pp. 45–58. Springer Nature Switzerland, Cham (2025). https://doi.org/10.1007/978-3-031-73716-9_4

23. Schwitanski, S., Oraji, Y.M., Pätzold, C., Jenke, J., Tomski, F., Müller, M.S.: RMASanitizer: generalized runtime detection of data races in remote memory access applications. In: Proceedings of the 53rd International Conference on Parallel Processing. ICPP '24, pp. 833–844. Association for Computing Machinery, New York, NY, USA (2024). https://doi.org/10.1145/3673038.3673109
24. Van der Wijngaart, R.F., Mattson, T.G.: The parallel research kernels. In: 2014 IEEE High Performance Extreme Computing Conference (HPEC), pp. 1–6 (2014). https://doi.org/10.1109/HPEC.2014.7040972

Review of MPI Continuations and Their Integration into PMPI Tools

Alexander Optenhöfel[1], Joachim Jenke[1](✉), Ben Thärigen[1],
and Joseph Schuchart[2]

[1] RWTH Aachen University, Aachen, Germany
alexander.optenhoefel@rwth-aachen.de,
{jenke,thaerigen}@itc.rwth-aachen.de
[2] Stony Brook University, Stony Brook, US
joseph.schuchart@stonybrook.edu

Abstract. Nonblocking communication in MPI significantly enhances high-performance computing by minimizing application time spent in MPI communication functions, enabling the overlap of computation and communication. Asynchronous programming models further enhance efficiency and adaptability in load balancing; however, the integration of MPI communication with these models remains insufficient. The MPI Continuations proposal, currently under discussion in the MPI Forum, aims to resolve the latter by introducing asynchronous completion for nonblocking communication. To ensure application developers can adopt this transformative feature, robust support in PMPI-based tools is essential. We have updated an early prototype to implement the latest discussion state from the MPI Forum. This shim library implementation of MPI Continuations is compatible with any MPI implementation. We describe potential pitfalls in implementing continuations, including a significant API issue that could lead to race conditions. We propose restrictions to prevent these issues and strengthen the robustness of the MPI Continuations proposal. Additionally, our analysis highlights the challenges PMPI-based tools will face with the new control flow, as MPI operations may now complete at nearly any point in a program. MPI progress threads and progress engines might become visible, requiring closer attention. Tools need to adapt by intercepting user-provided callback functions to monitor the completion of nonblocking communication effectively. Using the PMPI-based On-the-Fly Critical Path Tool used for performance analysis as an example, we demonstrate a clear path for integrating MPI Continuations into performance analysis tools, enhancing overall performance and adaptability in advanced computing applications.

1 Introduction

MPI, while primarily designed for distributed-memory platforms, is also applicable to shared-memory systems and their hybrids. It allows multiple processes to exchange messages seamlessly, regardless of whether they are on the same compute node. Initially, applications used shared memory as a fast interconnect between MPI processes, avoiding the need for different programming models. With the rise of large multicore processors, developers are adopting shared-memory programming in MPI applications to address memory limitations due to unnecessary data replication within a shared-memory node. Although MPI provides an interface for shared-memory programming through remote memory access, multithreading via models such as OpenMP, POSIX threads, and C++ threads remains dominant. MPI is mostly thread-agnostic, ensuring thread safety, but does not provide extensive support. Proposals like Endpoints [1] and Finepoints [2] aimed to enhance multi-threaded MPI performance.

OpenMP has a long history in high-performance computing (HPC) and has been used to parallelize bulk-synchronous applications that alternate between MPI communication and OpenMP computation. However, the introduction of tasking in OpenMP 3.0 has made task-level programming more relevant, blurring the lines between communication and computation phases. Asynchronous execution with tasks introduces new challenges in hybrid OpenMP+MPI approaches. Ensuring completion of MPI communication in OpenMP tasks via taskyield has shown to be unreliable due to insufficient guarantees from both models [9].

In this context, two competing publications [6,8] initiated discussions in the MPI forum, the standardization body of MPI. While the discussion led to a more concrete proposal text for the new feature MPI Continuations, none of the publication prototypes were updated yet. In this work, we update one of the initial implementation prototypes to reflect the current MPI Continuations proposal. Creating an up-to-date and widely usable prototype for MPI Continuations helps to detect implementation challenges and specification imprecisions early on. It also enables integrating support of continuations in PMPI tools, which are impacted by the new completion properties: With continuations, a tool can only observe the completion of nonblocking operations if the tool intercepts the calls to the application-provided callback function. PMPI has been part of MPI since the very beginning. Tool support is integral to ensure a wide adoption of the new feature in application codes. We implement the necessary workflow into the On-The-Fly Critical Path Tool (OTF-CPT) [7] which is used to analyze performance. To keep track of metrics along the critical path, the tool sends piggyback messages along with all application messages. To terminate the piggyback communication and employ the analysis in time, the tool needs to observe the completion of communication before the application. With this integration, we demonstrate the feasibility of tracking the completion of MPI operations in PMPI tools when the application uses continuations.

Overall, our work makes the following contributions:

- We update an earlier implementation to align with the current MPI Continuations proposal of the MPI forum and discuss potential implementation pitfalls. (see Sect. 3)
- We investigate the integration of MPI Continuations into PMPI-based tools. (see Sect. 4)
- We discuss ambiguities and problems with the current specification proposal and propose specific changes. (see Sect. 5)

2 Continuations

Currently, an application must ensure the completion of MPI nonblocking routines through either testing or waiting on the related request object of the operation. The need for explicit testing complicates the use of asynchronous multithreading paradigms, such as OpenMP tasks. Approaches that use taskyield to recurrently test for completion in tasks have even been shown to deadlock in specific scenarios [9].

```
1  omp_event_handle_t recv_ev;
2  #pragma omp task detach(recv_ev) depend(out: data)
3  {
4      MPI_Request req;
5      MPI_Irecv(data, ..., &req);
6      MPIX_Callback(&req, omp_fulfill_event, recv_ev);
7  }
8  #pragma omp task depend(in: data)
9      work_with(data);
```

Listing 1. Registering a callback for request completion binds the task dependency of the receive task to the completion of the receive operation; detaching from the task execution allow independent work to be scheduled; the second task depending on data to be received will only start after the operation completes

The upcoming feature, MPI Continuations, enables the asynchronous completion of MPI operations, thereby avoiding the pitfalls and overhead associated with repeated testing or waiting. The idea is to assign responsibility for completion to the MPI runtime and notify the application of completion via a callback. An abstract use case for this is outlined in Figure 1. In this example, the execution of the second OpenMP task comprising work_with(data) can only happen once data is released through the completion of the first OpenMP task. This completion is delayed until the event recv_ev. The idea is to link this event to the completion of the MPI operation that marks the actual point at which data, the task's output dependency, becomes available. This way, the dependent tasks can be scheduled as timely as possible once the event is invoked, which could conveniently happen in a callback that informs about the completion of the MPI operation involving data. Such a continuation callback is registered using MPIX_Callback in line 6 in the example, showcasing a use case of the proposed new MPI functionality. This function can be seen as a placeholder, but at the core, it registers a callback that should be invoked once the MPI operation it belongs to has completed, and that has a context on which it can work. The idea of MPI Continuations was proposed at the same time in two independent papers [6,8] under the names MPI_Detach and MPI_Continuations, respectively. Both approaches share the same general idea but differ in the exact definition of the API, which will be presented shortly in the following sections. The current MPI working draft is based on the Continuations paper.

2.1 Detach Proposal

Protze et al. [6] proposed three kinds of functions to detach the completion of an operation and attach a continuation: The abstract `MPIX_Callback` would either become `MPI_Detach`, `MPI_Detach_each`, or `MPI_Detach_all`. All functions get passed a continuation callback function and either one (detach) or a set of requests (detach-each, detach-all). For detach and detach-all, the callback is triggered once after the completion of all operation requests. For detach-each, the callback is triggered once for each operation request that is completed.

Detaching the completion gives ownership of the request to the MPI runtime; therefore, a detached request cannot be used in any MPI function while it is detached. This implies that the application can no longer test for completion, which might be important for progressing MPI communication. The Detach proposal suggests a generic function called `MPI_Progress`, which can be called from the application to actively advance progress. With repeated calls to the progress function, all completion callbacks for matched communication operations will eventually be called. The MPI Detach prototype is available as a shim library that can be transparently integrated into an application and is compatible with any MPI implementation.

2.2 Continuations Proposal

In addition to function calls similar to the above Detach functions, Schuchart et al. [8] also introduce a new type of MPI request: Continuation requests. When detaching a completion and attaching a continuation to an operation request, the corresponding continuation is also registered with a continuation request. The application can use the continuation request to test and wait for its completion by means of the usual `MPI_Wait` or `MPI_Test`. Through this, a weak progress guarantee for the registered operations and the continuation request itself is given since `MPI_Test` on a continuation request has the same effect as `MPI_Testall` on the registered operations. The same holds for `MPI_Wait` and `MPI_Waitall`, although the progress guarantees are only implied by the proposal, and possibly should be stated explicitly for clarification. As visualized in Fig. 1, each operation request can only have one continuation attached to itself, but multiple continuations can be registered with the same continuation request.

There exist two calls to detach the completion and attach a continuation: `MPI_Continue` and `MPI_Continueall`, which again are realizations of the abstract `MPIX_Callback` from Figure 1. Both functions receive a continuation callback, a continuation request, and either one or a set of operation requests, respectively. The continuation callback is triggered once all attached operation requests are completed. Additionally, a continuation request may also be attached to another continuation request.

The new continuation call also includes an MPI info object which allows to define specific changes of behavior for the continuations. Another difference to the Detach proposal is that only non-persistent operation requests transfer their ownership to the MPI runtime. Persistent requests stay valid and are allowed to be tested on from the application.

The initial MPI Continuations prototype was integrated into OpenMPI. Such implementation can directly access the internal data structures, easily distinguish between different kinds of requests, and detect the completion of a request by examining internal fields. The current proposal [5] for the MPI standard closely follows the design by Schuchart et al. and only makes minor changes for specific edge cases.

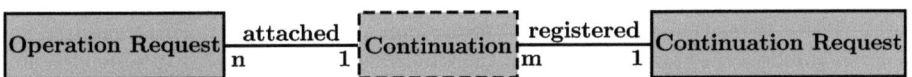

Fig. 1. Relation of continuation to operation and continuation request.

3 Continuations Library Implementation

Our Continuations library implementation is based on the shim-library implementation of MPI Detach [6]. It provides implementations for the additionally needed API function MPI_Continue_init and modifies the functions MPI_Detach and MPI_Detach_all to implement MPI_Continue and MPI_Continue_all. The MPI_Continue_init function initiates continuation requests. Once a continuation request has been created, the other two functions can be used to attach continuations to operations and register them with the continuation request. An application can pass this continuation request to any of the existing MPI completion functions to trigger progress and test for completion of all registered operations.

The Continuations library, therefore, also needs to change the behavior of these completion functions to handle continuation requests, which need to be distinguished from the *usual* requests. To this end, our Continuations library employs the MPI handle shim [3] to provide an abstraction from request handle objects that are used in MPI. The handle shim provides wrappers for any kind of MPI handle and maintains a one-to-one correspondence between the *application-facing* handles and the underlying *MPI-facing* handles. The wrapping of MPI handles is invisible to the application. The primary purpose of the MPI handle shim is to provide a framework for associating data with MPI handle objects and allow distinguishing persistent, non-persistent, and continuation requests. In the implementation of the completion function wrappers, the information from the wrapped handles enables us to distinguish between continuation requests and actual MPI requests, allowing us to treat them differently. For continuation requests, we invoke the internal function for progressing a continuation request. Other requests are just passed down to the MPI implementation for completion. Since our Continuations library is implemented as a shim layer on top of MPI, it can be used in combination with any existing MPI implementation.

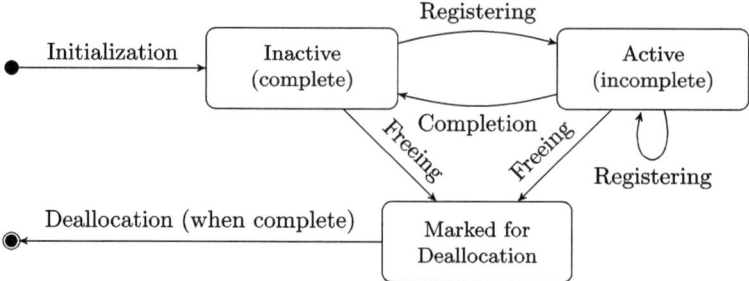

Fig. 2. State transition diagram for continuation requests. The terms *complete* and *incomplete* follow the terminology from the Continuations proposal, while *inactive* and *active* are more consistent with the current MPI standard.

3.1 Continuation Requests

The implementation must handle continuations created by the application. When the application issues a new continuation, it is registered to a continuation request. Therefore, relevant information is stored in thread-safe lists included in the continuation request data. For a more fine-grained synchronization, there are separate (sets of) lists used during the registering of new continuations and for accessing pending continuations when the continuation request is progressed. Before any continuations can be created, at least one continuation request has to be created first. Figure 2 shows the lifecycle of a continuation request and the states it can be in. On initialization, a continuation request is complete (or inactive, akin to persistent requests). When the first continuation is registered, it becomes incomplete (or active). More continuations can join while the continuation request is still incomplete, and it only becomes complete again once all pending continuations have been executed. The mechanism to explicitly progress and complete a continuation request is to pass it to an existing MPI test procedure (like MPI_Test). At all times, a continuation request can be freed using MPI_Request_free. It then gets marked for deallocation and is deallocated as soon as it is complete.

3.2 Nested Completion

A challenge arises during the use of nested continuation requests, i.e., a continuation request that is registered to another continuation request. In such a case, testing a continuation request will result in testing all nested continuation requests. With deeply nested continuation requests, this will lead to recursive testing. Additionally, info handles passed at the initialization of continuation requests can modify the behavior of continuations for the scope of a continuation request. The info key relevant in the case of recursive testing is max_poll, which sets the maximum number of continuations to be invoked at once, i.e., as part of one test call.

Figure 3 shows four nested continuation requests, where cr_i is always registered with cr_{i-1} for $i \in \{2, 3, 4\}$. Without `max_poll` limits, testing cr_1 will also test cr_2 and, in turn, also trigger testing of cr_3 and cr_4. cr_4 is observed to be complete, invoking its continuation callback. This completes cr_3, triggering a chain of continuation callbacks for cr_3 and cr_2 and finally completing cr_1.

The key `max_poll` can be specified differently for each continuation request and can introduce issues for naive testing implementations. Consider the following implementation illustrated in Fig. 3: In each nesting depth, we take the minimum of the current `max_poll` limit and passed-down limit. When passing down the limit, we conservatively subtract one since we cannot determine whether the nested continuation request will complete and trigger its continuation. In our example, the test triggered during testing cr_2 gets limit zero since the completion of cr_3 would already trigger the one allowed continuation call for cr_2. Consequently, cr_4 will never be reached and the completion of cr_1 and cr_2 can never be determined. This problem occurs when the nesting depth of continuation requests exceeds the poll limit and violates the weak progress guarantee of MPI, which states that requests must complete eventually if all conditions for completion are fulfilled.

The solution is to not reserve a space for the potential completion, but instead hold back completion of the request until the next test call executes successfully for the same situation. In this case, the first test of cr_1 triggers the completion callback for cr_4. A subsequent test then triggers the completion callbacks for cr_3 and cr_2 and signals the completion of cr_1.

3.3 Progress for Continuations

MPI leaves it open to how and when progress in communication is to be achieved. It only provides a weak guarantee that operations will be completed eventually when the completion criteria are fulfilled. The Continuations proposal does not change this. Instead, the option to let MPI handle the continuations for selected continuation requests is exposed by the info key `mpi_continue_thread`. By this, continuations can be allowed to execute outside of application threads if supported by an implementation. In our implementation, a thread dedicated to the

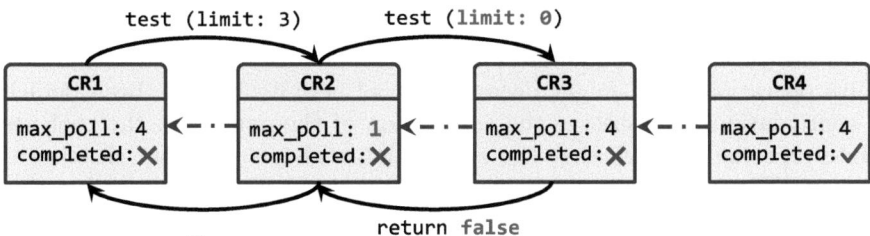

Fig. 3. Naive testing algorithm for nested continuation requests (CR). Due to the conservative approach of reserving a callback for the potential completion of the nested CR, the test will always fail.

completion of continuations is started as soon as a continuation request with `mpi_continue_thread` set to any is initialized. It then iterates over a list containing all continuation requests that use this setting and is put to sleep as long as there are no pending continuations registered with the requests in the list. During the finalization of MPI, the thread, if originally started, is then used to work off all remaining continuations and must join before finalization can succeed.

4 Tool Support

The usage of continuations has an impact on the control flow in an application. Crucially, the completion of nonblocking MPI operations is now linked to the invocation of callbacks as opposed to explicitly calling completion functions. PMPI tools that observe the completion of operations now need to instrument continuation callbacks to perform actions usually done in completion functions.

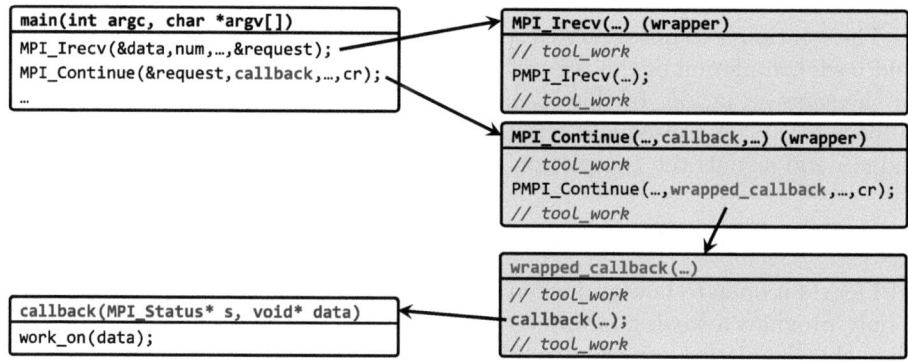

Fig. 4. Handling Continuation callbacks in tools

Figure 4 sketches the interaction of a PMPI tool with continuations. Application code is on the left, tool code on the right. First, the application initiates a nonblocking receive operation. The PMPI tool intercepts the respective call to `MPI_Irecv` and executes some additional code. The completion of the receive operation again might necessitate tool activity but has been detached via continuations. To observe the completion of the operation, the tool needs to intercept the callback that the application registers. Figure 4 sketches this workflow: The tool stores the original `callback` on its creation and passes a `wrapped_callback` containing the necessary tool code together with the original callback to MPI. When MPI observes the completion of the operation, it will call the `wrapped_callback`. The tool can observe the completion of the operation and execute the relevant code. Finally, the tool will call the original `callback` and notify the application. In addition to wrapping the callback, the tool will also need to wrap the callback data pointer passed to `MPI_Continue` and pass the application callback data pointer to `callback`.

The On-the-Fly Critical Path Tool (OTF-CPT) [7] is a PMPI-based tool to track different critical paths through an application for performance analysis. Lamport-like execution time clocks measure the critical path and need to be updated according to MPI synchronization. Therefore, the tool uses piggyback communication [10] for each communication performed by the application. To perform the necessary analysis, the OTF-CPT needs to detect the completion of MPI communication operations before the application does. The tool was one of the first tools built on top of the MPI handle shim library [3] to wrap MPI requests and store additional information with them. The MPI handle shim library by itself defines a completion callback. During creation of a request, the tool can select which code needs to execute during completion by selecting the right completion callback. The callback gets associated with the wrapped request object. This callback approach makes integration of continuations very comfortable. Inside the previously described `wrapped_callback`, we only need to call the tool completion callback before the app's continuation callback.

A new challenge we observed for PMPI tools is that a progress thread now might become visible to the tool. Depending on the configuration and the settings of the continuation request, the continuation callback might be called from a progress thread, which was not observed by the tool before. Tool-internal, thread-local data structures might not be properly initialized in such a case.

5 API Ambiguities and Proposed Adjustments

We propose and motivate changes to the current state of the MPI Continuations proposal. Consideration of necessary changes started when reviewing the potential of nested continuation requests. Section 3.2 already described considerations to be made when implementing testing of nested continuation requests. In this section, we go beyond implementation difficulties and recommend refining the proposal and the state conditions for continuation requests. We start by listing current definition ambiguities that should be eliminated, before describing correctness problems that motivate the introduction of a new state for requests.

5.1 Ambiguities

The current proposal still has some ambiguities in its definitions, mostly for implications for nested continuation requests (nested CRs). The ambiguities can be grouped into the following three categories:

Definition of Waiting and Testing: Usually, when the MPI standard [4] refers to *testing* or *waiting* of requests, it refers to explicit `MPI_Wait/Test` calls. This specifically excludes tests that the MPI runtime or progress engines might do. For nested continuation requests, this definition becomes fuzzy since testing or waiting on the outer request (e.g., via `MPI_Test`) requires recursive testing of the nested request. The question is now whether the specification's use of *testing* includes the recursive testing of the nested request. This becomes especially relevant for the `poll_only` info key, which allows execution of continuations only if the associated continuation request is *tested* or *waited* on. If the recursive testing does not count as *testing* but a user only explicitly tests the outer request, none of the requests will complete. The definition also influences the `max_poll` info key that influences how many continuations may be invoked upon testing the continuation request. If recursive testing does not count, the specified limit of nested continuation requests will not be considered when testing their parent's requests. In the following, we assume that recursive testing counts as testing.

Precedence of Info Keys for Nested CRs: The current proposal does not specify how info keys should be interpreted for nested continuation requests. Consider the `max_poll` info key. Our implementation discussion from Sect. 3.2 assumed that the smallest `max_poll` limit currently observed must be respected. One alternative interpretation is that only the limit of the explicitly tested continuation request has to hold, which corresponds to not counting recursive testing as *testing* described in the previous paragraph. Another interpretation is that only directly registered continuations count for the limit. In this case, for two nested continuation requests with limits 2 and 4, testing the outer continuation request can only trigger the execution of a maximum of two continuations registered with the outer request but can trigger in total up to 6 continuations since the inner request is tested as well and has a limit of 4.

Defining which info key takes precedence for nested continuation requests also influences the behavior of the `continue_thread` info key, which specifies whether continuations are allowed to be executed by non-application threads. Consider two nested continuation requests where the outer allows this while the inner does not. If the innermost info key takes precedence, a progress thread testing the outer request will also test the inner one. It would then need to explicitly avoid triggering a continuation for the inner request.

Imprecise Names of Info Keys: When discussing the implications of info keys, we also stumbled over two of the info key names. The `max_poll` key appears to restrict the number of requests to test but instead limits the number of executed continuation calls. A more suitable name might be `max_exec`. The `enqueue_complete` key indicates whether continuations for already completed requests are allowed to execute during the continue call or have to be *enqueued*. The value *true* makes sense since this forces continuations to be enqueued. However, the value *false* does not imply that continuations as above will always directly be executed in the continue call, but only that they are allowed to. A different name like `force_enqueue` might make this clearer.

5.2 Issues

To start, registering a continuation request with itself should be defined as erroneous. The request could never complete, and waiting for the request would deadlock. Broadening this problem, cyclic chains of nested continuation requests should also be defined as erroneous. While this can be seen as a static restriction, we will next motivate a more general restriction based on a new request state that is stronger and needed for multiple reasons.

```
1      MPI_Recv_init(&req);
2      MPI_Start(&req);
3      MPI_Continue(&req, creq);
4      MPI_Wait(&req);
5      MPI_Start(&req);
6      MPI_Wait(&creq);
```

Listing 2. Starting a persistent request that has been attached a continuation

The code example shown in Listing 2 raises questions resulting from different timings of the completion of a persistent receive operation. The persistent operation is started in line 2. The completion could happen during the call to MPI_Continue, in which case the callback would be triggered immediately. In this case, the MPI_Wait would return immediately due to the inactive request. Alternatively, the operation could complete in the MPI_Wait. In this case it is unclear whether the completion callback should trigger. We will discuss this and similar issues in the following.

Completing Persistent Requests: It is currently allowed to explicitly complete a persistent request using MPI_Wait/Test while it has a continuation attached to it. This allows a situation where one thread waits on the persistent request and another on the continuation request. This conflicts with MPI's current approach to multithreaded execution, which explicitly prohibits concurrent waiting or testing of requests [4, p. 516, l.38]. However, even if only one thread is used, there is an additional problem. Consider again the example in Listing 2 and assume that req is completed in line 4. Then it is unclear if a callback is executed before starting the operation again in line 5 as the callback is only invoked if the continuation request detects the completion of the operation in question. Consequently, a second send might be necessary to trigger the callback for the reactivated persistent operation when explicitly waiting on the continuation request in line 6. Depending on the configuration of the continuation request, the continuation could also trigger between the MPI_Wait in line 4 and the MPI_Start in line 5.

Activating Inactive Persistent Requests: Consider the registration of a continuation for a persistent request that is at that time inactive. Since the request is then considered completed, it is possible that the continuation is executed right away. However, this is not guaranteed and depends on the configuration of the corresponding continuation request and the MPI library implementation. If the operation identified through the persistent request is then started and the corresponding continuation request concurrently tested, it is hence unclear whether a continuation callback signals the completion of the inactive or the already started request. For this reason, starting a persistent operation with a continuation attached to it should be considered erroneous. Predictable results in such scenario are only possible for `mpi_continue_poll_only` where continuation can only happen during polling of the continuation request. With this setting, Listing 2 will need a second message to trigger the continuation in the final wait call.

Freeing Persistent Requests: The MPI standard allows to free persistent requests. After freeing a request, it cannot be used in completion calls. However, continuations can also be attached to inactive persistent requests. Without further restrictions, it would be possible to free a persistent request while having a continuation attached. Conceptually, such scenario is equivalent to freeing a persistent request while another thread waits for this request.

Registering with Nested Continuation Requests: Assume two continuation requests cr_1 and cr_2 where there is a continuation attached to cr_2 that is registered with cr_1. In this case, the registration of a new continuation with the nested cr_2 leads to an effect similar to the starting of a persistent request: cr_2 becomes incomplete, but the continuation for it might have already been triggered because it was complete beforehand. The state of cr_2 is therefore unclear after the execution of the continuation registered with cr_2 has been executed.

5.3 Recommendations

The ambiguities explained in Sect. 5.1 mostly concern nested continuation requests. We recommend a clarification on whether testing a continuation request includes nested testing. Otherwise, the meaning of the configuration key `poll_only` remains unclear. If nested testing is considered as testing, then defining a precedence order on the configuration keys `max_poll` and `continue_thread` is strongly recommended. Further, we find the names of the keys `max_poll` and `enqueue_complete` misleading and suggest new names like `max_exec` and `force_enqueue`, respectively.

A restriction on registering a continuation request with itself seems obvious but is missing from the proposal; such behavior should explicitly be forbidden. It should also be forbidden to free a persistent request that has a continuation attached to it because this might interrupt a thread that concurrently tries to complete this request.

The Completing State for Requests: The remaining issues addressed in Sect. 5.2 can be solved by introducing a third state for requests. Next to *incomplete* and *complete*, consider the state *completing* as depicted in Fig. 5. A request is in this state whenever it has a continuation attached to it or while it is passed to a completion function. Therefore, a request enters the state when passing the request to a call of any of the test, wait, or continue functions. After completion, the request returns into the *complete* state or is freed in case of non-persistent requests. After an unsuccessful test, the request returns to the *incomplete* state. While a continuation request is in the *completing* state, no new continuations can be registered with it. Note that this also solves the problem of cyclic chains explained at the beginning, as a continuation would have to be registered with a request that is currently *completing*. We propose this new state to apply for all kinds of requests. Requests in the *completing* state must not be passed to a start, wait, test, or free procedure.

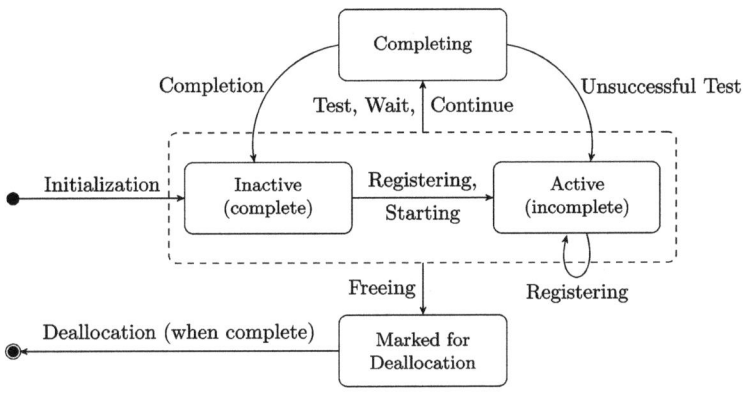

Fig. 5. Extended state transition diagram including the new *completing* state.

6 Evaluation

For the evaluation of the updated implementation, we repeat an experiment from the Detach paper [7] that evaluated the performance of MPI Detach for a distributed Blocked Cholesky factorization using OpenMP detached tasks. For our experiment, we adapted the code to use MPI Continuations by substituting `MPI_Detach(all)` calls with `MPI_Continue(all)` calls that all get registered with a single continuation request. We also start a dedicated progress thread in all executions. For our Continuations implementation we, therefore, use the appropriate info key during creation of the continuation request.

In the original experiment, the Detach library was treated as being part of the application code. In this setup, the tool observes communication completion by intercepting the completion calls from the Detach library, as depicted on the left in Fig. 6. For this work, we extended the OTF-CPT to support the prospective continuations API. In the new experiment, we treat the continuations library as being part of the MPI implementation. As shown on the right in Fig. 6, the OTF-CPT is placed in between the continuations library and the application.

All experiments are executed on exclusively reserved nodes of the CLAIX-2023 cluster with two Intel Xeon 8468 Sapphire Rapids processors and at least

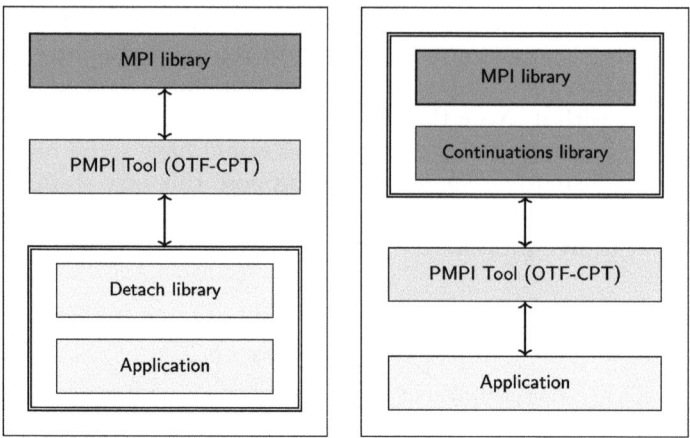

Fig. 6. Layering a PMPI tool with the Detach and Continuations implementation

256 GB of main memory. The nodes have hyper-threading disabled, and sub-NUMA clustering is enabled, splitting nodes into 8 NUMA domains of 12 cores each. The operating system is Rocky 9. We execute the code with 8, 16, and 32 processes and 12 threads in all cases.

Figure 7 shows the aggregated runtime across all threads for the strong-scaling experiment. The aggregated runtime corresponds to an execution time of about 160, 80, and 40 s for the different process counts. The slight increase in

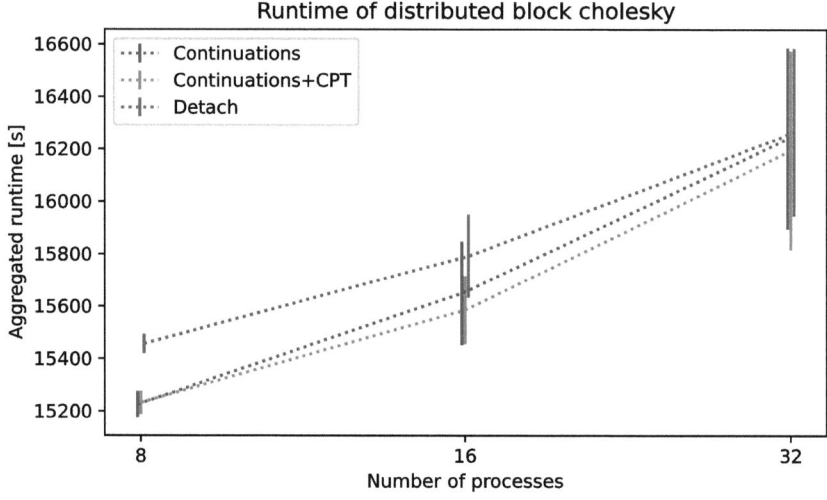

Fig. 7. Comparison of the initial Detach implementation with our updated implementation and OTF-CPT tool attached. For each of the different process counts the difference is less than one percent.

aggregated runtime for an increasing number of processes is caused by communicating more data for the more broadly distributed blocks and is consistent with the previous Detach experiments. Overall, the performance of the two implementations is nearly identical. Since the original detach implementation was shown to be efficient [6], we can also conclude that our continuations implementation is efficient and can, therefore, be used in future research on continuations.

7 Conclusions

The upcoming continuations feature in MPI facilitates the inclusion of asynchronous programming models into MPI by introducing asynchronous completion of MPI operations. To support the effective adoption of the new feature in applications, it is crucial to have a robust definition of MPI Continuations, implementations, and tool support early on. In this work, we updated an early prototype implementation of the continuations feature to align with the proposal currently being discussed by the MPI Forum. Our prototype can be easily used for various tests with existing MPI implementation since it is implemented as a shim layer on top of MPI. We also described potential pitfalls implementors might encounter. Implementing the prototype also revealed issues in the current proposal text, ranging from imprecise names and definitions for info keys to grave correctness issues like the possibility of cyclic continuations and a race condition for completing continuation requests. We proposed a new state for MPI Requests together with a set of rules to eliminate these correctness issues. Additionally, we discussed how MPI Continuations affect how PMPI-based tools handle the completion of operations. We adapted the PMPI-based On-The-Fly Critical Path Tool (OTF-CPT) to support MPI Continuations in its analysis to show the feasibility of PMPI support for continuations. Lastly, we also performed a brief overhead study of continuations and the tool, showcasing that the updated implementation matches the performance of the initial implementation and that the integration into the tool comes with negligible overhead.

References

1. Dinan, J., et al.: Enabling communication concurrency through flexible MPI endpoints. Int. J. High Perform. Comput. Appl. **28**(4), 390–405 (2014)
2. Grant, R.E., Dosanjh, M.G.F., Levenhagen, M.J., Brightwell, R., Skjellum, A.: Finepoints: partitioned multithreaded MPI communication. In: High Performance Computing, pp. 330–350 (2019)
3. Jenke, J., Knobloch, M., Hermanns, M., Schwitanski, S.: A shim layer for transparently adding meta data to MPI handles. In: Proceedings of the 30th European MPI Users' Group Meeting, EuroMPI 2023, Bristol, United Kingdom, September 11-13, 2023, pp. 6:1–6:9. ACM (2023). https://doi.org/10.1145/3615318.3615324
4. Message passing interface forum: MPI: a message-passing interface standard version 4.1 (2023). https://www.mpi-forum.org/docs/mpi-4.1/mpi41-report.pdf
5. Message passing interface hybrid working group: MPI continuations proposal (2021). https://github.com/mpiwg-hybrid/hybrid-issues/issues/6#issue-1030908230

6. Protze, J., Hermanns, M.A., Demiralp, A., Müller, M.S., Kuhlen, T.: MPI detach - asynchronous local completion. In: Proceedings of the 27th European MPI Users' Group Meeting. EuroMPI/USA '20, ACM (2020).https://doi.org/10.1145/3416315.3416323
7. Protze, J., Orland, F., Haldar, K., Koritzius, T., Terboven, C.: On-the-Fly calculation of model factors for multi-paradigm applications. In: Euro-Par 2022: Parallel Processing, pp. 69–84. Springer International Publishing (2022)
8. Schuchart, J., Samfass, P., Niethammer, C., Gracia, J., Bosilca, G.: Callback-based completion notification using MPI Continuations. Parallel Comput. **106**, 102793 (2021).https://doi.org/10.1016/J.PARCO.2021.102793
9. Schuchart, J., Tsugane, K., Gracia, J., Sato, M.: The impact of taskyield on the design of tasks communicating through MPI. In: Evolving OpenMP for Evolving Architectures, pp. 3–17 (2018)
10. Schulz, M., Bronevetsky, G., de Supinski, B.R.: On the performance of transparent MPI piggyback messages. In: Lastovetsky, A.L., Kechadi, M.T., Dongarra, J.J. (eds.) Recent Advances in Parallel Virtual Machine and Message Passing Interface, 15th European PVM/MPI Users' Group Meeting, Dublin, Ireland, September 7-10, 2008. Proceedings. Lecture Notes in Computer Science, vol. 5205, pp. 194–201. Springer (2008). https://doi.org/10.1007/978-3-540-87475-1_28

MPI Finally Needs to Deal with Threads

Joseph Schuchart[1](✉), Joachim Jenke[2], and Simon Schwitanski[2]

[1] Stony Brook University, Stony Brook, NY, USA
joseph.schuchart@stonybrook.edu
[2] RWTH Aachen University, Aachen, Germany
{jenke,schwitanski}@itc.rwth-aachen.de

Abstract. The Message Passing Interface (MPI) standard has long been a cornerstone of parallel computing, enabling multi-threaded processes to communicate effectively. However, integrating multi-threading with MPI is not as straightforward as it might seem. MPI must function optimally in a multi-threaded environment, which requires robust thread support. The description provided by MPI about how multiple application threads may interact with MPI forms a contract for guarantees that applications can rely on and that implementations must provide, and *vice versa*. We find that the definitions regarding multi-threaded behavior provided by MPI are imprecise, which leads to differing interpretations and potential over- or undercommitment of computational resources in order to provide their perceived semantics. We provide an analysis of relevant parts of the MPI standard dealing with multi-threading and provide proposals for definitions of concurrency, conflicts, and race conditions, which we hope will clarify the guarantees that are part of the contract between MPI multi-threaded applications and implementations.

1 Introduction

The MPI standard [12] provides communication primitives for point-to-point, collective, and one-sided communication between processes. The addressable entity within a communicator is a process (not a thread) and each process must participate exactly once in a collective operation on any given communicator whose group the process is a part of.

The consideration for threads in MPI reaches back almost two decades [18]. Yet, the descriptions of the semantics of multi-threading in MPI remain murky and imprecise, as we will discuss in this paper. Threads are thus only a second-class citizen: their support was added only in MPI 2.1 [11], 15 years after the initial release of MPI 1.0 [10]. Given the state of computer architectures at the time MPI was conceived, it is no surprise that threads entered the MPI standard only once multi-core CPUs had become widely available and started playing a major role in high-performance computing. However, this late addition has led to a patch-work of statements across the standard that define how multiple threads within a process may interact with MPI.

In modern operating systems on multi-core CPUs, it is likely that two or more threads execute MPI calls in parallel, i.e., more than one core may execute code of the MPI library at any given time. This requires MPI libraries to carefully protect internal data structures, either through mutual exclusion concepts (e.g., POSIX mutex) or atomic updates.

The serialization caused by synchronization between threads may have significant performance implications. MPI implementors thus have spent significant efforts to reduce the synchronization overhead [8] and more certain assertions provided by applications have provided opportunities to further reduce the required synchronization overhead.

At the same time, the way the standard describes the interaction between threads and MPI is essential for application developers to reason about what is permissible and what semantics can be safely expected. Recent discussions have shown that the standard's wording is far from unambiguous, potentially giving implementations more leeway than users expect.

Given the ubiquitous nature of multi-threaded applications, it is important that the MPI Forum revisits the relevant parts of the standard pertaining to multi-threaded usage of MPI to ensure that contract between MPI and the application is unambiguous.

We will argue that MPI should adopt a more stringent definition of terms related to multi-threaded execution and that it should clarify what guarantees users can expect and implementations have to provide. The main contributions of this paper are an analysis of the relevant parts regarding multi-threading in the MPI standard and proposed improvements to ensure precise rules for applications and implementations.

The remainder of the paper is structured as follows: Sect. 2 details the current state of multi-thread support in MPI and shortcomings in its definitions. Section 3 discusses missing features and Sect. 4 possible improvements to be considered by the MPI Forum. Section 5 briefly discusses related work.

2 Current State

The MPI standard already includes several paragraphs and definitions to incorporate threading support. This section gives an overview of the most important concepts, discusses shortcomings of some, and proposes potential improvements.

Generally, the MPI standard does not prescribe what a thread is in MPI but states in §11.6 that threads are expected to behave like POSIX threads:

> This section generally assumes a thread package similar to POSIX threads, but the syntax and semantics of thread calls are not specified here.

This generally includes the notion that the execution of threads may be suspended, that each thread maintains its own stack, program counter, and signal masks, and that threads execute concurrently.

2.1 Threading Levels

MPI defines four threading levels to help manage how multiple threads interact with MPI calls §11.2.1. Applications specify the threading-level during initialization of MPI, either when using the world-process model (i.e., using MPI_Init_thread) or when initializing a session. The threading levels are:

- MPI_THREAD_SINGLE: Only one thread will execute. No threading is used, making this the simplest level.
- MPI_THREAD_FUNNELED: Only the main thread will make MPI calls, but other threads can be created. This allows for a simple threading model where the main thread handles all communication.
- MPI_THREAD_SERIALIZED: Multiple threads can make MPI calls, but only one thread at a time can make calls. This level allows for a simpler programming model without requiring complex synchronization.
- MPI_THREAD_MULTIPLE: Multiple threads can make MPI calls simultaneously. This level allows the most flexibility but requires careful management of resources and potential race conditions.

For the context of this paper, the threading levels MPI_THREAD_SERIALIZED and MPI_THREAD_MULTIPLE are relevant as they allow applications to interact with MPI from multiple threads.

2.2 Thread-Compliant Implementations

In §11.6.1, the MPI standard defines the two main requirements of a "thread-compliant" implementation:

> 1. All MPI calls are thread-safe, i.e., two concurrently running threads may make MPI calls and the outcome will be as if the calls executed in some order, even if their execution is interleaved.
> 2. Blocking MPI calls will block the calling thread only, allowing another thread to execute, if available. The calling thread will be blocked until the event on which it is waiting occurs. Once the blocked communication is enabled and can proceed, then the call will complete and the thread will be marked runnable, within a finite time. A blocked thread will not prevent progress of other runnable threads on the same process, and will not prevent them from executing MPI calls.

The first point requires MPI implementations to support threads calling into MPI without prior synchronization, i.e., without an order imposed by the application. It should be noted that this text is oblivious to the topic of MPI thread levels. A reasonable interpretation would be to assume that a "thread-compliant" implementation is only required if MPI_THREAD_MULTIPLE was specified.

The second point requires implementations to allow forward-progress of other threads even if one or more threads are waiting for a communication operation to complete. In particular, a thread may not hold a lock while waiting for a communication to complete if that lock may prevent other threads from completing their MPI operations. This is important to account for transitive dependencies between threads, e.g., where Thread A on Process X waits for a message from Process Y that in turns depends on a message from Thread B on Process X.

2.3 Thread-Safe Functions

The MPI standard states in §11.6:

> Regardless of whether or not the MPI implementation is thread compliant, a subset of MPI functions must always be thread-safe. A complete list of such MPI functions is given in Table 11.1. When a thread is executing one of these routines, if another concurrently running thread also makes an MPI call, the outcome will be as if the calls executed in some order.

The functions listed in Table 11.1 of the standard can also be called before `MPI_Init` and after `MPI_Finalize`. For the functions `MPI_Initialized` and `MPI_Finalized`, it is crucial that they can be called before and after `MPI_Init` and `MPI_Finalize`. The functions `MPI_Get_version` and `MPI_Get_library_version` are trivially thread-safe, since they just provide a constant string and are therefore stateless.

Similarly, routines for error handler management (e.g., `MPI_Errhandler_free`, `MPI_Add_error_code`, `MPI_Remove_error_code`) operate on global state of the MPI implementation that can be protected through a single mutex.

The thread-safety of `MPI_Info_set` is less clear. In particular, the text can be interpreted in two ways. The wide interpretation is that all calls to `MPI_Info_set` are thread-safe, no matter what info object is used. This is the interpretation used by Open MPI, which provides support for concurrent modifications or modifications and queries of info object by protecting the underlying data structure and using reference-counted string. Interestingly, this protection is only available in Open MPI if MPI has been initialized with `MPI_THREAD_MULTIPLE`.

A narrower interpretation is that calls to `MPI_Info_set` are generally thread-safe if they are not conflicting, i.e., they are not accessing the same info object. This interpretation is brought forward by the MPICH documentation[1]:

> The MPI standard defined a thread-safe interface but this does not mean that all routines may be called without any thread locks. For example, two threads must not attempt to change the contents of the same `MPI_Info` object concurrently. The user is responsible in this case for using some mechanism, such as thread locks, to ensure that only one thread at a time makes use of this routine.

MPICH does not appear to protect its info objects from concurrent modifications. This discrepancy likely leads to applications avoiding multi-threaded accesses to info objects. The MPI Forum should clarify whether "thread-safe"

---

[1] https://www.mpich.org/static/docs/v3.3/www3/MPI_Info_set.html.

here applies only to the state of the MPI library or whether it extends to conflicting accesses to info objects.

2.4 Erroneous Multi-threading Usage

Local Buffer Race. The MPI standard in §3.6 states for non-blocking operations that

> A nonblocking send call indicates that the system may start copying data out of the send buffer. The sender should not modify any part of the send buffer after a nonblocking send operation is called, until the send completes.
> A nonblocking receive call indicates that the system may start writing data into the receive buffer. The receiver should not access any part of the receive buffer after a nonblocking receive operation is called, until the receive completes.

In §3.4, it is further specified that

> In a multi-threaded implementation of MPI, the system may de-schedule a thread that is blocked on a send or receive operation, and schedule another thread for execution in the same address space. In such a case it is the user's responsibility not to modify a communication buffer until the communication completes. Otherwise, the outcome of the computation is undefined.

However, the restriction not to "modify" the communication buffer until completion is not sufficient for receive operations: the outcome is undefined if the application accesses the buffer in *any* way (read or write) before the receive has completed. Further, the sentence is part of the description of the MPI blocking send family of functions, but actually affects any MPI operation with accesses to user-provided buffers. An advice early on should replace the fragmented statements by clearly stating that any *conflicting* access to buffers currently used by MPI may lead to undefined outcomes. This will ensure that any buffer races are problematic, whether they come from the same thread that started the operation or from different threads. It will also make sure that the advice applies to all communication, not just point-to-point operations.

Concurrent Use of Collectives. In §6.14, the MPI standard lays out some rules for multi-threaded use of collective operations:

> Finally, in multi-threaded implementations, one can have more than one, concurrently executing, collective communication initialization call at an MPI process. In these situations, it is the user's responsibility to *ensure that the same communicator is not used concurrently by two different collective communication initialization calls at the same MPI process*. Collective communication initialization calls include all calls for blocking collective operations, all initiation calls for nonblocking collective operations, and all initialization calls for persistent collective operations.

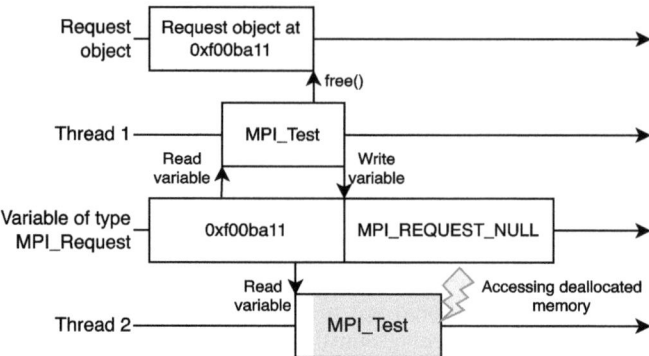

Fig. 1. Two threads attempting to test the same non-persistent request handle. Thread 1 completes the request and frees the request object. Thread 2 holds a stale handle to the freed request object because it did not see the completion of the request by Thread 1.

Concurrent Completion of Requests. For nonblocking operations, the concurrent completion of requests by different threads is classified as erroneous in §11.6.2:

> A program in which **two threads block**, waiting on the **same** request, is erroneous. Similarly, the **same request** cannot appear in the array of requests of **two concurrent** MPI_{WAIT|TEST}{ANY|SOME|ALL} calls. In MPI, a request can only be completed once. Any combination of wait or test that violates this rule is erroneous.

This explicitly forbids concurrent *waiting* on a request with MPI_Wait. Otherwise, one thread posting a wait could complete the communication, but before the request is released and set to MPI_REQUEST_NULL, another thread may also start to wait on the same request before it is released. Consequently, this simplifies request completion since MPI implementations do not have to add synchronization measures for potentially concurrent waits.

The formulation of the restriction in the standard, however, does not cover concurrent *testing* on a request with MPI_Test (or a combination of MPI_Test and MPI_Wait) which could also complete the communication and run into the same problem. This ambiguity may lead to the assumption that different threads may be allowed to call MPI_Test concurrently on the same request. In that case, MPI implementations would have to permit and guard concurrent testing on the same request, which may negatively impact performance.

In practice, the issue is that any non-persistent request object will be freed by the MPI implementation once the operation has completed and completion has been detected through a call to any of the test or wait functions. The request handle will thus be replaced by MPI_REQUEST_NULL. There thus exists a race condition on the *handle* of the request, where two threads read the handle value from the *same or different* variable, release the request, and update the variable holding the handle value to `MPI_REQUEST_NULL`. Thus, one thread may read a stale handle value for which the underlying request object has been released already or will be released while the thread is using the handle to access the request object. This may lead to accesses of unallocated memory.

This is exemplified in Fig. 1 where two threads concurrently test the same request handle (stored in the same variable) for completion. Thread 1 finds the operation complete, frees the request object, and sets the variable to `MPI_REQUEST_NULL`. Thread 1 reads the handle value before Thread 1 resets it and proceeds to access the referenced but now released MPI object.

To support such behavior, the MPI implementation would have to employ a global lock to ensure mutual exclusion. In the example shown in Fig. 1 an atomic swap on the variable would be feasible but that would i) incur significant overheads; and ii) fail to support cases where the same handle is stored in different variables, i.e., the race condition on the *MPI handle* would persist.

It has been proposed in previous discussions, that the first sentence in the above quote from §11.6.2 implies that `MPI_Test` is potentially not thread-safe.[2] However, we argue that implementation-internal thread-safety and the absence of race conditions on user-controlled handles are orthogonal issues and that a thread-safe implementation may assume that a correct program is free of race-conditions.

Therefore, the standard should also explicitly forbid concurrent *testing* on the same request to avoid ambiguities.

Conflicting Messages. While processes in MPI can be clearly distinguished by their rank, this is not the case for the threads within an MPI process. This leads to additional challenges in scenarios with concurrent communication calls as described in §3.5:

> If a process has a single thread of execution, then any two communications executed by this process are ordered. On the other hand, if the process is multi-threaded, then the semantics of thread execution may not define a relative order between two send operations executed by two distinct threads. The operations are logically concurrent, even if one physically precedes the other. In such a case, the two messages sent can be received in any order. Similarly, if two receive operations that are logically concurrent receive two successively sent messages, then the two messages can match the two receives in either order.

In other words, when two threads within an MPI process post a receive call with a matching message envelope concurrently, either thread can receive the message. It has been established that this formulation is ambiguous[3] and that two interpretations exist:

---

[2] "Change in thread safety in MPI 4.1" (#846): https://github.com/mpi-forum/mpi-issues/issues/846.

[3] "'Logically concurrent' isn't" (#117): https://github.com/mpi-forum/mpi-issues/issues/117.

1. Two messages that match the same receive operation sent from two different threads are matched in the order in which they were posted. If the threads are serialized through some synchronization at the application level then they are not logically concurrent and the messages must be matched in the order in which they were posted. We consider this the *stronger* interpretation.
2. The same two messages sent from two threads are *logically concurrent* even if they have been serialized by the application. This interpretation focuses on the part that states "the semantics of thread execution may not define a relative order between two send operations executed by two distinct threads. The operations are logically concurrent [...]". We consider this the *weaker* interpretation.

While this behavior is not necessarily harmful for an application, users may avoid those situations by using distinct communicators at each thread or encode a custom thread identifier in the message tag. As noted earlier, §11.6.1 states

> It is the user's responsibility to prevent races when threads within the same application post conflicting communication calls. The user can make sure that two threads in the same process will not issue conflicting communication calls by using distinct communicators at each thread.

It can thus be argued that the weaker interpretation is legitimate because applications may work around this issue. A counter-argument is that the use of distinct communicators prevents the matching of messages between any threads, which may be the application's intent, and that the different semantics between single- and multi-threaded execution is counter-intuitive for applications. It should also be noted here that the "`mpi_assert_allow_overtake`" info key on communicators allows applications to disable strict message ordering if they can guarantee that the application will execute correctly in the absence of strict message ordering. The weaker interpretation asserts that this only applies to messages originating from the same thread.

It should also be noted that the standard does not clearly define what MPI procedures are relevant when considering concurrent operations. While it is ambiguous for blocking operations, it is less clear for non-blocking and persistent operations. It is, however, reasonable to assume that for nonblocking and persistent point-to-point and collective operations the point of relevant concurrency is the starting procedure call while for partitioned operations it is the initialization procedure call.

2.5 Definition of Concurrency

MPI provides a definition of concurrency in the text quoted above: "[...]" the semantics of thread execution may not define a relative order between two send operations executed by two distinct threads. The operations are logically concurrent, even if one physically precedes the other. This text neglects the possible ordering of events using synchronization events and—as stated above—suggests

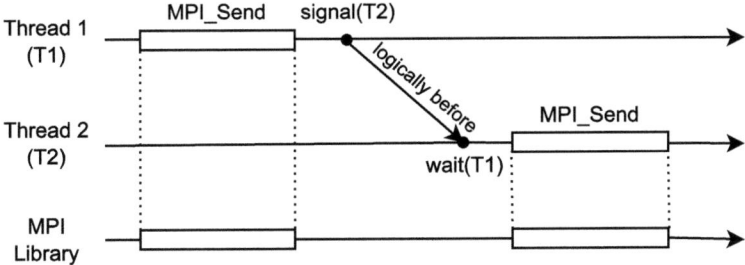

Fig. 2. Logically ordered MPI_Send calls via thread synchronization. T2 waits for a signal from T1 such that T1's MPI_Send is logically ordered before T2's MPI_Send. Such thread synchronization may be a mutex, condition variable, or a thread barrier.

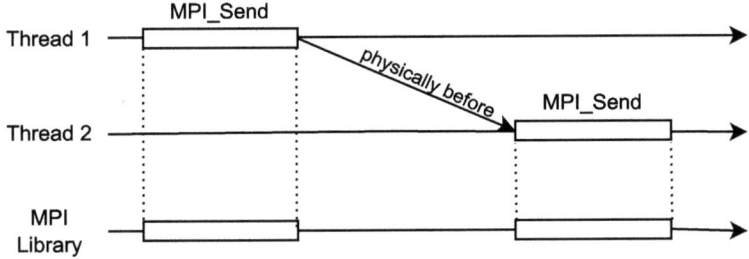

Fig. 3. Physically ordered MPI_Send calls. There is no synchronization construct between the threads (logically concurrent), but the timing still ensures a physical order.

that *any* MPI calls from multiple threads may indeed be treated as logically concurrent.

Lamport [9] defined logical concurrency based on the happens-before order $\xrightarrow{hb}$ between events in parallel entities (such as threads or processes). It is the smallest relation satisfying the following three properties:

1. Whenever an event a occurs before an event b on the *same* parallel entity, then $a \xrightarrow{hb} b$.
2. When a parallel entity sends in event a a signal to another parallel entity that waits (blocks) for it in an event b, then $a \xrightarrow{hb} b$.
3. Whenever $a \xrightarrow{hb} b$ and $b \xrightarrow{hb} c$, then $a \xrightarrow{hb} c$.

To determine the happened-before relation, logical clocks may be used, which are advanced, piggybacked, and merged through certain (synchronization) events, e.g., an MPI message, a POSIX mutex, or an atomic update. Based on those logical clocks [6], the happened-before relation can be determined for any parallel entity, e.g., for processes or threads.

From MPI's view it is irrelevant whether the logical clock is advanced through MPI or some other measure by the application. As long as the application can ensure the $\xrightarrow{hb}$ relation, it is reasonable to expect that two threads calling into MPI are considered neither physically nor logically concurrent. A logical order,

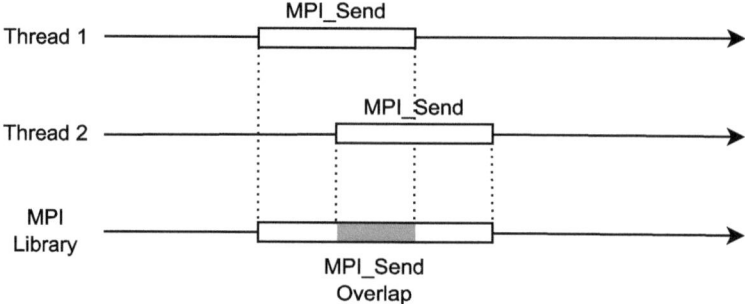

Fig. 4. Logically and physically concurrent `MPI_Send` calls. The calls are both active at the same time and overlap for a certain time frame.

i.e., $\xrightarrow{hb}$ relation, between two events implies a physical order between those events, but not vice versa. Figure 2 shows an example where one application thread synchronizes with another application thread, establishing a logical order of the two `MPI_Send` calls. Figure 3 shows the same example with no logical order, but the physical order (due to the timing of the calls) still ensures that the calls are not concurrent. In both cases, the MPI implementation observes a physical order of the calls to `MPI_Send` and should assume that this order has been established intentionally.

In Fig. 4, no order is established and the calls can be considered logically and physically concurrent. The MPI implementation does not observe a physical order and must thus choose an order itself.

It is important to note that the MPI implementation has no way of observing whether or not a logical order of threads entering the MPI library has been established by the application. It can only observe the physical order of threads entering, leaving, or passing a certain point in the MPI library. This observation will be important in Sect. 4.1 when improving the definition of logical concurrency.

3 Missing Features

3.1 Concurrency Guarantees for User Functions

In §6.9.5, the MPI standard defines the properties of user-defined reduction functions, including the choice of commutativity, allowed MPI procedure calls (`MPI_ABORT` being the only permissible procedure to call), and the expected behavior of the function in terms of the element-wise reduction of an input vector and an output vector.

However, the standard does not mention the interaction between threads and user-defined reduction operators. It is undefined which thread will invoke the reduction operator (e.g., whether an application can rely on thread-local data) and whether the reduction operator may be invoked concurrently from multiple threads within the MPI implementation, i.e., whether or not the reduction callback has to be thread-safe.[4] This is relevant for third-party language bindings where concurrent invocation of callbacks may not be supported.

Moreover, it is undefined whether the user function callback itself may have side-effects, e.g., whether or not it may distribute the reduction across multiple threads, e.g., using `#pragma omp taskloop` followed by `#pragma omp taskwait`. This is relevant in cases where the callback is invoked on threads that are not controlled by the application, e.g., threads that are not known to the OpenMP runtime.

3.2 Concurrent Commit of Types

In §5.1.9, the standard explicitly allows for already committed types to be passed to `MPI_Type_commit`:

> `MPI_TYPE_COMMIT` will accept a committed datatype; in this case, it is equivalent to a no-op.

3 However, it is unspecified whether concurrent threads may commit the same MPI datatype concurrently, since both threads will potentially see the datatype as not yet committed. We suggest including a clarification of the behavior in this case.

4 Proposed Improvements

This section outlines the proposed changes for the MPI standard, building from a definition of concurrency over conflicting access to what "thread-safety" should mean in the context of MPI.

4.1 Definition of Concurrency

In order to define the behavior under multi-threaded applications, it is important to define the concept of concurrency. As was pointed out in Sect. 2.4, the current definition of "logical concurrency" and "physical concurrency" are insufficient and have caused more confusion than clarity.

Based on Lamport's happens-before relationship, the standard should clearly define when two threads are considered concurrent in MPI. It is important that such definition considers the *user's* perception of the established rules handling the interaction of threads and MPI. Following the principle of least astonishment [15], two calls to MPI procedures should be considered concurrent only if no happens-before relation between the two events can be established. Thus, the effect of two MPI procedure calls within a process should be the same no

---

[4] "Threading guarantees of `MPI_User_function`" (#64): https://github.com/mpi-forum/mpi-issues/issues/64.

matter whether they were issued by the same thread or two threads that have established an order through synchronization primitives.

The text in §11.6.1 should thus be changed to

> If a process has a single thread of execution, then any two communications executed by this process are ordered, **i.e., they have an established happens-before relation**. On the other hand, if the process is multi-threaded, **then two operations are considered logically concurrent only if the application has not established a happens-before relation (i.e., strict ordering) between the two messages**. In such a case, two messages sent can be received in any order. Similarly, if two receive operations that are logically concurrent receive two successively sent messages, then the two messages can match the two receives in either order.
> **The same principle can be extended to MPI procedure calls: two MPI procedure calls are considered "logically concurrent" only if no happens-before relation between them has been established.**

3 The improved definition provides guidance to both users and implementors about when two operations can be considered *logically concurrent*.

Since the mechanism through which an ordering between threads has been established may not be visible to MPI, the MPI implementation must operate under the following two assumptions:

1. The application *has established* a happens-before relationship between two MPI procedure calls. The implementation must adhere to any ordering imposed by the application.
2. The application *may not have established* a happens-before relationship between two MPI procedure calls. This means that two calls to MPI may happen logically and even physically concurrent and the implementation must be able to choose an order.

An obvious way for implementations to conform to these requirements is through an atomic increment of a sequence counter attached to the communicator.

The principle of least astonishment supports the stronger interpretation outlined in Sect. 2.4. Assuming that application developers care about correctness first and performance second (and not vice versa), extending hints such as the "mpi_assert_allow_overtake" to limit the non-overtaking property to the scope of a single thread should be considered. A similar proposal was made to limit the scope of RMA operation semantics (e.g., flush) to individual threads [16].

Based on this notion of concurrency, we can derive all subsequent rules governing concurrent activities in multi-threaded applications.

4.2 Definition of Conflicting Access

As discussed in Sect. 2.4, rules about concurrent accesses to buffers used by incomplete MPI operations are spread throughout the document and only partially cover the relevant conflicts. We propose the following text to describe undefined outcome of concurrent accesses to memory buffers:

> Two logically concurrent memory accesses are *conflicting* if they access overlapping memory regions and at least one of them potentially modifies the content in that region. For example, such conflicting accesses may occur if a thread reads the content of a buffer that is used by an incomplete receive operation or if a thread writes to a buffer that is used by an incomplete send operation. Such conflicting accesses may occur with any MPI operation. The outcome of such behavior is undefined.

4.3 Definition of Handle-Equality

In §2.5.1, the MPI standard requires that

> In addition to their use by MPI calls for object access, handles can participate in assignments and comparisons.

However, the standard does not define when two MPI objects are the same. This is owed partially to the conflation of MPI objects (communicators, requests, ...) and their handles (MPI_Comm, MPI_Request, ...) throughout the text. The standard should establish clearly that two handles (i.e., two variables of type MPI_Request) represent the same MPI object if their value is identical.

It is important to clarify that all MPI procedures act on *MPI objects* and that the handles representing them are the equivalent to pointers in the C language. This will help avoid any misconceptions about whether two variables of the same handle type with the same value represent the same or different entities.

The standard should thus be amended as follows:

> In addition to their use by MPI calls for object access, handles can participate in assignments and comparisons. **Two handles refer to the same MPI object if their type and value are identical.**

It is important to note that we do not require the comparison of *MPI objects*. The comparison of handles (i.e., pointers or public facing identifiers) is sufficient to establish whether two variables reference the same MPI object.

4.4 Definition of Thread-Safety

As discussed in Sect. 2.2, the MPI standard defines two main requirements for a "thread-compliant" implementation: i) multiple threads must be allowed to enter MPI calls concurrently with the outcome being "as if executed in some order"; and ii) no threads blocked in MPI may block other threads from progressing.

However, the MPI standard does not specify the extent to which this thread-safety applies. Generally, thread-safety requires some form of protection of shared state to prevent corruption from concurrent updates. Such state can be grouped into three categories:

1. **Global or session-specific state**, including network handles and memory caches. Such state is typically not associated with any particular MPI object and its life-time spans multiple MPI objects and operations.
2. **MPI objects**, such as communicators, files, windows, and requests. These objects are typically allocated and released through distinct MPI procedure calls and they carry state that is either hidden (e.g., message sequence counters in communicators) or user-observable (e.g., entries of an info object, state of a request) through query functions.
3. **MPI handles**, such as MPI_Comm or MPI_Request. Handles represent MPI objects and are stored in application-controlled variables. The release of an MPI object typically entails the reset of the used handle to one of the null-handles like MPI_REQUEST_NULL.

It is clear that any "thread-compliant" implementation must protect the first category of state, i.e., protect global or session-specific state from corruption due to concurrent updates.

However, as we have pointed out in Sect. 2.3, interpretations of whether the second category must be protected diverge: the question of whether info objects can be modified concurrently is answered differently by different implementations. Such divergence is generally to the detriment of the user and points to a failure of the MPI standard to provide clear definitions. Managing concurrent updates of MPI objects generally involves fine-grained locks on these objects. Such protection is, however, limited to the life-time of the object and does not extend beyond its life-time.

The third category involves application-controlled variables, i.e., memory locations that hold the handles for MPI objects. Including this category in the thread-safety guarantees would require implementations to protect updates to variables of type MPI_Request in a call to MPI_Test to avoid race conditions on this variable, i.e., to ensure that two threads calling MPI_Test on the same request variable atomically read and write that variable to ensure that no thread uses a stale handle to reference an MPI object that has been released. This might incur significant overheads (from atomic updates or global locks) from catering to edge cases that are not relevant for the majority of MPI applications. It is thus important to carefully find a balanced approach.

It should be clear that "thread-safe" (or "thread-compliant") should not mean the absence of *any* race conditions. We propose that thread-safety in the context of MPI must include the first two categories of state, but not the third. This enables concurrent starting of operations, to the extent that is allowed by the operations, e.g., excluding starting concurrent collective operations on the same communicator. However, it does not include concurrent release of objects due to the lack of protection for reading stale handles (category 3).

Below, we present two possible adaptations of the MPI standard.

Wide: Disallow Concurrent Release. The MPI standard should thus be changed as follows. The paragraph in §11.6.1 "Multiple threads completing the same request" should be removed and replaced by

> A program in which two threads concurrently pass the same MPI handle to MPI procedures and one of them may release the MPI object (i.e., replace the MPI handle value) is erroneous. For example, a non-persistent request can only be completed once and a communicator can only be freed once.

This has some interesting implications. For one, it codifies that concurrent updates to info objects are valid as long as the info object remains valid. More importantly, however, it implies that persistent requests can be checked for completion concurrently, since they are not released by test and wait calls. However, it should be noted that concurrent start calls are not permissible because calls to MPI_Start may replace the request handle (the request argument is not const) and thus the original could be released eventually.

Narrow: Only Allow Concurrent Modification of Non-User Observable State. As an alternative, we propose a slightly stricter rule. Instead of allowing all concurrent MPI procedure calls that do not replace the MPI handle value, this proposal allows only concurrent MPI procedure calls that do not change the user-observable state of an MPI object. This preserves the possibility for concurrent MPI point-to-point operations (since the sequence number is not user-observable) but would disallow concurrent wait or test as the request status is user-observable.

Among other things, this rule would prohibit concurrent setting of info objects on MPI objects such as communicators, files, and windows (since they are user-observable state). It would also prohibit concurrently setting info keys on an info object and would thus be in line with the MPICH interpretation.

The proposed wording would be

> A program in which two threads concurrently pass the same MPI handle to MPI procedures **and one of them may alter the user-observable state of the MPI object or the handle itself** is erroneous. For example, a request can only be completed once and a communicator can only be freed once.

5 Related Work

The issue of efficient multi-threaded communication has been a long-standing topic within the MPI Forum. MPI endpoints had been proposed to limit the scope of communication to individual threads [5]. Various optimizations have been developed in MPI implementations over time [3,14,19,20] and ways to efficiently manage the integration of threads and MPI have been proposed [17]. Ultimately, the topic of MPI endpoints has been abandoned [21]. A recent proposal for stream integration would provide similar resource isolation between threads [22].

Other communication libraries such as LCI [2,13], GASPI [7], and GASnet(-EX) [1] provide communication abstractions targeting multi-threaded programming models. OpenSHMEM introduced the concept of contexts, which provide for thread-isolation of network resources [4].

6 Conclusions

In this paper, we outlined the current state of thread support in the MPI standard and how the existing wording can lead to differing interpretations of the required thread support. We found that the current definition of concurrency is insufficient and have proposed wording that, we hope, is unambiguous. Based on this definition, we propose further improvements to clarify race conditions in the MPI API. We propose that thread-safety does not mean that MPI has to cope with any and all race conditions that may arise in the use of the MPI interface and instead focus on a sensible subset that covers the vast majority of users without incurring significant overheads.

References

1. Bonachea, D., Hargrove, P.H.: GASNet-EX: a high-performance, portable communication library for Exascale. In: Hall, M., Sundar, H. (eds.) LCPC 2018. LNCS, vol. 11882, pp. 138–158. Springer, Cham (2019). https://doi.org/10.1007/978-3-030-34627-0_11 ISBN 978-3-030-34627-0
2. Dang, H.V., et al.: A lightweight communication runtime for distributed graph analytics. In: 2018 IEEE International Parallel and Distributed Processing Symposium (IPDPS), pp. 980–989 (2018). https://doi.org/10.1109/IPDPS.2018.00107
3. Dang, H.V., Seo, S., Amer, A., Balaji, P.: Advanced thread synchronization for multithreaded MPI implementations. In: 2017 17th IEEE/ACM International Symposium on Cluster, Cloud and Grid Computing (CCGRID), pp. 314–324 (2017). https://doi.org/10.1109/CCGRID.2017.65
4. Dinan, J., Flajslik, M.: Contexts: a mechanism for high throughput communication in OpenSHMEM. In: Proceedings of the 8th International Conference on Partitioned Global Address Space Programming Models, PGAS 2014, Association for Computing Machinery, New York, NY, USA (2014). ISBN 978145033247, https://doi.org/10.1145/2676870.2676872
5. Dinan, J., et al.: Enabling communication concurrency through flexible MPI endpoints. Int. J. High Perform. Comput. Appl. **28**(4), 390–405 (2014). https://doi.org/10.1177/1094342014548772. ISSN 1094-342
6. Fidge, C.: Logical time in distributed computing systems. Computer **24**(8), 28–33 (1991). ISSN 1558-081, https://doi.org/10.1109/2.84874
7. Grünewald, D., Simmendinger, C.: The GASPI API specification and its implementation GPI 2.0. In: 7th International Conference on PGAS Programming Models, vol. 243, p. 52 (2013)
8. Hjelm, N., Dosanjh, M.G.F., Grant, R.E., Groves, T., Bridges, P., Arnold, D.: Improving MPI multi-threaded RMA communication performance. In: Proceedings of the 47th International Conference on Parallel Processing, ICPP 2018, Association for Computing Machinery, New York, NY, USA (2018). ISBN 978145036510, https://doi.org/10.1145/3225058.3225114, https://doi.org/10.1145/3225058.3225114

9. Lamport, L.: Time, clocks, and the ordering of events in a distributed system. Commun. ACM **21**(7), 558–565 (1978). https://doi.org/10.1145/359545.359563. ISSN 0001-078
10. Message Passing Interface Forum: MPI: A Message-Passing Interface Standard Version 1.0 (1994). https://www.mpi-forum.org/docs/mpi-1.0/mpi-10.ps. Accessed 24 Apr 2025
11. Message Passing Interface Forum: MPI: A Message-Passing Interface Standard Version 2.1 (2008). https://www.mpi-forum.org/docs/mpi-2.1/mpi21-report.pdf. Accessed 24 Apr 2025
12. Message Passing Interface Forum: MPI: A Message-Passing Interface Standard Version 4.1 (2023). http://mpi-forum.org/docs/mpi-4.1/mpi41-report.pdf. Accessed 24 Apr 2025
13. Mor, O., Bosilca, G., Snir, M.: Improving the scaling of an asynchronous many-task runtime with a lightweight communication engine. In: Proceedings of the 52nd International Conference on Parallel Processing. ICPP 2023, pp. 153–162, , Association for Computing Machinery, New York (2023). ISBN 979840070843, https://doi.org/10.1145/3605573.3605642
14. Patinyasakdikul, T., Eberius, D., Bosilca, G., Hjelm, N.: Give MPI threading a fair chance: a study of multithreaded MPI designs. In: 2019 IEEE International Conference on Cluster Computing (CLUSTER), pp. 1–11 (2019). https://doi.org/10.1109/CLUSTER.2019.8891015
15. Saltzer, J.H., Kaashoek, M.F.: Principles of computer system design: an introduction (2009). ISBN 978-0-12-374957-4
16. Schuchart, J., Niethammer, C., Gracia, J., Bosilca, G.: Quo vadis MPI RMA? Towards a more efficient use of mpi one-sided communication (2021). https://arxiv.org/abs/2111.08142
17. Si, M., Peña, A.J., Balaji, P., Takagi, M., Ishikawa, Y.: MT-MPI: multithreaded MPI for many-core environments. In: Proceedings of the 28th ACM International Conference on Supercomputing. ICS 2014 pp. 125–134., Association for Computing Machinery, New York (2014). ISBN 978145032642, https://doi.org/10.1145/2597652.2597658
18. Skjellum, A., Protopopov, B., Hebert, S.: A thread taxonomy for MPI. In: Proceedings Second MPI Developer's Conference, pp. 50–57 (1996). https://doi.org/10.1109/MPIDC.1996.534094
19. Tang, H., Yang, T.: Optimizing threaded MPI execution on SMP clusters. In: Proceedings of the 15th International Conference on Supercomputing. ICS 2001, pp. 381–392. Association for Computing Machinery, New York (2001). ISBN 158113410, https://doi.org/10.1145/377792.377895
20. Zambre, R., Chandramowlishwaran, A., Balaji, P.: Scalable communication endpoints for MPI+threads applications. In: 2018 IEEE 24th International Conference on Parallel and Distributed Systems (ICPADS), pp. 803–812 (2018). https://doi.org/10.1109/PADSW.2018.8645059
21. Zambre, R., Chandramowliswharan, A., Balaji, P.: How I learned to stop worrying about user-visible endpoints and love MPI. In: Proceedings of the 34th ACM International Conference on Supercomputing. ICS 2020, pp. 1–13. ACM (2020). https://doi.org/10.1145/3392717.3392773
22. Zhou, H., Raffenetti, K., Guo, Y., Thakur, R.: MPIX stream: an explicit solution to hybrid MPI+X programming. In: Proceedings of the 29th European MPI Users' Group Meeting. EuroMPI/USA 2022, pp. 1–10. Association for Computing Machinery, New York (2022). ISBN 9781450397995, https://doi.org/10.1145/3555819.3555820

Performance Analysis of Open MPI on AMR Applications over Slingshot-11

Maxim Moraru[1(✉)], Howard Pritchard[1], Derek Schafer[2], Galen Shipman[1], and Patrick Bridges[2]

[1] Los Alamos National Laboratory, Los Alamos, NM 87545, USA
{moraru,howardp,gshipman}@lanl.gov
[2] Department of Computer Science, University of New Mexico, Albuquerque, USA
{dschafer1,patrickb}@unm.edu

Abstract. The HPE Slingshot interconnect is used on numerous supercomputers, including the top two supercomputers on the TOP500. Recently, HPE open-sourced the software stack for Slingshot introducing new opportunities for exploring alternative MPI implementations on HPE's Cray supercomputers. This work investigates the performance implications of using Open MPI, as opposed to the traditionally bundled Cray MPICH, on systems equipped with Slingshot-11 interconnects. We focus our analysis on Adaptive Mesh Refinement (AMR) applications in this work, as they exhibit a wide variety of communication patterns, including dynamically changing communicating peers. Based on profiling and analysis of these AMR applications, we designed a targeted microbenchmark to capture key communication patterns in AMR that can benefit from Open MPI on Slingshot-11 systems. We demonstrate that Open MPI can improve the overall execution time of AMR-based scientific applications by up to 11%. Deeper analysis using our communication pattern benchmark reveals one aspect of this performance difference. Open MPI has a much lower latency than Cray MPICH in bursty halo exchanges among even a moderately small number of processes.

Keywords: MPI · Performance evaluation · AMR applications · Slingshot interconnect

1 Introduction

The Message Passing Interface [7] (MPI) has been the predominant runtime for executing scientific applications on distributed computing systems, playing a central role in High-Performance Computing (HPC) for several decades. Currently, numerous MPI implementations and variants exist, each providing specialized optimizations that may significantly influence application performance depending on the underlying architecture and execution context. One significant example is Cray MPICH [13], a vendor-optimized MPI implementation, designed by

Hewlett Packard Enterprise (HPE). Cray MPICH has been fine-tuned to leverage the features of the HPE Slingshot interconnect [6], aiming to optimize MPI application performance on HPE Cray supercomputer systems.

Multiple US national laboratories rely on Cray systems equipped with Slingshot interconnects, such as El Capitan, Venado, and Perlmutter, to run scientific applications and advance research across a variety of scientific domains. HPE recently made publicly available the source code for the CXI OFI libfabric [11] provider and the underlying libcxi [12] library. This has facilitated more flexible testing of alternative MPI implementations on systems using the Slingshot interconnect.

In this study, we evaluate and compare the performance of Cray MPICH and Open MPI [8] over Slingshot 11 (SS11) using Eulerian and Lagrangian adaptive mesh refinement (AMR) applications. Our assessment includes multiple configurations of Open MPI, exploring their relative efficiency and scalability. Additionally, we highlight the key differences between the two MPI implementations by proposing a new micro-benchmark designed to stress the tag matching algorithm. Our results shows that while Cray MPICH delivers better performance on micro-benchmarks, Open MPI delivers comparable, and sometimes better performance on these AMR applications. This underscores the value of flexibility in MPI selection and the need for guidance to help developers match MPI implementations to the specific communication patterns and requirements of their applications.

The rest of the paper is organized as follows. Section 2 outlines how Open MPI can be configured to use the CXI provider on SS-11-based systems. Section 3 reviews related work, highlighting prior efforts to enable CXI support in Open MPI and to evaluate its performance. Section 4 presents our performance results on the Intel MPI Benchmarks and AMR applications. Section 5 investigates the observed performance gap, providing a detailed analysis. Finally, Sect. 6 summarizes our findings and outlines directions for future work.

2 Background

In this work, we focus on systems equipped with SS11 interconnects and OFI libfabric. The vendor supports a OFI Libfabric provider - CXI - which allows applications to access the SS11 HPC features such as RDMA, network based atomic operations, hardware message tag matching, and collective offload. Therefore, for our experiments we build libfabric with the CXI provider and configure Open MPI with libfabric support. Note that, the CXI provider is only supported by newer Open MPI versions (starting with v5.0.0).

Open MPI is structured around a Modular Component Architecture (MCA) design [17]. Key parts of the implementation are structured as MCA *frameworks*. For example, MPI collectives are implemented within a *collectives* framework. Different components of this framework implement different collective algorithms or target specialized hardware or software. Framework components can be built at compile time and in some cases are selectable at application runtime.

There is a Point-to-point Messaging Layer (PML) framework. It contains a collection of components which use different lower level network APIs to transmit and receive MPI messages. The lower level software must present an MPI-like interface supporting tagged messages and MPI's message ordering semantics. MPI processes must use the same PML in order to exchange MPI messages. There is a PML component for UCX and a CM component which supports use of portals4, PSM2, and OFI libfabric via a Matching Transport Layer(MTL) framework. In addition, an PML ob1 component provides an Open MPI internal implementation for message delivery. The PML ob1 can also interface to OFI libfabric. Thus, there are different options for running Open MPI on the SS11 network.

The PML component is critical for the performance of AMR applications, since most of those applications rely on individual point to point messaged for their communication patter. In this paper, we consider two PML components:

- **PML ob1** - delegates the data transfer to one or more Byte Transfer Layer (BTLs) components. This allows it to select an optimal combination of available BTLs at runtime, enabling more efficient communication depending on the data transfer type (e.g. intra or inter-node messages). Tag matching is done within PML ob1.
- **PML cm** - uses a single low-level transport interface provided by the MTL. The MTL allows for direct use of the network transport layers, allowing PML cm to support MPI tag matching semantics. An assumption in the design of the MTL framework was that targeted network APIs such as OFI libfabric, PSM2, etc. provide optimal message transmission between MPI processes.

The CXI provider supports three different modes for tag matching: software, hardware and hybrid. In contrast, PML ob1 only supports the software mode, as it handles tag matching internally. The CXI provider routes all messages through the SS11 Cassini network adaptor irrespective of whether the libfabic endpoints involved are collocated on the same node or not.

3 Related Work

Given that the support for the CXI provider in Open MPI is relatively recent, there are a few studies that addressed both enabling the CXI support in Open MPI [4,16] and evaluating the Open MPI performance on SS11-based systems [3, 15].

Notably, Shehata [16] et al. proposed a new provider called LINKx aimed at overcoming the limitation of CXI libfabric provider concerning intra-node message delivery no.ted above. Indeed, LINKx is able to combine - from the perspective of the consumer of the libfabric API - multiple libfabric providers into a single one, and thus be able to take advantage of specific optimizations depending on the context (e.g. use CXI for inter and SHM for intra-node communication). The LINKx provider was integrated into libfabric, starting with 2.0.x. Currently, it only supports linking the libfabric shared memory provider and another provider for inter-node traffic. The libfabric documentation mentions that future releases will allow linking any number of providers.

While these studies have made significant contributions toward enabling an efficient implementation of OpenMPI on Cray systems, there is no work that highlights a category of real applications that might benefit from those efforts. Most of the related work only presents results on micro-benchmarks, and the few papers that analyzed the performance on scientific applications, concluded that Cray MPICH outperforms the other implementations. Therefore, in this paper we would like to underline the key differences between the two MPI libraries by analyzing a different category of scientific applications.

4 Evaluation and Analysis

In this section, we first describe the SS11 system on which all experiments were conducted. We then describe the set of configurations we explore in our experimental setup. A configuration corresponds to a specific MPI implementation coupled with different build-time flags and runtime parameters. Finally. we present the obtained results on MPI micro-benchmarks and scientific applications.

4.1 Experimental Platform

All experiments presented in this paper were conducted on the HBM and DDR partitions of the Rocinante supercomputer, a scaled-down replica of the Crossroads system. Rocinante is the first large-scale deployment of Intel's Sapphire Rapids CPUs. The partitions are composed of nodes equipped with two SS11 network cards, 112 physical cores and the corresponding memory type (HBM or DDR).

4.2 Methodology

To explore the performance potential of Open MPI, we examined a range of different build-time and runtime configurations, as well as multiple versions of libfabric in order to identify the most effective setup for our specific workloads.

We used Spack [9] for building Open MPI 5.0.6 with different versions of libfabric and different configurations. The two main configurations that we use in this work are depicted in Fig. 1. We intentionally omitted non-essential Spack built instructions. The first configuration we considered relies on the libfabric instance already available on the system (i.e. the one used by Cray MPICH). This ensures that Open MPI benefits from any potential system-specific optimizations with which libfabric may have been configured, enabling a fair and consistent comparison with Cray MPICH. The second configuration allow us to evaluate the performance of the LINKx provider, as well as to compare the two versions of libfabric. We made sure to build Open MPI with the XPMEM support in order to fully expose the performance capabilities of LINKx.

Additionally, for each of the builds we select different runtime configurations (e.g. the PML component). Below are the environmental variables that we set at runtime to customize Open MPI for leveraging different components and providers:

- PML ob1 runtime configuration

```
OMPI_MCA_pml=ob1
OMPI_MCA_btl="self,sm,ofi"
FI_PROVIDER=cxi
OMPI_MCA_btl_ofi_mode=2
FI_CXI_RX_MATCH_MODE=software
```

- PML cm runtime configuration

```
OMPI_MCA_pml=cm
FI_CXI_RX_MATCH_MODE=software|hardware|hybrid
```

- LINKx runtime configuration

```
FI_LNX_PROV_LINKS="shm+cxi"
OMPI_MCA_opal_common_ofi_provider_include="shm+cxi:lnx"
OMPI_MCA_mtl=ofi
FI_SHM_USE_XPMEM=1
FI_CXI_RX_MATCH_MODE=software
```

As with the previously presented build instructions, we omit non-essential environment variables to maintain clarity and focus. The runtime configuration described above allow us to run with the LINKx provider and with the ob1 and PML cm implementations. To run with Cray MPICH, we use the default environment on the system and set the matching mode.

Note that the main branch of libfabric changed the syntax for selecting the LINKx provider at runtime. One needs to manually specify each individual link via the FI_LNX_PROV_LINKS variable (e.g., set it to shm+cxi:cxi0|shm+cxi:cxi1).

4.3 Micro-bechmarks

We start our comparison between Cray MPICH and Open MPI by running the well known Intel MPI Benchmarks [5] (IMB). We analyze both the inter and intra-node communication latency and the performance of Alltoall, a collective that is routinely used in the literature to reveal performance differences among tag-matching algorithms. To ensure consistent results and avoid variability-induced bias, we ran the micro-benchmarks on the same set of nodes using identical process bindings. The results are depicted in Fig. 2, in a log-log scale and averaged over 10 runs. To keep the graphs uncluttered, we display only the best-performing matching mode for each configuration.

For intra-node communication and smaller buffer sizes, we observed PML ob1 consistently and significantly outperforming the other Open MPI configurations. We also observed PML cm outperforming the other configurations in inter-node communication, though with a less significant delta. The LINKx provider showed impressive performance improvements in intra-node communication and

Open MPI configured with the system libfabric.

```
specs:
- openmpi@5.0.6
packages:
  openmpi:
    require: fabrics=ofi,cma schedulers=slurm
  libfabric:
    externals:
    - spec: libfabric@1.15.2.0
      prefix: <prefix_to_sys_libfabric>
```

Open MPI configured with libfabric built via Spack (+LINKx and XPMEM support).

```
specs:
- openmpi@5.0.6
packages:
  util-linux-uuid:
    require: @2.40.1
  xpmem:
    externals:
    - spec: xpmem@2.6.2
      prefix: <prefix_to_sys_xpmem>
  openmpi:
    require: fabrics=ofi,cma schedulers=slurm
  libfabric:
    require: ^libfabric@2.1.0 fabrics=cxi,shm,lnx,xpmem
```

Fig. 1. Spack configurations used for the Open MPI builds.

with larger buffers. However, for inter-node communication it performed noticeably worse than the other configurations (similarly to PML ob1). Cray MPICH seemed to be the best well-rounded option, showing very good performance in both intra-node and inter-node communication.

The results presented for the Alltoall micro-benchmark were collected by running with one process per nodes for a total of 32 nodes. For the Alltoall collective, we have not noticed a significant difference among the different configuration, other than that PML ob1 seems to perform slightly worse for larger buffer sizes. Similarly, we have not observed a difference in performance between the system libfabric and the 2.1 version, except for a small difference with PML cm, where the system libfabric performed marginally better in inter-node communication for smaller buffer sizes.

4.4 AMR Applications

This sections highlights the performance differences between Open MPI and Cray MPICH on two production, multi-physics simulation codes. In this section we will not be able to present results with the LINKx provider because these

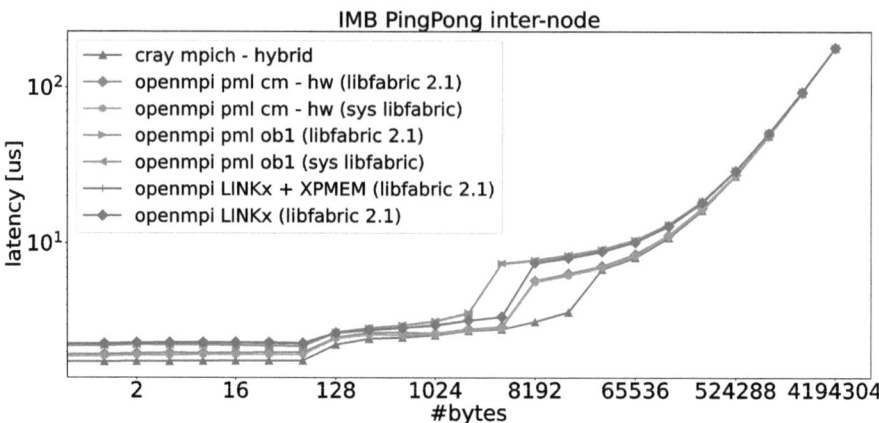

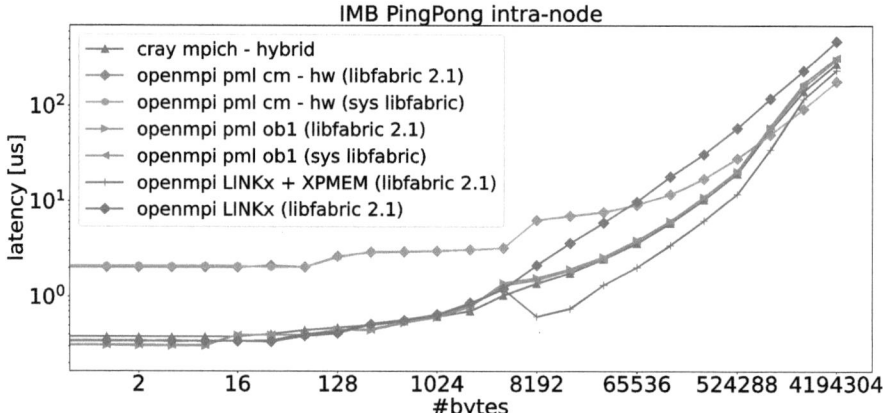

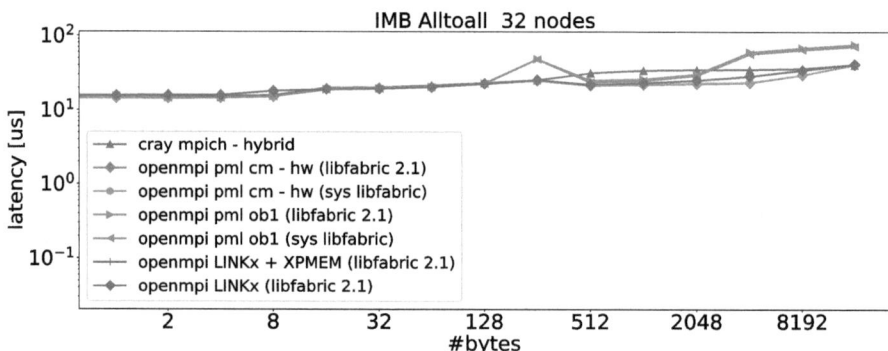

Fig. 2. Highlight the performance differences between Cray MPICH and Open MPI on the Intel MPI Benchmarks. **(lower is better)**

applications terminate with segmentation faults when run with it. The issue has been reported on the libfabric GitHub repository. Therefore the LINKx provider is omitted from all subsequent evaluation tests.

Parthenon-VIBE [10]. Parthenon is an open-source, performance-portable framework for block-structured AMR applications. In this paper we focus on a particular application included in the Parthenon repository called Parthenon-VIBE, which solves the Vector Inviscid Burgers' Equation. Parthenon's halo exchange code uses non-blocking point-to-point communication. Each process has a different set of neighbors that can change after a refinement or derefinement phase. In Parthenon-VIBE, the communication is pairwise-symmetric: every process sends exactly as many messages as it receives, and each sent message is paired with an incoming message of identical size.

For all our experiments we run with a 3D cube mesh, two level of refinements, and a block size of $16 \times 16 \times 16$. We performed out a weak-scaling study on up to 32 nodes and with 112 processes per node. We make sure we assigned to each node an equivalent workload while maintaining a cubic mesh (identical extent in every spatial direction).

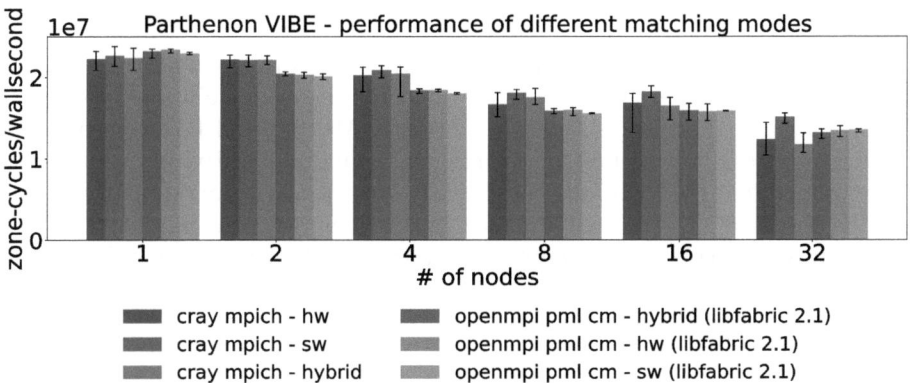

Fig. 3. Comparison of the performance differences between matching modes on SS11 with Cray MPICH and PML cm. **(higher is better)**

Our first experiment consisted of running Parthenon-VIBE with different matching modes. Figure 3 shows the obtained results for both Cray MPICH and PML cm, averaged over 10 runs with min and max bars. The x-axis represent the number of nodes and the y-axis the zone-cycles per second (higher is better). By analyzing the plot we can make three observations. First, Cray MPICH outperforms PML cm with any of the matching modes. Second, for Cray MPICH, the software matching mode outperformed the alternatives by more than 20% and was markedly more stable (i.e., it showed lower variance across the runs). Third, the performance of PML cm appears unaffected by the choice of matching mode, as all three variants yield comparable results. For clarity, we only show the results obtained with libfabric 2.1, but we obtained similar results with the system libfabric.

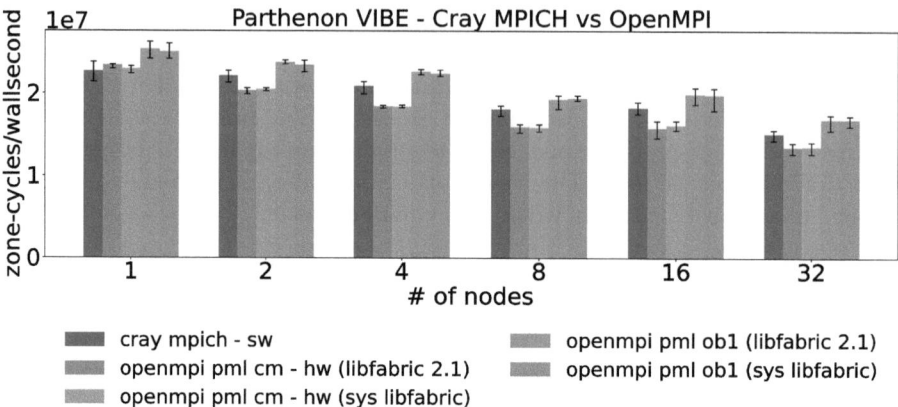

Fig. 4. Performance difference between Open MPI and Cray MPICH on Parthenon VIBE. **(higher is better)**

Next, we compare the performance of Cray MPICH to Open MPI by running with the exact same Parthenon setup. We include the results obtained with both libfabric 2.1 and the system libfabric. For Cray MPICH and PML cm, we only report the results for the best-performing matching mode. By analyzing Fig. 4 we can notice that the PML ob1 consistently outperforms Cray MPICH in every run. We observed a 6–11% performance gap, varying with the number of nodes. Performance was comparable between our runs with the system libfabric and the 2.1 version, but their stability differed: the system libfabric occasionally segfaulted, whereas 2.1 ran reliably.

FLAG. [14] is an arbitrary Lagrangian-Eulerian (ALE) multiphysics, unstructured mesh simulation code. Among its many features is an AMR capability which allows a user to specify conditions under which a zone should be refined by sub-dividing the zone in to child zones. For best results, it is recommended that AMR be used in conjunction the application's load rebalancing capability.

In initial comparisons of Cray MPICH and Open MPI, it was observed that for non-AMR, pure lagrangian or ALE benchmarks, the performance of the code was very similar when using either the vendor MPICH or Open MPI with either the PML ob1 or the PML cm. However, strong scaling AMR benchmark problems showed that the amount of time spent in the load rebalancing component was significantly larger using Open MPI with the PML cm and somewhat larger when using the PML ob1 compared to Cray MPICH, particularly as the scalability limit for a given problem size was being approached.

We were unable to use the LINKx provider owing to the same problems noted above. No results are reported for the system libfabric as many of the flag

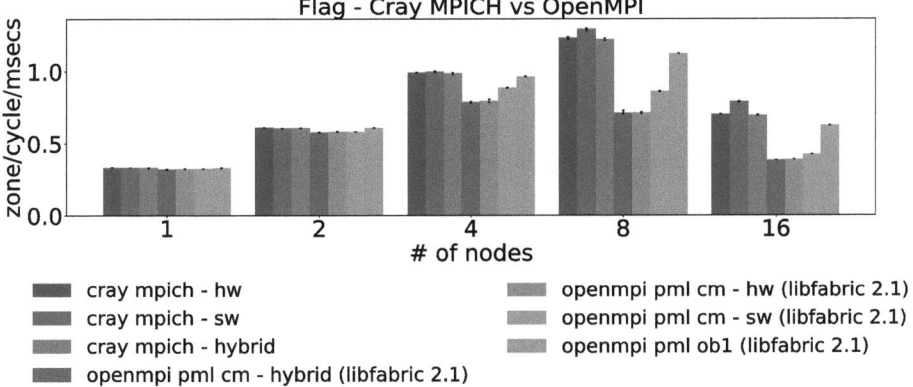

Fig. 5. Performance difference between Open MPI and Cray MPICH on Flag for a single-material Richtmyer-Meshkov instability problem.(**higher is better**)

regressions tests fail when using this older version (1.15.0) of libfabric. These runs were made on DDR memory nodes as there was insufficient memory on the HBM nodes to run the problem using one and two nodes.

In Fig. 5 we present the results obtained on the Richtmyer-Meshkov instability problem starting with approximately two million zones. The x-axis shows the number of nodes used for a given set of calculations and the y-axis shows the zone/cycle/msecs (higher is better). The results show that Cray MPICH using software tag matching gives the best performance, with the PML ob1 giving better results than the PML cm when using Open MPI. Hardware tag matching is not likely to benefit the application as the majority of point to point messaging routines use MPI_Probe on the receive side. At eight nodes, the PML ob1 is 16% slower than Cray MPICH and 28% slower at 16 nodes. Results were quite consistent from run-to-run. Across a variety of problems and node counts, the PML ob1 gave consistently better performance than the PML cm.

5 Performance Analysis

Parthenon. To analyze the performance gap observed on Parthenon when using Open MPI with PML ob1 versus Cray MPICH, we first collected profiling data with kokkos-tools [2]. By measuring the time spent in each application region we found that the main performance difference in communication comes from the halo exchange. Cray MPICH spends on average 20% more time in this phase than Open MPI. This observation contradicts our earlier micro-benchmark results, in which Cray MPICH always matched or out-performed Open MPI performance for point to point communication.

To understand this discrepancy, we manually instrumented Parthenon to record, at each iteration, the number of processes involved in the halo exchange and the total number of send or receive requests posted (Parthenon's communication pattern is symmetric). Figure 6 shows data collected from a 32 node run.

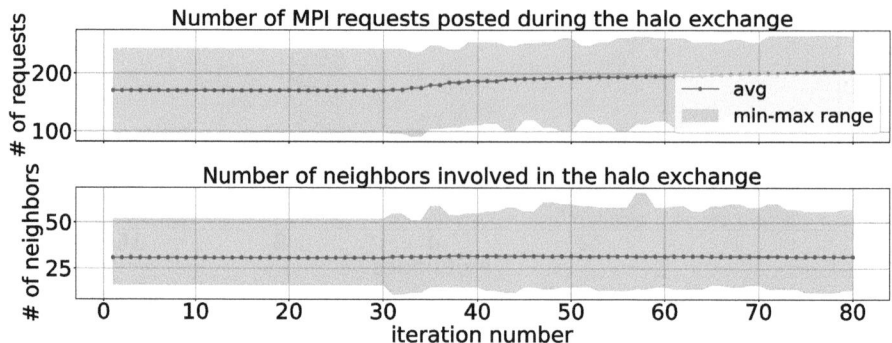

Fig. 6. Halo-exchange communication pattern in Parthenon: for each iteration, the figure highlights the number of non-blocking MPI send/receive requests and the number of neighbor processes engaged.

Depending on the iteration, each process communicates with 13 to 60 neighbors and receives between 100 and 200 messages per iteration (up to 300 with the two-node run), using about 35 distinct MPI tags on average.

Guided by these observations, we implemented a micro-benchmark (Listing 1.1) designed to highlight a key difference between the Cray MPICH and Open MPI implementations. In this benchmark, all processes except one, post a fixed number of send requests with tags in a random order, shuffled with the Fisher-Yates shuffle algorithm. The root process posts the corresponding receives with tags in sequential order. At the end, the root process measures the time required to receive all messages. The goal of the proposed micro-benchmark is to further accentuate the difference between Open MPI and Cray MPICH in a bursty context.

To the best of our knowledge, no existing micro-benchmark mimics such a bursty, many-to-one communication pattern. The closest is the Shuffle micro-benchmark proposed in the MadMPI [1] suite, in which one process posts a number of sends with shuffled tags while the another process posts the corresponding receives with tags in sequential order. The limitation of this benchmark is that it can be run with only two processes and therefore may not reveal the matching differences between Open MPI and Cray MPICH. Indeed, PML ob1 maintains an individual matching queue per peer. Because each process communicates with only one peer, the Shuffle micro-benchmark cannot reveal the potential benefits of OpenMPI's per-peer matching algorithm.

Figure 7 reports the results obtained with the bursty benchmark, averaged over five runs and in a log-log scale. We present the results with 30 and 250 send requests per neighbor. The first plot reproduces a communication pattern close to that of Parthenon, based on the profiling data presented earlier. For example, for the 16 node run, there are 15 senders each issuing 30 requests, so process 0 receives 450 tagged messages. The second plot shows how the matching mode impacts the performance when the request count becomes extremely high, push-

Performance Analysis of Open MPI on AMR Applications over Slingshot-11   117

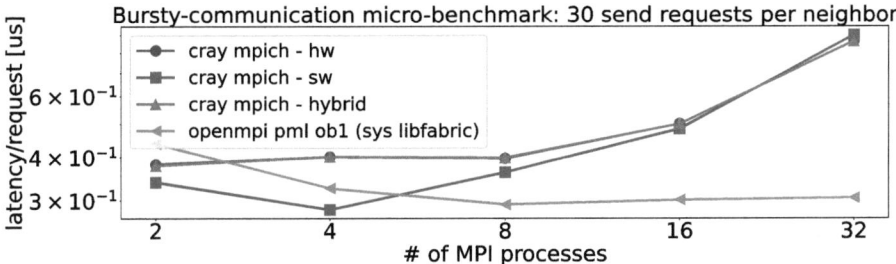

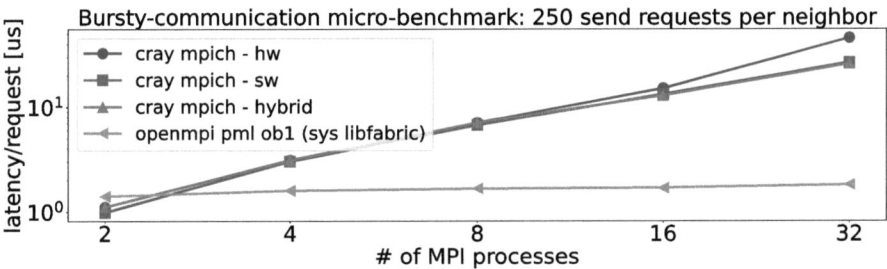

Fig. 7. Performance difference between Open MPI and Cray MPICH in handling multiple concurrent requests from different peers. **(lower is better)**

ing the hardware toward resource exhaustion. All the experiments were executed on the exact same nodes and using the same bindings to eliminate hardware variability. In the figures, the x-axis shows the total number of processes (one per node) participating in the micro-benchmark, and the y-axis reports the average time required to process a single request. Perfect scaling would appear as a horizontal line, showing a constant per-request time regardless of the number of nodes.

By analyzing the plots, we can make multiple observations. First, the performance of PML ob1 is significantly less affected by the number of neighbors, keeping the time per request almost constant. This behavior is consistent with PML ob1's matching algorithm, which in this case keeps the number of requests per peer constant. Second, Cray MPICH's per-request time grows as the number of neighbors increases. Therefore, starting with seven neighbors and 210 simultaneous requests, Open MPI outperforms Cray MPICH. Third, when running on two nodes (or four nodes with 30 send requests), Cray MPICH is faster than Open MPI. This matches our results obtained with the Shuffle benchmark (not presented in this paper). Fourth, once the number of simultaneous requests exceeds 7 750, the software and hybrid matching modes outperform the hardware mode. This drop in performance can indicate resource exhaustion on the hardware side. Because Cray MPICH's matching scheme is proprietary, its details are unclear. Nevertheless, our results show that Open MPI handles bursty many-to-one traffic more efficiently, exposing a clear performance gap between the two runtimes.

Listing 1.1. Bursty-communication micro-benchmark

```
warm_up();
if (comm_world_rank != 0) { /* senders (neighbors) */
    shuffle = shuffled_tags();
    for (int rep = 0; rep < repetitions; rep++) {
        MPI_Barrier(MPI_COMM_WORLD);
        for (int i = 0; i < nb_of_mpi_requests; i++) {
            int tag = shuffle[i];
            MPI_Isend(&sbuf[i], 1, MPI_CHAR, 0,
                tag, MPI_COMM_WORLD, &sreqs[i]);
        }
        MPI_Waitall(nb_of_mpi_requests, sreqs, MPI_STATUSES_IGNORE);
    }
} else { /* receiver */
    for (int rep = 0; rep < repetitions; rep++) {
        MPI_Barrier(MPI_COMM_WORLD);
        double start = MPI_Wtime();
        for (int src = 1; src < size; src++) {
            int offset = (src - 1) * nb_of_mpi_requests;
            for (int i = 0; i < nb_of_mpi_requests; i++) {
                int tag = i;
                MPI_Irecv(&rbuf[offset + i], 1, MPI_CHAR, src,
                    tag, MPI_COMM_WORLD, &rreqs[offset + i]);
            }
        }
        MPI_Waitall(num_senders * nb_of_mpi_requests,
            rreqs, MPI_STATUSES_IGNORE);
        double end = MPI_Wtime();
        total_time += (end - start);
    }
}
```

FLAG. The time report generated by the FLAG application showed that the main difference in timings between Cray MPICH and Open MPI was in the dynamic load balance section of the application. Further analysis of timings in this section of application revealed that a large number of eight byte allreduce operations (∼2400) were being done in the recursive bisection algorithm for simulation cycles where rebalancing was carried out. The default allreduce algorithm in the Open MPI 5 release stream for an eight byte message size and 1760 MPI processes is a four stage set of hierarchical operations - two reductions followed by two broadcasts. However, for the number of processes used per node and at higher node counts, a simpler, single-level recursive doubling algorithm gives better performance (selected by disabling the *han* collective component). *Hpctoolkit* [18] showed that the simpler algorithm was taking about the same time as the hierarchical algorithm on average, but with a much smaller standard deviation in the time spent in the operation at each process. Similar behavior, although not as large, is observed using the IMB Allreduce micro-benchmark at these process counts (Fig. 8). Using the recursive doubling allreduce algorithm, the application performance difference between Cray MPICH and Open MPI narrows to 1% slower at 8 nodes, 22% slower at 16 nodes. Although the hierarchical algorithm gives better results in the unit test, it involves substantially more data structures when in operation, competing in the case of use in the application for space in the first level instruction and data caches.

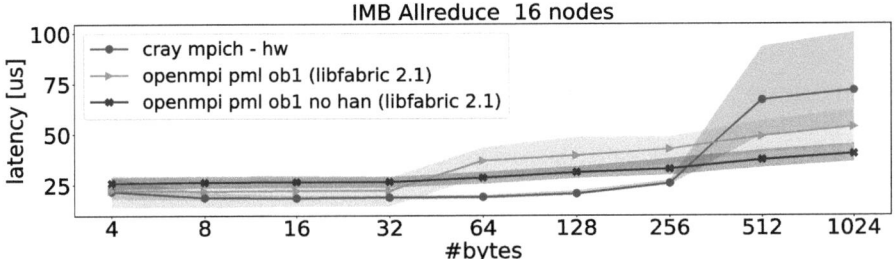

Fig. 8. Comparison of Cray MPICH and Open MPI with and without hierarchical collectives in the Intel MPI Allreduce benchmark. **(lower is better)**

6 Conclusion

This study provides a detailed evaluation of Open MPI and Cray MPICH performance on SS-11-based systems using AMR applications as representative workloads. Our findings show that Open MPI, when configured with PML cm, performs significantly worse than both Cray MPICH and Open MPI using the PML ob1 implementation. This is mainly because of poor performance of PML cm for intra-node communication.

Across our experiments, Cray MPICH generally outperformed or matched Open MPI, particularly in all microbenchmarks and in one of the AMR applications. However, in scenarios characterized by bursty communication patterns, such as those found in the Parthenon application, Open MPI demonstrated better performance than Cray MPICH, even though it did not perform as well on the raw microbenchmarks.

To investigate this performance gap between Open MPI and Cray MPICH, we profiled the Parthenon application. Our analysis showed that the Open MPI is able to handle a large number of simultaneous messages from many peers more efficiently, which is particularly relevant in bursty communication phases. Based on these findings, we designed a synthetic benchmark that reflects this behavior and helps isolate the communication pattern where Open MPI with PML ob1 shows an advantage.

In conclusion, while Cray MPICH remains the preferred default for AMR applications on supercomputers equipped with Slingshot-11 interconnects, Open MPI can offer clear benefits in certain contexts. Moreover, with the emergence of the LINKx provider, Open MPI's potential on Slingshot-11 systems becomes increasingly compelling and merits further exploration.

Acknowledgments. This material is based upon work supported by the Department of Energy, National Nuclear Security Administration under contract number 89233218CNA000001. LA-UR-25-24969 Approved for public release; distribution is unlimited. This work was also supported by the U.S. Department of Energy under the Predictive Science Academic Alliance Program (PSAAP-III), Award #DE-NA0003966.

References

1. MadMPI benchmark suite. https://pm2.gitlabpages.inria.fr/releases. Accessed 12 May 2025
2. Kokkos tools: Profiling and debugging utilities for kokkos (2025). https://github.com/kokkos/kokkos-tools. Accessed 12 May 2025
3. Beebe, M., et al.: A performance analysis of gpu-aware mpi implementations over the slingshot-11 interconnect. In: 2024 IEEE High Performance Extreme Computing Conference (HPEC), pp. 1–7. IEEE (2024)
4. Bernholdt, D.E., et al.: Taking the mpi standard and the open mpi library to exascale. Int. J. High Perfor. Comput. Appl. **38**(5), 491–507 (2024). https://doi.org/10.1177/10943420241265936
5. Corporation, I.: Intel MPI Benchmarks. https://github.com/intel/mpi-benchmarks. Accessed 12 May 2025
6. De Sensi, D., Di Girolamo, S., McMahon, K.H., Roweth, D., Hoefler, T.: An in-depth analysis of the slingshot interconnect. In: SC20: International Conference for High Performance Computing, Networking, Storage and Analysis, pp. 1–14 (2020). https://doi.org/10.1109/SC41405.2020.00039
7. Forum, M.P.: Mpi: a message-passing interface standard (1994)
8. Gabriel, E., et al.: Open MPI: goals, concept, and design of a next generation MPI implementation. In: Kranzlmüller, D., Kacsuk, P., Dongarra, J. (eds.) EuroPVM/MPI 2004. LNCS, vol. 3241, pp. 97–104. Springer, Heidelberg (2004). https://doi.org/10.1007/978-3-540-30218-6_19
9. Gamblin, T., et al.: The spack package manager: bringing order to hpc software chaos. In: Proceedings of the International Conference for High Performance Computing, Networking, Storage and Analysis, pp. 1–12 (2015)
10. Grete, P., et al.: Parthenon–a performance portable block-structured adaptive mesh refinement framework. Int. J. High Perfor. Comput. Appl. **37**(5), 465–486 (2023)
11. Grun, P., et al.: A brief introduction to the openfabrics interface. In: Proceedings of 22nd International Symposium High Performance Interconnects (2015)
12. Hewlett Packard: libcxi - the cxi library. https://github.com/hewlettpackard/shs-libcxi. Accessed 12 May 2025
13. HPE: Cray MPICH documentation. https://cpe.ext.hpe.com/docs/24.03/mpt/mpich/index.html. Accessed 12 May 2025

14. Kenamond, M., Kuzmin, D., Shashkov, M.: A positivity-preserving and conservative intersection-distribution-based remapping algorithm for staggered ale hydrodynamics on arbitrary meshes. J. Comput. Phys. **435** (2021). https://doi.org/10.1016/j.jcp.2021.110254. https://www.osti.gov/biblio/1771097
15. Khorassani, K.S., Chen, C.C., Ramesh, B., Shafi, A., Subramoni, H., Panda, D.K.: High performance mpi over the slingshot interconnect. J. Comput. Sci. Technol. **38**(1), 128–145 (2023)
16. Shehata, A., Naughton, T., Bernholdt, D.E., Pritchard, H.: Bringing hpe slingshot 11 support to open mpi. Concurr. Comput. Pract. Exp. **36**(22), e8203 (2024)
17. Squyres, J.M., Lumsdaine, A.: The component architecture of open MPI: enabling third-party collective algorithms. In: Getov, V., Kielmann, T. (eds.) Proceedings, 18th ACM International Conference on Supercomputing, Workshop on Component Models and Systems for Grid Applications, pp. 167–185. Springer, St. Malo (2004). https://doi.org/10.1007/0-387-23352-0_11
18. Tallent, N., Mellor-Crummey, J., Adhianto, L., Fagan, M., Krentel, M.: Hpctoolkit: performance tools for scientific computing. J. Phys. Conf. Ser. **125**(1), 012088 (2008). https://doi.org/10.1088/1742-6596/125/1/012088

Examining MPI and its Extensions for Asynchronous Multithreaded Communication

Jiakun Yan[1](✉), Marc Snir[1], and Yanfei Guo[2]

[1] University of Illinois Urbana-Champaign, Urbana, IL 61801, USA
{jiakuny3,snir}@illinois.edu
[2] Argonne National Laboratory, Lemont, IL 60439, USA
yguo@anl.gov

Abstract. The increasing complexity of HPC architectures and the growing adoption of irregular scientific algorithms demand efficient support for asynchronous, multithreaded communication. This is most pronounced with Asynchronous Many-Task (AMT) systems. Such communication was not a consideration during the initial MPI design. The MPI community has recently introduced several extensions to address these new requirements. This work evaluates two such extensions, the Virtual Communication Interface (VCI) and the Continuation extensions, in the context of an established AMT runtime, HPX. We begin by using an MPI-level microbenchmark, modeled from HPX's low-level communication mechanism, to measure the peak performance potential of these extensions. We then integrate them into HPX to evaluate their effectiveness in real-world scenarios. Our results show that while these extensions can enhance performance compared to standard MPI, areas for improvement remain. The current continuation proposal limits the maximum multithreaded message rate achievable in the multi-VCI setting. Furthermore, the recommended one-VCI-per-thread mode proves ineffective in real-world scenarios due to the attentiveness problem. These findings underscore the importance of improving intra-VCI threading efficiency to achieve scalable multithreaded communication and fully realize the benefits of recent MPI extensions.

Keywords: Multithreaded communication · Asynchronous communication · Task parallelism · VCI · continuation

1 Introduction

High-performance computing (HPC) architectures are becoming increasingly heterogeneous with extensive on-node parallelism and deep memory hierarchies. Modern compute nodes often feature over 100 CPU cores and multiple accelerators. Meanwhile, scientific applications are adopting more adaptive or sparse algorithms [20,26] to achieve higher resolution and scalability. These trends challenge the traditional Bulk-Synchronous Parallel (BSP) model, in which all processes operate in lockstep with evenly distributed workloads.

Asynchronous Many-Task (AMT) systems have emerged as a compelling alternative. In these systems, applications are expressed as task dependency graphs, and the runtime manages task scheduling, dependencies, and communication, usually operating with one multithreaded process per socket or node. AMT runtimes employ oversubscription, asynchronous execution, and communication-computation overlap to outperform hand-tuned BSP implementations in irregular workloads [1,14,40].

AMTs exhibit different communication characteristics from BSP applications [28,42]. Messages are typically finer-grained and dominated by point-to-point communication rather than global collectives. Communication patterns are highly dynamic, with many outstanding operations, and most threads (logically or physically) can generate or consume messages. These characteristics fall outside the traditional design and optimization focus of MPI.

This paper investigates how well existing MPI and recent extensions can support AMT's communication requirements through a case study of an established AMT runtime, HPX. While our focus is on AMTs, their communication challenges are increasingly common in applications with data-dependent execution, beyond the traditional BSP domain. To remain broadly relevant, MPI must evolve to meet these demands.

Building on the analysis of communication requirements of AMT presented in [42], we focus on two critical features shown to impact application-level performance significantly: (1) scalable handling of many concurrent communication operations, and (2) effective replication of communication resources to reduce contention. We first use an MPI-level microbenchmark, modeled from HPX's low-level communication mechanism, to evaluate the raw capabilities and limitations of the tested extensions, and then integrate them into HPX to assess their practicality and system-level effectiveness.

Specifically, our evaluation is based on MPICH [31] and primarily involves two MPI extensions:

- *The Virtual Communication Interface (VCI) Extension* [44]: a mechanism to mitigate thread contention by replicating internal communication resources and mapping them to distinct communicators.
- *The Continuations Extension* [37]: a callback-based completion mechanism designed to reduce the overhead of managing large numbers of pending operations.

Our results reveal both these extensions' advantages and current limitations and motivate recommendations for evolving MPI standards and implementations to better support asynchronous multithreaded runtimes.

The rest of the paper is organized as follows. Section 2 provides background on the MPI threading model and the extensions we study. Section 3 describes how we integrate the VCI and continuation extensions into the HPX parcelport logic, including our modifications to the existing extensions. Section 4 presents our MPI-level microbenchmark and the fundamental performance characteristics of the extensions. Section 5 then evaluates the extensions in the context of the HPX runtime, using both microbenchmarks and a real-world astrophysics application, OctoTiger [14]. Section 6 presents related work. Finally, Sect. 7 concludes the paper and discusses suggestions for improving MPI support for AMT systems.

2 Background

2.1 MPI Threading Level

The MPI specification [30] defines four levels of thread support, in increasing order: MPI_THREAD_SINGLE, MPI_THREAD_FUNNELED, MPI_THREAD_SERIALIZED, and MPI_THREAD_MULTIPLE. MPI_THREAD_MULTIPLE offers the highest level of thread support, allowing multiple threads to invoke MPI functions simultaneously. This model is the most intuitive approach for writing multithreaded MPI programs and is preferred by many users [7]. Most AMT systems such as HPX [23], Legion [6], and Charm++ [24] rely on MPI_THREAD_MULTIPLE. However, efficient support for this thread level has historically been lacking in many MPI implementations [35], primarily due to contention on internal MPI data structures and underlying network resources. This work focuses on optimizing and evaluating MPI extensions, specifically in the context of MPI_THREAD_MULTIPLE.

2.2 MPICH VCI

The Virtual Communication Interface (VCI) extension [44] is a mature mechanism in MPICH for addressing the MPI multithreaded efficiency issue through resource replication. When enabled, the MPICH runtime will associate a distinct set of communication resources (VCIs) with every MPI communicator, allowing each thread to communicate on dedicated resources with minimal contention. It also has advanced options for mapping communications to different VCI using message tags. MPICH recommends that multithreaded applications allocate a separate VCI/communicator for each thread. However, as we will demonstrate in this paper, this setup does not always yield optimal performance in real-world scenarios.

The design and implementation of VCI have been covered in detail in [44,46]. As a brief overview, a VCI represents a relatively independent set of communication resources needed on the critical path of MPI communication routines. It primarily includes a UCP worker (when using the UCX [38] backend) or an OFI domain (when using the OFI [33] backend), which further encapsulates resources related to network hardware interfacing, memory registration, tag matching, and progressing. MPICH employs a per-VCI spinlock to ensure thread safety, allowing concurrent operations across VCIs but serializing accesses within each VCI.

2.3 MPI Continuations Proposal

The MPI Continuations Proposal [36] aims to provide an efficient mechanism for managing multiple pending communication operations. In standard MPI, the only way to track pending operations is to wait for or test the request object corresponding to each communication operation. However, in event-driven systems such as AMTs, threads may post many communication operations concurrently, and the runtime must react when any individual operation completes. `MPI_Testsome` is unsuitable for this use case as it is typically implemented as a loop over the input request array, and maintaining the request array is inconvenient and expensive. Instead, such systems typically maintain lists of MPI requests (i.e., request pools) and use `MPI_Test` to opportunistically probe requests in the pool until one or more completed ones are found. A thread polls the pool when it becomes idle [13,27,41].

To avoid the polling overhead and the thread synchronization required to manage shared request pools, the continuation proposal introduces an API that allows MPI clients to attach callback functions to individual requests and register them with a *continuation request*. The application then polls only this continuation request to drive progress, and callbacks are invoked automatically when corresponding communication operations complete. [37] implements this proposal on a test branch of OpenMPI and integrates it into PaRSEC, operating in a mode where a single communication thread handles all MPI calls.

In this work, we implement the continuation proposal in MPICH and evaluate it in the context of HPX, where all worker threads can produce and consume messages concurrently. This context provides a more realistic test case for multithreaded communication. We further investigate how well the continuation mechanism integrates with multi-VCI configurations and assess its effectiveness in managing completion overhead in these scenarios.

3 Extend HPX Parcelport with MPI Extensions

In this section, we will describe the design of HPX's low-level communication layer, known as *parcelport*, and detail how we integrate the two MPI extensions into the parcelport implementation. We also discuss the modifications made to the continuation extension to better support multi-VCI scenarios.

3.1 Background

We first briefly describe the HPX communication stack and the original MPI parcelport implementation. Please refer to [42] for a more detailed description.

HPX Application Interface. HPX provides a rich set of APIs for developing parallel and distributed applications. At the core of its distributed programming model is a Remote Procedure Call (RPC) mechanism. Users can register functions or class methods as `Actions`, and allocate globally accessible objects. Any HPX process can then invoke these actions remotely, either on another process or on a global object.

HPX Communication Stack Overview. Currently, HPX has three fully functioning communication backends: TCP, MPI, and LCI [41]. HPX's communication stack is organized into two layers. The *upper layer* is shared by all backends and handles essential services such as action argument (de)serialization, global object address resolution, message aggregation, and termination detection. Below it, the *parcelport layer* is backend-specific and implements the actual data transfer protocol.

In HPX, messages are transmitted in the form of *parcels*, each representing one or multiple remote action invocations and (logically) consisting of one non-zero-copy (NZC) chunk and an optional set of zero-copy (ZC) chunks. The NZC chunk contains control metadata, while the ZC chunks hold bulk data. This design avoids expensive memory copying by separating metadata from large payloads. Since ZC chunks must be deserialized into memory layouts compatible with C++ data structures, the upper layer pre-allocates appropriate receive buffers before the parcel is fully received.

Each parcelport must implement two core functions: (1) a non-blocking `send_parcel` function to send parcels and invoke a callback when complete, and (2) a `background_work` function that checks for incoming parcels and progresses outstanding communication. The `background_work` function is frequently invoked by idle threads and notifies the scheduler whether communication made forward progress. It passes the received parcels to the upper layer by enqueuing or immediately executing the encapsulated tasks.

Baseline MPI Implementation. The original MPI parcelport transfers an HPX parcel using a sequence of MPI messages, consisting of a header followed by one or more data messages. The header contains metadata, such as NZC size, number of ZC chunks, and the MPI tag used for the follow-ups, and may piggyback the NZC chunk if it is small enough. Each remaining chunk is sent in a separate message.

All communications are non-blocking. Header and data messages use `MPI_Isend`, with a common tag for header messages and a distinct tag for each parcel. A single `MPI_Irecv` (pre-posted with `MPI_ANY_SOURCE` and the header tag) listens for incoming headers. Upon receiving one, the receiver posts additional `MPI_Irecv`'s for the corresponding data messages, using buffer allocations from the upper layer as needed.

To simplify synchronization, each parcel has at most one active `MPI_Isend` or `MPI_Irecv` at a time; the following message is posted only after the current one completes. Messages from different parcels may proceed concurrently. The MPI request handles for pending sends and receives (except the preposted receive) are stored in two STL deques (*request pools*). The `background_work` function is responsible for polling the preposted receive request and the request pools using `MPI_Test`. The request pools are polled in a round-robin fashion.

Because any HPX worker may call `send_parcel` and `background_work`, the parcelport must be thread-safe. MPI is initialized with `MPI_THREAD_MULTIPLE`, and all polling operations are guarded by an HPX lock. The parcelport will use non-blocking `try-lock` whenever possible. In the case of blocking waiting, the HPX lock will deschedule the underlying user-level threads to avoid wasting CPU cycles.

3.2 Replication of Communicators

The baseline implementation uses a single communicator. In MPICH, this maps to a single set of internal communication resources and is protected by a single spinlock. This causes severe thread contention for the lock if multiple threads access it simultaneously to post sends/receives or test corresponding requests. The VCI extension in MPICH enables us to replicate internal communication resources by mapping them to distinct communicators. We thus enhance the baseline MPI parcelport with the ability to split communication traffic into a configurable number of communicators. We will call this enhanced parcelport the *MPIx parcelport*.

We must ensure the send and receive operations for the same MPI message are posted with the same communicator. Therefore, we construct a static mapping from HPX worker threads to MPI communicators during parcelport initialization. We assign HPX worker threads to communicators in an order that ensures most adjacent threads are assigned the same communicator, thereby improving locality. When the upper layer invokes the `send_parcel` function of the parcelport layer on a worker thread, the following MPI send and receive calls for that parcel will use the communicator associated with this thread. The header message carries the index of this communicator.

With multiple VCIs, the MPIx parcelport will pre-post one `MPI_Irecv` for incoming header messages for each communicator. Worker threads will poll for completed communications using `background_work` only for their communicator. When the continuation extension is not used, the request pools are replicated per communicator, and the `background_work` function will poll the request pools associated with their communicator.

The current MPICH implementation employs a hybrid progress model in the case of multiple VCIs: a progress call (happening implicitly inside `MPI_Test` and all blocking MPI functions) will primarily progress the VCI that is associated with the calling operation, but it will also progress all VCIs once in a while (every 255 VCI-local progress calls). This provides stronger progress guarantees [45], but also increases contention between threads. As a result, we set the `MPIR_CVAR_CH4_GLOBAL_PROGRESS` to `false` to turn off the occasional global progress. Section 4.3 analyzes the performance impact of this setting.

3.3 Replacing Request Polling with Callbacks

The Continuations Proposal allows clients to attach a callback function to an operation request. In the MPIx parcelport, after we post a `MPI_Isend` for a header or follow-up message or a `MPI_Irecv` for a follow-up message, we attach a callback function to the resulting request. The callback function will push a completion descriptor to a preallocated completion queue. Essentially, we use the continuation callback to implement a queue-based completion mechanism. The background_work function will poll the completion queue for any completed operation and react accordingly. We share the completion queue among all threads to improve load balancing. The completion queue uses a state-of-the-art atomic queue implementation (LCRQ [29]).

We do not directly invoke the HPX completion logic in the callback because HPX can invoke arbitrary user tasks and even destroy the current user-level thread, which can lead to reduced performance and even deadlocks. The queue-based design decouples the upper-level complexity from the low-level communication logic.

One side effect of sharing the queue across threads is potential contention during follow-up MPI_Isend and MPI_Irecv operations, as these may be issued by threads not originally associated with the relevant communicator. However, such contention only occurs for large parcels, which are assumed to be relatively infrequent and less contention-sensitive. Prior experiments have shown that the benefits of using a shared queue typically outweigh this overhead.

Complication with Continuation Requests: While the core mechanism of the Continuations Proposal is to attach callback functions to individual MPI operation requests, it is not the entire proposal. To ensure progress and allow more controls over callback execution, the proposal also introduces a persistent *continuation request* object. All continuations (requests with attached callbacks) must be registered with a continuation request. The continuation request is marked complete when all the registered continuations have executed; the continuation request can be tested for completion, and has to be explicitly restarted with MPI_Start before newly attached continuations can be executed again. In MPICH, an atomic counter per continuation request tracks the total number of pending requests to determine whether the continuation request is complete.

The continuation proposal expects users to test the continuation requests to drive the MPI progress engine. In a multi-VCI setup, when a continuation request is tested, the MPI runtime must determine which VCI(s) to make progress on. MPICH adopts the following strategy for selecting the VCI(s) to make progress: Each continuation request maintains a per-VCI atomic counter to track the number of pending operations on that VCI; when testing the continuation request, the MPICH implementation will only make progress on VCI(s) with active associated operations (along with occasional global progress).

In many scenarios, the continuation request functionality adds unnecessary overhead: progress can be guaranteed using other MPI calls, and each communication completion already invokes a client-defined callback. From the client's perspective, there is no need to test for the completion of multiple handler invocations explicitly. Therefore, we extend the existing continuation proposal with the option to disable the usage of the continuation request, by setting the cont_request argument to MPI_REQUEST_NULL in the MPIX_Continue function. In this case, we can avoid the overhead of atomically counting the pending callbacks and completing/restarting the continuation request. We evaluate the performance implications of this optimization in Sect. 4.4.

In HPX, we adopt this optimization and skip the allocation of continuation requests entirely. HPX worker threads periodically poll their pre-posted receives, which automatically invokes the progress engine for the corresponding VCI. It is a lovely coincidence that HPX does not need to do anything additional to ensure the progress of all pending communications attached to continuation callbacks. For other clients where this is not the case, the MPICH runtime provides a non-standard function `MPIX_Stream_progress` to invoke the progress engine of a specific VCI explicitly.

4 MPI-Level Microbenchmark

We begin with a multithreaded active message ping-pong microbenchmark to evaluate the basic performance characteristics of the mechanisms used in the MPIx parcelport, independent of the HPX runtime. To do so, we isolate the active message layer from the MPIx parcelport implementation in HPX and use it to construct a standalone microbenchmark. The active message layer uses pre-posted receives for incoming messages and manages the pending sends with request pools, with the option to leverage the VCI and continuation requests. The benchmark runs on two nodes, each hosting a single MPI process with a configurable number of threads. Threads are pinned to individual cores, and each thread performs a fixed number of ping-pong iterations with a corresponding peer thread on the remote node. All communications use the active message services provided by the extracted layer.

The isolated active message layer organizes the relevant MPI resources (including a communicator, a preposted receive request, and a request pool) into a logical unit called a *device*. All threads share a single device in the baseline (standard MPI) configuration. With the VCI extension enabled, each thread is assigned a private device, mapped to a distinct VCI. With the continuation extension, request pools are replaced with callbacks.

4.1 Experiment Setup

We run all the experiments in this section and Sect. 5 on SDSC Expanse and NCSA Delta. Table 1 summarizes the platforms' configurations. The two platforms have similar CPUs but have different network hardware and software stacks. Expanse uses HDR InfiniBand with Mellanox ConnectX-6 NICs, while Delta uses HPE Slingshot-11 with HPE Cassini NICs. On InfiniBand, MPICH can use either UCX [38] or OFI [33] as the network backend, while on Slingshot-11, MPICH can only use OFI. We use a customized version of MPICH 4.3.0 that implements the continuation proposal. This version is currently available in a pull request on the MPICH GitHub repository[1].

---

[1] https://github.com/pmodels/mpich/pull/7164.

Table 1. Platform Configuration.

Platform	SDSC Expanse	NCSA Delta
CPU	AMD EPYC 7742	AMD EPYC 7763
sockets/node	2	2
cores/socket	64	64
NIC	Mellanox ConnectX-6	HPE Cassini
Network	HDR InfiniBand (2x50Gbps)	Slingshot-11 (200Gbps)
Software	MPICH 4.3.0 UCX 1.17.0 Libfabric 1.21.0 OpenMPI 4.1.3 Libibverbs 43.0	MPICH 4.3.0 Cray MPICH 8.1.27 Libfabric 1.15.2.0 SSHOT2.1.3

4.2 Overall Performance with Multiple VCIs

We begin by evaluating the performance impact of using multiple VCIs with different MPICH network backends and compare the results to those of system-installed MPI implementations (OpenMPI and Cray-MPICH) and standard MPICH without VCI extensions.

As shown in Fig. 1, the MPICH VCI extension improves the multithreaded performance of MPI, outperforming both the system-installed MPI (OpenMPI and Cray-MPICH) and standard MPICH itself. When comparing the best-performing multi-VCI configurations against the best standard MPI configurations using 32 threads per process, we observe speedups of 10x on Expanse and 8x on Delta. Reduced thread contention through replicated communication resources is the primary cause of the speedup. However, the performance gain depends on the underlying network backend, revealing a trade-off between UCX and OFI. While UCX has better base performance, it scales poorly when the number of threads/VCIs exceeds 16. On Expanse with 64 threads (and 64 VCIs), MPICH with the OFI backend outperforms the UCX backend by 4×.

In the standard MPI configuration shown in Fig. 1, all threads share a single device (i.e. a communicator, a preposted receive, and a request pool). For comparison, we also evaluated a variant where each thread has its own device, still using standard MPI. However, it results in even lower performance than the shared device case. With multiple outstanding pre-posted receive requests, there is more contention for the blocking lock of the VCI.

We have also compared the continuation extension's performance against plain request polling. However, we found no performance difference between the two approaches in either the multi-VCI or the standard MPI cases. This is expected, as in this ping-pong microbenchmark, each thread has only one send request and one receive request to poll simultaneously.

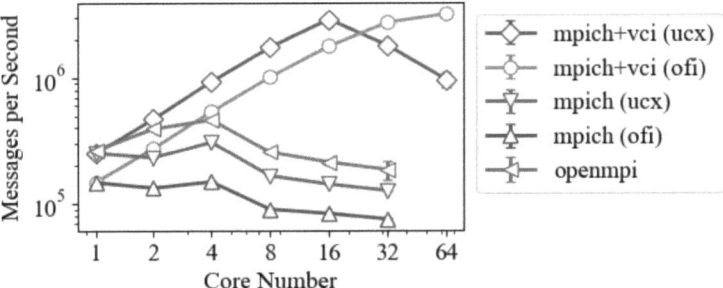

(a) Experiment Results on Expanse with 1-64 threads per process.

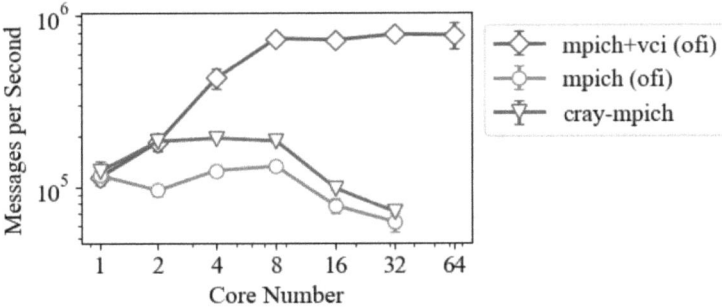

(b) Experiment Results on Delta.

Fig. 1. Performance impacts of the VCI extension compared to other MPI variants with 1–64 threads per process.

In addition to the VCI and the continuation extensions, the *mpix* results shown in Fig. 1 were measured with two special options: (1) the global progress was disabled with MPIR_CVAR_CH4_GLOBAL_PROGRESS set to 0, and (2) we disabled the usage of the continuation request by passing MPI_REQUEST_NULL as the *cont_request* argument to the MPIX_Continue function. We discuss these two additions and their performance impact in the next two sections.

4.3 Global Progress with Multiple VCIs

As discussed in Sect. 3.2, MPICH employs an occasional global progress strategy by default for stronger MPI progress semantics, at the cost of increased thread contention across VCIs. Figure 2 shows the performance impact. We evaluate two variants (configured by the MPIR_CVAR_CH4_GLOBAL_PROGRESS control variable): one with occasional global progress enabled (the default option) and the other with it disabled (the option used by HPX). We observe that performance significantly improves when we disable the global progress option, even though it only performs one global progress every 255 per-VCI progress tests. The message rate improves by 4.5x on Expanse and 40% on Delta.

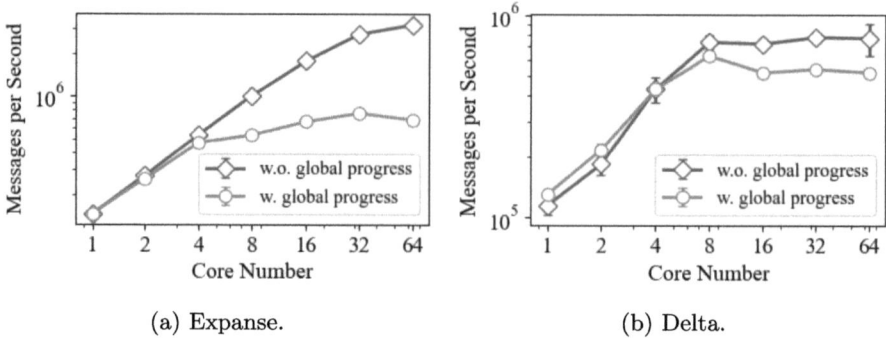

Fig. 2. Performance impacts of the global progress requirement with 1–64 threads per process.

4.4 Continuation with Multiple Threads

As discussed in Sect. 3.3, the continuation request gives users more control over the progress and completion of pending MPI operations but also adds overhead. Figure 3 shows its performance impact. We evaluate two variants with/without the continuation requests. The variant with the continuation request allocates one continuation request per VCI, so there will be no contention on the VCI progress engines. The performance is improved when we disable the continuation request (by passing `MPI_REQUEST_NULL` as the `cont_request` argument to the `MPIX_Continue` function). With 64 threads, the performance improves by 64% on Expanse and 27% on Delta. This indicates that the atomic operations and the logic for completing and restarting continuation requests cause a noticeable overhead.

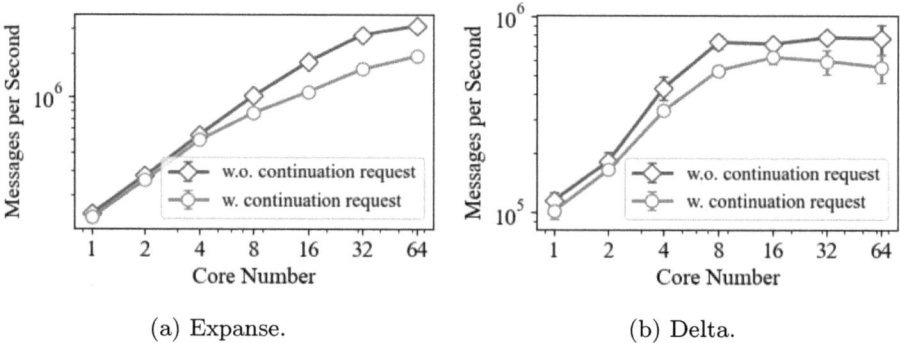

Fig. 3. Performance impacts of the continuation request with 1–64 threads per process.

4.5 Summary

The VCI extension greatly improves the maximum message rate achievable in multithreaded scenarios. However, the two existing network backends in MPICH (UCX and OFI) have limitations. The global progress requirement of the MPI specification and the continuation request construct of the existing continuation proposal can also hurt the performance.

5 HPX Evaluation

In this section, we evaluate the performance impacts of the VCI and continuation extensions on the MPIx parcelport. We do this using two major benchmarks: an HPX microbenchmark, with a flood of messages between two nodes, which tests the maximum throughput of message processing; and an astrophysics application, OctoTiger [14], which tests the impact on a real-world application. [42] describes in detail the HPX flooding microbenchmark.

For the HPX microbenchmark, we report the achieved message rate for two payload sizes: 8 bytes and 16 kilobytes. With 8-byte payloads, the header message can piggyback the application data, and every parcel uses one MPI message. With 16-kilobyte payloads, every parcel uses two MPI messages: one header message and one data message. For the OctoTiger benchmark, we show the total execution time of the application with 20 iterations on 32 nodes. We run two OctoTiger processes per node and 63 threads per process, reserving 1 CPU core per socket for OS activities.

We also include the performance number of the LCI parcelport [41] for comparison. LCI [43] is an experimental communication library specifically designed for efficient asynchronous and multithreaded communication. Its interface and runtime are designed with AMT in mind, enabling a more direct communication path between the network and application layers. We include the LCI parcelport as a reference point representing achievable performance when programming directly against the native network API, unconstrained by the MPI standard.

5.1 Overall Performance

We first compare the MPIx parcelport (*mpix*) with the existing LCI parcelport (*lci*) and the original MPI parcelport (*mpi*) in HPX.

Figure 4 shows the experimental results with varying numbers of MPICH VCIs or LCI devices. We show the results of the LCI parcelport (*lci*), the MPIx parcelport with continuation (*mpix*), the MPIx parcelport with request polling (*mpix_req*), and the old MPI parcelport (*mpi*). We observe that *mpix* greatly shrinks the performance gap between *lci* and *mpi*, especially on Expanse at higher device counts. *lci* is expected to outperform MPI-based approaches as it features a full redesign from the network layer up to suit AMT needs. The performance of *mpi* is much worse than that of *mpix*, showing the performance benefit of the VCI extensions.

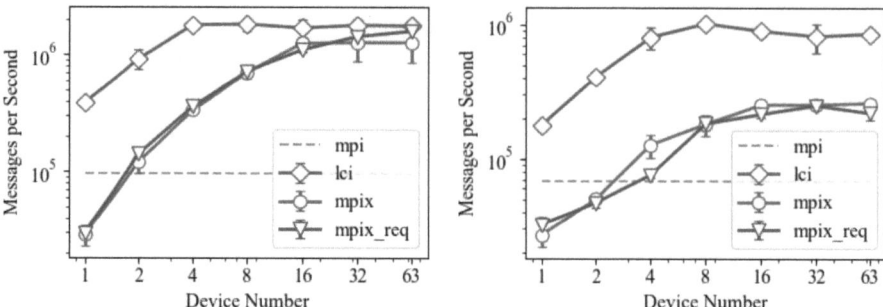

(a) Message Rate (8B) achieved with the flooding microbenchmark on Expanse.

(b) Message Rate (8B) achieved with the flooding microbenchmark on Delta.

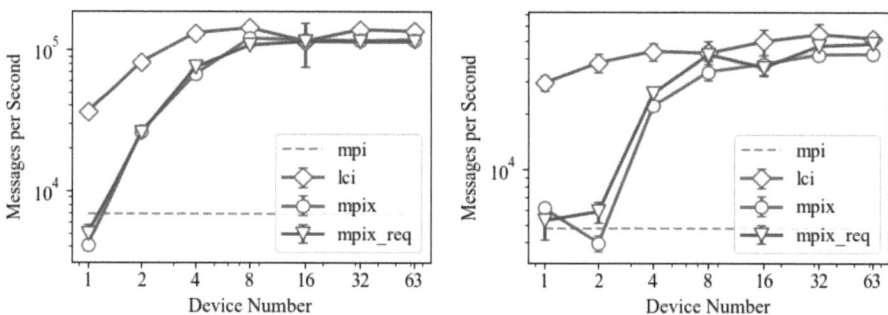

(c) Message Rate (16KiB) achieved with the flooding microbenchmark on Expanse.

(d) Message Rate (16KiB) achieved with the flooding microbenchmark on Delta.

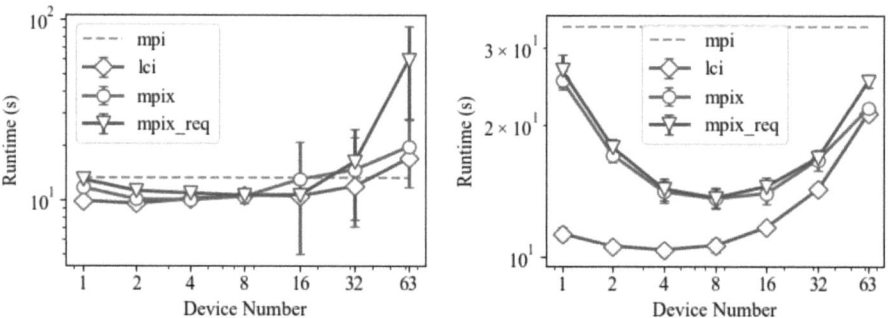

(e) Octo-Tiger time per step with 32 nodes on Expanse.

(f) Octo-Tiger time per step with 32 nodes on Delta.

Fig. 4. Performance impacts of using multiple VCIs and continuation. *lci* uses LCI. *mpi* uses the original MPI parcelport. *mpix* uses MPICH with the VCI and continuation extensions.

Continuation-based programming simplifies development compared to managing and polling request pools, offering clear programmability benefits. It also yields a 5% performance improvement for OctoTiger on Expanse but shows no measurable gains in other scenarios, contrary to our expectations. This suggests that the overhead of request polling is less significant than anticipated.

A prior study of the LCI parcelport [42] observed that a lightweight polling mechanism is indeed beneficial compared to the request polling mechanism, seemingly contradicting the observation here. However, LCI has a more thread-efficient runtime than MPICH, as LCI uses atomic-based data structures while MPICH uses a per-VCI spinlock to ensure thread safety. As a result, the contention due to lock-based request polling is relatively more significant with the LCI parcelport; this effect is hidden in the *mpix* case as MPICH's per-VCI spinlock is already coarse-grained. As a result, we believe the continuation extension will be beneficial when the MPICH runtime gets rid of the coarse-grained per-VCI spinlock and uses a more efficient lock-free data structure.

5.2 Investigate the Slowdown with Too Many VCIs

It is commonly believed that using one VCI per thread yields optimal multithreaded performance. However, our results show that using too many VCIs can degrade performance in real-world applications. We have observed this in the Octo-Tiger benchmark, where performance deteriorates with more than 16 VCIs. We also see a similar upward curve with the LCI parcelport. We further investigated why too many MPICH VCIs or LCI devices worsen performance. We identify **the attentiveness problem** as the main reason.

With too many VCIs, each VCI may not get enough attention from the threads. For 63 threads and 63 VCIs, each VCI only gets one thread to poll it. If the thread gets stuck executing a long-running task, it will not poll the corresponding VCI, and pending communications on that VCI will not be processed, even though other threads may be idle and waiting for work. With fewer VCIs, more threads poll each VCI, and pending communications on that VCI will be processed more quickly. On the other hand, there is more contention.

We implement a new progress strategy (*random*) in the MPIx parcelport and the LCI parcelport to verify this hypothesis and explore a potential fix. In the *random* strategy, each thread randomly picks a VCI to poll from all available VCIs. This way, even if a thread gets stuck executing a long-running task, other threads can still progress the pending communications on that VCI. Correspondingly, we name the previous strategy as *local*, as each thread only polls its own VCI.

Figure 5 shows the performance impact of the *random* progress strategy. We notice that it greatly improves the performance of the LCI parcelport. However, it does not improve the performance of the MPIx parcelport. Instead, it worsens it on Expanse. This is due to the different threading efficiency of the two communication runtimes. In MPICH, every progress call will block waiting for the per-VCI spinlock, while in LCI, the progress call is non-blocking and always

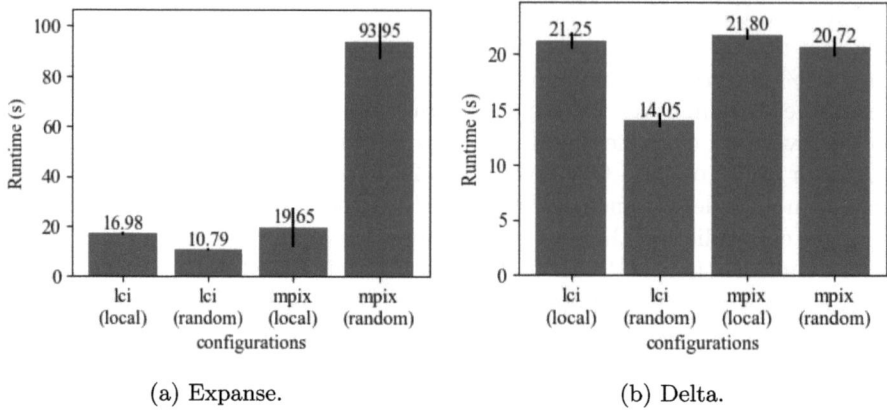

Fig. 5. Performance impacts of the *random* progress strategies on OctoTiger execution time with 63 threads per process and 1 VCI per thread.

employs a try-lock wrapper around the low-level network resources [43]. Profiling confirms that MPICH gets stuck in the VCI spinlock more often with the *random* strategy.

5.3 Summary

The VCI extension shows great performance benefits across the HPX microbenchmark and the real-world application. The continuation extension does not show much performance benefits compared to per-VCI request polling with the current MPICH implementation. The recommended usage of one VCI per thread may not work with real-world applications where tasks both compute and communicate due to the attentiveness problem.

6 Related Work

Multiple efforts have sought to improve MPI performance in multithreaded environments. Prior work [2,3,5,17,34] has focused on reducing lock contention and minimizing the scope of critical sections within the MPI runtime. Other approaches [11,21,22,25] leverage user-level threads, task systems, or process-in-process techniques to enhance MPI on many-core processors and irregular workloads. More recently, [45,46] proposed using VCI to replicate low-level network resources, thereby removing the need for runtime-level serialization. The VCI mechanism has since become the recommended approach for improving multithreaded performance in MPICH, representing a major milestone in MPI implementation-level optimization. Similar optimizations have also been adopted in OpenMPI [34].

A complementary line of research has focused on extending the MPI interface to support multithreaded execution better. [16] proposed the endpoints extension, which decouples threads from ranks and enables threads within a process to issue non-contending MPI calls with different endpoints. More recent MPIX Stream [47] and thread communicator [48] extensions revive and refine the endpoint model. These interface-level extensions help users better convey thread-level parallelism to the MPI runtime. Under the hood, the MPI runtime still relies on VCIs for better multithreaded performance.

Beyond the MPI ecosystem, several other communication libraries have been developed to support asynchronous and multithreaded communication. GASNet and GASNet-EX [9,10] provide low-level active messages and RMA operations for library developers and compiler-generated codes. At a higher level, PGAS models like UPC [18], UPC++ [4], and OpenSHMEM [12] expose global memory abstractions with one-sided RMA operations. LCI [43] proposes new interface and runtime designs to enhance multithreaded communication performance and simplify asynchronous programming.

In contrast to these efforts, our work does not propose new MPI extensions or communication libraries. Instead, we focus on evaluating the practical effectiveness of existing mechanisms, specifically the VCI and continuation extensions, and identifying their limitations. Our analysis complements prior work, offering detailed insights into how current MPI features can be better utilized and where future improvements are needed.

7 Conclusion and Discussion

In this paper, we evaluated the effectiveness of the VCI and continuation extensions in MPICH using both MPI-level and HPX-level benchmarks. Our results show that the VCI extension can significantly improve the performance of multithreaded applications. The continuation extension, while beneficial for programmability, currently shows limited performance benefit.

Contrary to the common recommendation of assigning one VCI per thread, we found that excessive use of VCIs can degrade performance in real-world applications. We identified the attentiveness problem as the primary cause: when too many VCIs are in use, the MPI runtime may fail to poll them frequently enough, leading to increased latency and missed progress opportunities. Our findings highlight intra-VCI threading efficiency as a critical factor. Improving it not only resolves the attentiveness issue by enabling more efficient polling across threads, but also allows users to meet their multithreaded communication needs with fewer VCIs, which will also boost scalability by reducing resource usage.

Improved intra-VCI efficiency also helps demonstrate the benefits of the continuation extension. Continuations eliminate the need for explicit polling of shared request pools, thus removing the associated thread contention. However, if intra-VCI operations rely on coarse-grained locks, internal contention can obscure these gains. With more efficient intra-VCI handling, continuations can better realize their potential of minimizing overhead and avoiding contention.

While it is known to be challenging to design a threading-efficient VCI due to the non-overtaking requirement and the need to support wildcard receives, recent MPI info keys such as *allow_overtaking* and *no_any_tag/source* offer a practical path forward. When these keys are set, MPI runtimes can safely adopt more scalable designs. Task systems, some of the primary users of asynchronous multithreaded communication, can often tolerate these relaxations [42]. However, they still require support for *any_source* receives, which may necessitate additional info keys. One possible approach is to propagate *any_source* information to the sender side, as suggested in prior work [15].

In addition, our evaluation has revealed limitations in two commonly used communication middlewares: UCX and libfabric. Specifically, UCX shows performance degradation when more than 16 UCP workers are used, and libfabric delivers lower absolute performance. Prior work on LCI [43] has demonstrated that multithreaded performance comparable to MPI-everywhere (one process per core) is achievable when building directly on top of the libibverbs [32] layer. Addressing these performance constraints in the underlying middleware is essential for MPI implementations to fully realize scalable multithreaded communication.

We believe these insights offer practical guidance for improving multithreaded communication performance in MPICH and other MPI implementations, and we hope they inform future runtime and interface design.

Acknowledgements. This work used Expanse at San Diego Supercomputer Center [39] and Delta at National Center for Supercomputing Applications [19] through allocations CCR130058 and CIS250465 from the Advanced Cyberinfrastructure Coordination Ecosystem: Services & Support (ACCESS) program [8], which is supported by U.S. National Science Foundation grants #2138259, #2138286, #2138307, #2137603, and #2138296.

References

1. Abdulah, S., et al.: Boosting earth system model outputs and saving petabytes in their storage using exascale climate emulators. In: Proceedings of the International Conference for High Performance Computing, Networking, Storage, and Analysis. SC '24. IEEE Press (2024). https://doi.org/10.1109/SC41406.2024.00008
2. Amer, A., et al.: Lock contention management in multithreaded MPI. ACM Trans. Parallel Comput. **5**(3), 12:1–12:21 (2019). https://doi.org/10.1145/3275443. https://dl.acm.org/doi/10.1145/3275443
3. Amer, A., Lu, H., Wei, Y., Balaji, P., Matsuoka, S.: MPI+threads: runtime contention and remedies. In: Proceedings of the 20th ACM SIGPLAN Symposium on Principles and Practice of Parallel Programming, PPoPP 2015, pp. 239–248. Association for Computing Machinery (2015). https://doi.org/10.1145/2688500.2688522. https://dl.acm.org/doi/10.1145/2688500.2688522
4. Bachan, J., et al.: UPC++: a high-performance communication framework for asynchronous computation. In: 2019 IEEE International Parallel and Distributed Processing Symposium (IPDPS), pp. 963–973 (2019). https://doi.org/10.1109/IPDPS.2019.00104

5. Balaji, P., Buntinas, D., Goodell, D., Gropp, W., Thakur, R.: Toward efficient support for multithreaded MPI communication. In: Lastovetsky, A., Kechadi, T., Dongarra, J. (eds.) EuroPVM/MPI 2008. LNCS, vol. 5205, pp. 120–129. Springer, Heidelberg (2008). https://doi.org/10.1007/978-3-540-87475-1_20
6. Bauer, M., Treichler, S., Slaughter, E., Aiken, A.: Legion: expressing locality and independence with logical regions. In: SC '12: Proceedings of the International Conference on High Performance Computing, Networking, Storage and Analysis, pp. 1–11 (2012). https://doi.org/10.1109/SC.2012.71
7. Bernholdt, D.E., et al.: A survey of MPI usage in the US exascale computing project. Concurr. Comput. Pract. Exp. **32**(3), e4851 (2020). https://doi.org/10.1002/cpe.4851. https://onlinelibrary.wiley.com/doi/abs/10.1002/cpe.4851
8. Boerner, T.J., Deems, S., Furlani, T.R., Knuth, S.L., Towns, J.: Access: advancing innovation: Nsf's advanced cyberinfrastructure coordination ecosystem: services & support. In: Practice and Experience in Advanced Research Computing 2023: Computing for the Common Good, pp. 173–176 (2023). https://doi.org/10.1145/3569951.3597559
9. Bonachea, D., Hargrove, P.H.: GASNet-EX: a high-performance, portable communication library for exascale. In: Hall, M., Sundar, H. (eds.) LCPC 2018. LNCS, vol. 11882, pp. 138–158. Springer, Cham (2019). https://doi.org/10.1007/978-3-030-34627-0_11
10. Bonachea, D., Jeong, J.: Gasnet: a portable high-performance communication layer for global address-space languages. CS258 Parallel Comput. Arch. Proj. Spring **31**, 17 (2002)
11. Carribault, P., Pérache, M., Jourdren, H.: Enabling low-overhead hybrid MPI/OpenMP parallelism with MPC. In: Sato, M., Hanawa, T., Müller, M.S., Chapman, B.M., de Supinski, B.R. (eds.) IWOMP 2010. LNCS, vol. 6132, pp. 1–14. Springer, Heidelberg (2010). https://doi.org/10.1007/978-3-642-13217-9_1
12. Chapman, B., et al.: Introducing OpenSHMEM: SHMEM for the PGAS community. In: Proceedings of the Fourth Conference on Partitioned Global Address Space Programming Model. PGAS '10. Association for Computing Machinery, New York (2010). https://doi.org/10.1145/2020373.2020375
13. Chatterjee, S., et al.: Integrating asynchronous task parallelism with MPI. In: 2013 IEEE 27th International Symposium on Parallel and Distributed Processing, pp. 712–725. IEEE (2013). https://ieeexplore.ieee.org/abstract/document/6569856
14. Daiß, G., et al.: Asynchronous-many-task systems: Challenges and opportunities–scaling an amr astrophysics code on exascale machines using kokkos and hpx. arXiv preprint arXiv:2412.15518 (2024)
15. Dang, H.V., Snir, M., Gropp, W.: Towards millions of communicating threads. In: Proceedings of the 23rd European MPI Users' Group Meeting, EuroMPI '16, pp. 1–14. Association for Computing Machinery, New York (2016). https://doi.org/10.1145/2966884.2966914
16. Dinan, J., et al.: Enabling communication concurrency through flexible mpi endpoints. Int. J. High Perfor. Comput. Appl. **28**(4), 390–405 (2014)
17. Dózsa, G., et al.: Enabling concurrent multithreaded MPI communication on multicore petascale systems. In: Keller, R., Gabriel, E., Resch, M., Dongarra, J. (eds.) EuroMPI 2010. LNCS, vol. 6305, pp. 11–20. Springer, Heidelberg (2010). https://doi.org/10.1007/978-3-642-15646-5_2
18. El-Ghazawi, T., Smith, L.: UPC: Unified parallel C. In: Proceedings of the 2006 ACM/IEEE Conference on Supercomputing, SC '06, p. 27–es. Association for Computing Machinery, New York (2006). https://doi.org/10.1145/1188455.1188483

19. Gropp, W., Boerner, T., Bode, B., Bauer, G.: Delta: balancing gpu performance with advanced system interfaces (2023)
20. Hofmeyr, S., et al.: Terabase-scale metagenome coassembly with metahipmer. Sci. Rep. **10**(1), 10689 (2020)
21. Hori, A., et al.: Process-in-process: techniques for practical address-space sharing. In: Proceedings of the 27th International Symposium on High-Performance Parallel and Distributed Computing, HPDC '18, pp. 131–143. Association for Computing Machinery, New York (2018). https://doi.org/10.1145/3208040.3208045
22. Huang, C., Lawlor, O., Kalé, L.V.: Adaptive MPI. In: Rauchwerger, L. (ed.) LCPC 2003. LNCS, vol. 2958, pp. 306–322. Springer, Heidelberg (2004). https://doi.org/10.1007/978-3-540-24644-2_20
23. Kaiser, H., et al.: HPX - the C++ standard library for parallelism and concurrency. J. Open Source Softw. **5**(53), 2352 (2020)
24. Kale, L.V., Krishnan, S.: CHARM++: a portable concurrent object oriented system based on C++ **28**(10), 91–108. https://doi.org/10.1145/167962.165874. https://dl.acm.org/doi/10.1145/167962.165874
25. Kamal, H., Wagner, A.: FG-MPI: fine-grain MPI for multicore and clusters. In: 2010 IEEE International Symposium on Parallel and Distributed Processing, Workshops and Phd Forum (IPDPSW), pp. 1–8 (2010). https://doi.org/10.1109/IPDPSW.2010.5470773
26. Ltaief, H., et al.: Toward capturing genetic epistasis from multivariate genome-wide association studies using mixed-precision kernel ridge regression. In: SC24: International Conference for High Performance Computing, Networking, Storage and Analysis, pp. 1–12 (2024). https://doi.org/10.1109/SC41406.2024.00012
27. Mei, C., et al.: Enabling and scaling biomolecular simulations of 100 million atoms on petascale machines with a multicore-optimized message-driven runtime. In: SC '11: Proceedings of 2011 International Conference for High Performance Computing, Networking, Storage and Analysis, pp. 1–11 (2011)
28. Mor, O., Bosilca, G., Snir, M.: Improving the scaling of an asynchronous many-task runtime with a lightweight communication engine. In: Proceedings of the 52nd International Conference on Parallel Processing, ICPP '23, pp. 153–162. Association for Computing Machinery (2023). https://doi.org/10.1145/3605573.3605642. https://dl.acm.org/doi/10.1145/3605573.3605642
29. Morrison, A., Afek, Y.: Fast concurrent queues for x86 processors. In: Proceedings of the 18th ACM SIGPLAN Symposium on Principles and Practice of Parallel Programming, PPoPP '13, pp. 103–112. Association for Computing Machinery, New York (2013). https://doi.org/10.1145/2442516.2442527
30. MPI Forum: MPI: a message passing interface standard (2023). https://www.mpi-forum.org/docs/mpi-4.1/mpi41-report.pdf
31. MPICH Developers: MPICH: High-Performance Portable MPI. https://www.mpich.org (nd)
32. NVIDIA: Rdma aware networks programming user manual (2025). https://docs.nvidia.com/networking/display/rdmaawareprogrammingv17
33. (OFIWG), O.W.G.: Libfabric programmer's manual (2023)
34. Patinyasakdikul, T., Eberius, D., Bosilca, G., Hjelm, N.: Give MPI threading a fair chance: a study of multithreaded MPI designs. In: 2019 IEEE International Conference on Cluster Computing (CLUSTER), pp. 1–11 (2019). https://doi.org/10.1109/CLUSTER.2019.8891015. https://ieeexplore.ieee.org/abstract/document/8891015

35. Patinyasakdikul, T., Luo, X., Eberius, D., Bosilca, G.: Multirate: a flexible mpi benchmark for fast assessment of multithreaded communication performance. In: 2019 IEEE/ACM Workshop on Exascale MPI (ExaMPI), pp. 1–11 (2019). https://doi.org/10.1109/ExaMPI49596.2019.00006
36. Schuchart, J.: MPI continuations proposal (2021)
37. Schuchart, J., Samfass, P., Niethammer, C., Gracia, J., Bosilca, G.: Callback-based completion notification using MPI continuations. Parallel Comput. **106**, 102793 (2021). https://doi.org/10.1016/j.parco.2021.102793. https://www.sciencedirect.com/science/article/pii/S0167819121000466
38. Shamis, P., et al.: UCX: an open source framework for HPC network APIs and beyond. In: 2015 IEEE 23rd Annual Symposium on High-Performance Interconnects, pp. 40–43 (2015). https://doi.org/10.1109/HOTI.2015.13
39. Strande, S., et al.: Expanse: computing without boundaries: Architecture, deployment, and early operations experiences of a supercomputer designed for the rapid evolution in science and engineering. In: Practice and Experience in Advanced Research Computing 2021: Evolution Across All Dimensions. PEARC '21. Association for Computing Machinery, New York (2021). https://doi.org/10.1145/3437359.3465588
40. Yadav, R., et al.: Legate sparse: distributed sparse computing in python. In: Proceedings of the International Conference for High Performance Computing, Networking, Storage and Analysis. SC '23. Association for Computing Machinery, New York (2023). https://doi.org/10.1145/3581784.3607033
41. Yan, J., Kaiser, H., Snir, M.: Design and analysis of the network software stack of an asynchronous many-task system – the LCI parcelport of HPX. In: Proceedings of the SC '23 Workshops of The International Conference on High Performance Computing, Network, Storage, and Analysis, SC-W '23, pp. 1151–1161. Association for Computing Machinery, New York (2023). https://doi.org/10.1145/3624062.3624598
42. Yan, J., Kaiser, H., Snir, M.: Understanding the communication needs of asynchronous many-task systems–a case study of HPX+LCI. arXiv preprint arXiv:2503.12774 (2025)
43. Yan, J., Snir, M.: Lci: a lightweight communication interface for efficient asynchronous multithreaded communication. arXiv preprint arXiv:2505.01864 (2025)
44. Zambre, R., Chandramowliswharan, A., Balaji, P.: How i learned to stop worrying about user-visible endpoints and love MPI. In: Proceedings of the 34th ACM International Conference on Supercomputing. ICS '20. Association for Computing Machinery, New York (2020). https://doi.org/10.1145/3392717.3392773
45. Zambre, R., Chandramowliswharan, A., Balaji, P.: How I learned to stop worrying about user-visible endpoints and love MPI. In: Proceedings of the 34th ACM International Conference on Supercomputing, ICS '20, pp. 1–13. Association for Computing Machinery (2020). https://doi.org/10.1145/3392717.3392773. https://dl.acm.org/doi/10.1145/3392717.3392773
46. Zambre, R., Sahasrabudhe, D., Zhou, H., Berzins, M., Chandramowlishwaran, A., Balaji, P.: Logically parallel communication for fast MPI+threads applications **32**(12), 3038–3052 (2021). https://doi.org/10.1109/TPDS.2021.3075157. https://ieeexplore.ieee.org/document/9411740

47. Zhou, H., Raffenetti, K., Guo, Y., Thakur, R.: MPIX stream: an explicit solution to hybrid MPI+X programming. In: Proceedings of the 29th European MPI Users' Group Meeting, pp. 1–10 (2022)
48. Zhou, H., Raffenetti, K., Zhang, J., Guo, Y., Thakur, R.: Frustrated with MPI+Threads? Try MPIxThreads! In: Proceedings of the 30th European MPI Users' Group Meeting, pp. 1–10 (2023)

Extending the SPMD IR for RMA Models and Static Data Race Detection

Semih Burak[1](✉), Simon Schwitanski[1], Felix Tomski[1], Jens Domke[2], and Matthias Müller[1]

[1] Chair for High Performance Computing, IT Center, RWTH Aachen University, Aachen, Germany
burak@itc.rwth-aachen.de
[2] RIKEN Center for Computational Science, Kobe, Japan

Abstract. Modern multi-node systems necessitate parallel programming models (PPMs) like MPI to facilitate execution and communication among multiple processing elements. These single program, multiple data (SPMD) PPMs offer features such as RMA or accelerator support. However, SPMD program tools, such as those for correctness checks or performance optimization, are typically developed for specific PPMs or rely on tool-internal abstractions. To overcome this limitation, the SPMD IR was introduced as an intermediate representation (IR) within a multi-layer program representation and realized as a dialect in MLIR (LLVM).

This work extends the SPMD IR by incorporating, among others, capabilities for RMA and related completion mechanisms. These enhancements increase compatibility with MPI and SHMEM, while newly integrating support for NVSHMEM. By leveraging traits in MLIR, SPMD IR provides an extensible approach for implementing SPMD program analysis.

The applicability of the SPMD IR is demonstrated through the use case of static local data race detection. It is implemented in a generalized fashion, covering not only RMA but also non-blocking communication in general, and is independent of specific API calls, offering increased extensibility. Using a comprehensive set of micro-benchmark suites and proxy apps, the SPMD IR is evaluated against both static and dynamic tools. Overall, the SPMD IR verification distinguishes itself with extensive PPM support and high detection accuracy. Notably, it is the first tool capable of detecting data races across SHMEM, NVSHMEM, and their hybrid combinations (with MPI).

Keywords: MLIR · Static Analysis · Correctness · MPI · SHMEM · NVSHMEM

1 Introduction

Single program, multiple data (SPMD) parallel programming models (PPMs), such as MPI [25], have become the de-facto standard for executing parallel programs on modern multi-node HPC cluster systems. These models enable efficient

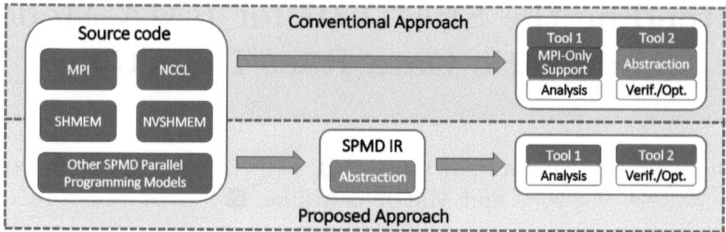

Fig. 1. Illustrates how (static) tools would work on parallel programming models including input with or without a unifying SPMD IR in-between.

execution and communication among many processing elements on distributed-memory systems. Besides MPI, other SPMD PPMs, such as SHMEM [35] and NCCL [34], provide similar functionalities with distinct features. NCCL focuses on inter-GPU communication involving CUDA [33] stream semantics, and SHMEM operates based on the partitioned global address space (PGAS) principle.

Remote-memory access (RMA), also known as one-sided communication, is an essential part of the (OPEN)SHMEM specification along with its related completion mechanisms. Due to its inherently lower communication overhead compared to point-to-point communication [5,10,21,37], RMA has gained increasing attention also from the AI community [8,9,36] for inter-GPU communication through NVSHMEM [32,38]. However, this benefit comes at the cost of heightened risk for correctness issues, such as data races. That is why tools like RMAsanitizer [44] and PARCOACH [2,39] have been developed.

PARCOACH offers data race detection through static [39] and dynamic analysis [2]. However, its support is limited to MPI. RMAsanitizer, on the other hand, is a dynamic tool designed specifically to identify RMA-related data races and builds upon MUST [14,43]. It employs a tool-internal PPM abstraction, enabling support for MPI, SHMEM, and GASPI [11]. The situation of such SPMD program tools is illustrated in Fig. 1. In the upper part, it shows how current tools either support only one PPM, like MPI, or rely on built-in abstractions. Extending a tool's capability for another PPM requires expert knowledge of the tool.

To address these problems posed by the diversity and increasing numbers of PPMs, previous work [7] introduced the SPMD IR. This intermediate representation (IR) aims to unify SPMD PPMs and reduce the need to reimplement tools for each PPM and their combinations. Unlike partial abstractions, such as the one in RMAsanitizer for RMA, the SPMD IR seeks to encompass entire PPMs. Adding tool support for another PPM is reduced to providing the necessary transformations to the SPMD IR. Initial work on the SPMD IR laid the foundation for a unified representation of SPMD PPMs, demonstrating its potential through a toolchain implementation. However, it focused primarily on collective communication and operations related to process or communicator management, as showcased by the use case of collectives verification.

Proving an IR's utility requires broader application scenarios, which is why this work introduces a significant extension to the SPMD IR together with the use case of static local data race detection. Unlike the initial focus, data race detection requires adequate representation and handling of additional SPMD features, such as non-blocking communication, completion mechanisms, and data management. This enables showing whether the SPMD IR is expressive enough to represent essential parts of modern PPMs, providing a robust basis for comprehensive evaluation.

This paper makes the following contributions:

- Designing a unifying extension for the SPMD IR that can represent one-sided communication and related synchronization and completion features of SPMD PPMs for distributed-memory, PGAS, and GPU programs (Sect. 3.1).
- Implementing a prototype of the IR extension and necessary analyses and transformations as compiler passes in MLIR, featuring analysis of GPU kernels and GPU-initiated API calls and thereby support for NVSHMEM (Sect. 3.2).
- Providing a generalized, extensible static approach on local data race detection to the SPMD IR, supporting PPMs besides MPI and combined analysis for RMA and non-blocking communication in general (Sect. 4).
- Showcasing an evaluation of the proof-of-concept compared to PARCOACH and RMAsanitizer/MUST, extending RMARaceBench [42], and assessing the applicability of the SPMD IR on three proxy apps (incl. performance) (Sect. 5).

2 Background to MLIR

Intermediate representations (IRs) are purpose-built components playing a crucial role in compilation by facilitating optimizations, analyses, and transformations. Modern compilation chains typically involve multiple IRs, starting from high-level representations and progressively lowering them to machine code. IRs can give rise to derived data structures, which are more efficient for specific algorithms or lightweight for analysis.

LLVM IR [19] is a widely used, well-established IR that serves as a common target for various programming languages in the LLVM toolchain, including C/C++, Fortran, and Julia. This unified representation layer enables the generalized application of optimization and analysis passes, eventually leading to the generation of target-specific machine code and binaries.

The multi-level intermediate representation (MLIR) [20] is a novel compiler framework and part of LLVM. It is successfully and extensively used both in DSL-based toolchains [30,49] and full compilation pipelines for high-level languages, such as the new Fortran compiler flang [6,24]. Similarly, ongoing work aims to develop a new clang compiler that introduces a high-level MLIR layer, called CLANG IR [23], positioned between clang's AST and LLVM IR.

A key difference between LLVM IR and MLIR lies in their extensibility. LLVM IR defines a fixed set of low-level operations and types. In contrast, MLIR supports the extension of existing dialects or the creation of new ones through customizable operations, attributes, types, and traits, while also integrating the LLVM dialect to maintain equivalent expressiveness and smooth transition.

In MLIR, a *dialect* is essentially a namespace that groups related operations and types. An *operation* is the most fundamental element of an IR and can have

```
1  MPI_Comm_rank(MPI_COMM_WORLD, &rank);
2  MPI_Win_fence(0, win);
3  if (rank == 0)
4      MPI_Put(buf, bufLen, MPI_INT, 1, ..., win);
5  buf[0] = 42; // data race !
6  MPI_Win_fence(0, win);
```

Fig. 2. An RMA example code snippet in C containing a local data race.

```
1  %_ = func.call @MPI_Comm_rank(%commWorld, %rankPtr) : (i32,llvm.ptr) -> i32
2  %rank = llvm.load (%rankPtr) : (llvm.ptr) -> i32
3  %rankIsZero = arith.cmpi (%rank, %c0) {eq} : ...
4  %_ = func.call @MPI_Win_fence(%c0, %win) : (i32, i32) -> i32
5  scf.if (%rankIsZero) : ...
6      %err3 = func.call @MPI_Put(%buf, %bufLen, %mpiInt, %c1, ..., %win):...
7  llvm.store (%c42, %buf) : ... // write to buf[0]; data race!
8  %_ = func.call @MPI_Win_fence(%c0, %win) : ...
```

Fig. 3. Figure 2 represented in MLIR, where Rank 0 *puts* data to Rank 1. Red highlights the dialects, orange the values, and blue the types. Some code is left for brevity.

multiple typed operand and result *values* in static single assignment (SSA) form, i.e., assigned exactly once, similar to LLVM IR. These values represent dynamic (runtime) information, while *attributes* are used for static (compile-time) data. *Traits* abstract common properties and implementation details of MLIR objects such as operations or types, e.g., the Collective trait in the SPMD IR. Unlike attributes, which are specified at compile-time, traits are defined at dialect-definition-time, i.e., during the design of the IR itself, prior to any compilation.

Operations may also contain *regions*, which in turn consist of blocks that host additional operations. The execution logic and return value within and among those is to be specified by the operation. For example, the scf.if has two regions (then and else), only one of which is executed based on a boolean operand. Since dialects are defined with common features such as traits, attributes, or types and allow defining or implementing interfaces, analysis or transformation passes can be designed to work with one or even multiple dialects. This nested structure allows for flexible and hierarchical IR designs. Each stage of the compilation pipeline can employ specialized dialects, performing specific analyses and optimizations before lifting or lowering the representation as needed.

The C code in Fig. 2 shows an MPI example, in which Rank 0 transfers data to Rank 1 using RMA, containing a local data race with the local write in Line 5. Figure 3 illustrates the MLIR representation obtained by transforming Fig. 2 through clang and LLVM IR. This example demonstrates the intermixing of dialects within MLIR. The arith dialect handles arithmetic operations and defining constants, while the func dialect represents function behavior. The scf (structured control flow) dialect provides high-level control structures such as loops and branches, similar to those in high-level programming languages. Additionally, low-level operations like memory allocation are handled here by the llvm dialect, illustrating the seamless integration of high- and low-level abstractions.

```
1  %commWorld = spmd.commWorld () {execKind = "All"}: () -> !spmd.comm
2  %rank, %_= spmd.getRankInComm (%commWorld){...} : ... -> (i32,!spmd.error)
3  %rankIsZero = arith.cmpi (%rank, %c0) {...} : ...
4  %_ = spmd.fence (%win, %c0) {...} : ...
5  scf.if (%rankIsZero) {isMV = true, ...} : ...
6    %_ = spmd.put (%buf, %bufLen, %typeI32, ..., %win, ...)
       {isBlocking = false, execKind = "Static", executedBy = [0]}
       : (!llvm.ptr, i64, !spmd.datatype, ..., !spmd.win, ...) -> ...
7  llvm.store (%c42,%buf) {...} : ... // write to buf[0]; data race!
8  %_ = spmd.fence (%win, %c0) {...} : ...
```

Fig. 4. Shows Fig. 3 transformed to the SPMD IR. Some code is left out for brevity.

Lines 1–3 retrieve the process's rank and compare it to zero. Line 4 starts a synchronization epoch, followed by a one-sided data transfer from Rank 0 to Rank 1 (Lines 5–6). In Line 7, a local write occurs at index zero, causing a data race, as the synchronization epoch is only closed afterwards in Line 8.

The flexibility to use multiple special-purpose dialects within a single IR, each capable of embedding domain-specific information or high-level semantics, motivated the implementation of the SPMD IR in MLIR. This approach allows SPMD-related parallelism and PPM details to be represented without sacrificing the ability to maintain other aspects of the program or requiring the development of an entirely separate compiler framework.

3 SPMD IR

Figure 3 illustrates that specific semantic information related to MPI is not directly encoded in the IR. For instance, commWorld is represented as an integer (i32) constant, but its specific value or even type may vary across MPI implementations. Similarly, the datatype argument mpiInt for MPI_Put is also represented as an integer constant, which lacks semantic clarity. Although the new ABI [13,25] for MPI aims to address cross-implementation differences, it does not ensure that essential semantic information is directly accessible to the compiler. This limitation is further evident in the MPI_Comm_rank call, where the rank is assigned via a pointer rather than being returned directly. Such a design complicates analysis and optimization for a static tool because the memory side effects are ambiguous.

This is where SPMD IR (Single Program, Multiple Data Intermediate Representation) comes into play. The SPMD IR manifests the idea of unifying and providing enriched semantic information of SPMD PPMs such as MPI or SHMEM. It is realized in form of a newly introduced spmd dialect in MLIR, allowing a multilayer program representation. SPMD IR enhances the compiler's understanding by explicitly representing API calls and values of SPMD PPMs with appropriate operations, types, and constants, possibly facilitating further optimizations and analyses. Special SPMD-specific values such as a communicator or window are assigned dedicated types, ensuring that their semantic roles are preserved. Calls that generate new values, e.g., MPI_Comm_rank, are transformed into IR operations that directly return these values. Memory side effects, e.g., read-only or write, are defined for each operand, clearly defining the input-output behavior. Additionally, the SPMD IR enriches the IR with traits and attributes to capture key characteristics of operations such as collective or non-blocking behavior.

Beyond this, the SPMD IR incorporates the multi-value (MV) analysis, which identifies if control-flow operations depend on values that remain consistent across executing processes (single-) or not (multi-value) [1]. Further, the SPMD IR extends this analysis by classifying each operation in the IR based on the execution-kind and executing-rank analysis, distinguishing between cases with compile-time known ranks and those determined at runtime.

Figure 4 presents an excerpt of the resulting IR of transforming the example from Fig. 3 to the SPMD IR. While operations such as for arithmetic or control-flow are kept in their previous forms and dialects, SPMD-related API calls and values are converted to their counterparts in the spmd dialect. For instance, the rank is directly returned by the getRankInComm operation, and the world communicator, the window, and former mpiInt operand received their dedicated types and representations. Furthermore, each operation is annotated with its execution kind, with executing ranks specified for static cases (cf. Line 6) and multivaluedness captured for conditionals (cf. Line 5).

In summary, SPMD IR leverages MLIR's modern framework to express SPMD PPM semantics for compile-time analyses. It provides a unifying approach that can serve as a layer above individual SPMD dialects and enhances the IR with critical semantic information.

3.1 Extensions

Table 1 provides an overview of the current capabilities of SPMD IR in representing SPMD PPM features, including the necessary transformations to it. It also indicates which model supports each feature. This work introduces support for managing windows, RMA communication, and related completion mechanisms. Furthermore, basic support for partitioned and persistent communication is provided (not shown in Table 1). Altogether, the SPMD IR encompasses key management functionalities related to processes, devices, communicators, memory, requests, windows, and streams. It supports point-to-point, collective, RMA, (basic) partitioned, and persistent communication and their related synchronization and completion mechanisms together with non-blocking semantics.

An example for the SPMD IR unification is the put operation. It abstracts over MPI_Put, MPI_Rput, shmem_TYPE_put[_nbi], shmem_putmem[_nbi], and nvshmem_TYPE_put[_nbi]. For RMA completion, locks are available for covering MPI RMA. OPENSHMEM's quiet is mapped to a flushAll, and barrier_all to a fence, in correspondence to MPI. However, an OPENSHMEM fence is *not* mapped to the same operation as MPI_Win_fence. Due to semantic differences, a separate operation called fenceOrdering is introduced to represent the ordering of RMA operations without guaranteeing their remote or local completion. In the SPMD IR, MPI's window feature is kept for unification purposes, which is why a default window is created for use in RMA operations by SHMEM or NVSHMEM. This default window spans over the whole target buffer communicated with.

Table 1. Coverage of SPMD concepts in the SPMD IR, new additions highlighted in gray. Check marks indicate supported features by a programming model.

Concept	MPI	SHMEM	NCCL	NVSHMEM	SPMD IR Operations
Management					
Process & Device	✓	✓	✓	✓	init, finalize, getSizeOfComm, getRankInComm, getDeviceInComm, abort
Communicator	✓	✓	✓	✓	commSplit, commDestroy, commSplitStrided, commWorld, commNode
Memory	✓	✓	✓	✓	malloc, realloc, free
Request	✓				created by respective communication operations
Window		✓			winCreate, winAlloc, winFree
Stream			✓	✓	created, e.g., by CUDA; used as operands
Communication					
Point-to-Point	✓		✓		send, recv
Collective	✓	✓	✓	✓	bcast, {all}reduce, {reduce}Scatter, barrier
RMA	✓	✓		✓	put, get, {get}Accumulate, {compareAnd}Swap
Sync. & Completion					
Non-blocking	✓	✓	✓	✓	wait{All,Some,Any}, test{All,Some,Any}
RMA	✓	✓		✓	fenceOrdering, flush{All}, lock{All}, unlock{All}

Regarding types, window and lock values now have their dedicated types. Notably, the type of communicated data is no longer restricted to `memref` types. The SPMD IR now allows any `addressLike` type, currently llvm pointers and `memref` types. This adjustment ensures compatibility with MLIR generated from LLVM IR, where `memref` types may not be readily available. In terms of attributes, this work adds `isLocal` and `isReadyMode` to distinguish former API calls with similar functionality, as done by the existing `isBuffered` and `isBlocking` attributes. For instance, `isLocal` separates `MPI_Win_flush_local` and `MPI_Win_flush`, and `isReadyMode` `MPI_Rsend_init` and `MPI_Ssend_init`.

The SPMD IR categorizes operations using traits such as P2P (point-to-point) or `ProcessManagement`. This work extends this further by introducing traits like `RMA`, `Sync`, and `Communication`, enabling an API-independent approach for data race detection (cf. Sect. 4). The `Collective` trait is now the primary marker for executing the collectives verification [7], increasing extensibility.

Two features of OPENSHMEM are currently not covered by the SPMD IR: contexts and point-to-point signaling or wait operations. Detecting data races in the presence of point-to-point synchronization is particularly challenging for static tools, as it requires reasoning about inter-process synchronization and the actual values of variables, which becomes even more difficult in the presence of dynamic control flow (cf. Sect. 4.1 for a discussion on remote race detection). Additionally, NVSHMEM largely adheres to the OPENSHMEM 1.3 specification, which predates the introduction of contexts in version 1.4. For MPI, the Post-Start-Complete-Wait RMA synchronization model is not supported due to similar reasons as for point-to-point synchronization in SHMEM. These restrictions have led to deferring support for these three features to future work.

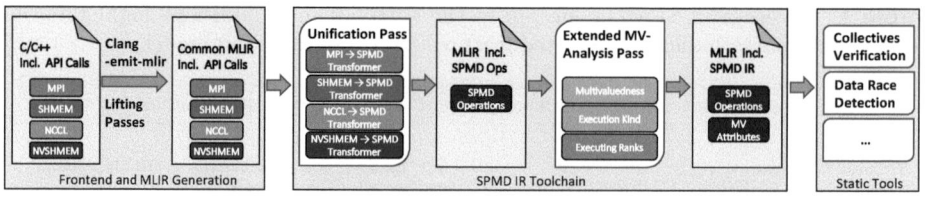

Fig. 5. The new workflow for the SPMD IR that uses LLVM IR in-between the input C/C++ code and MLIR in the frontend.

3.2 Toolchain Workflow

The starting point is a program written in C/C++. In order to obtain a program representation in MLIR there are currently two possible approaches: Polygeist [27] and through LLVM IR. The previous workflow [7] relied on Polygeist for MLIR generation, which directly outputs MLIR at a high level of abstraction. However, it has a limited applicability—especially for complex programs—due to its prototypical stage and limited supported programming language features. That is why this workflow has been replaced with an LLVM IR-based approach, shown in Fig. 5. This new workflow aligns with other MLIR-based prototypes, such as the SYCL-MLIR compiler [50]. C/C++ code is first translated to LLVM IR using clang, followed by a conversion from LLVM IR to the llvm dialect of MLIR. This conversion is directly supported by the MLIR framework, leveraging a one-to-one mapping between LLVM IR and the llvm dialect. Once there, a series of MLIR passes transform the low-level llvm operations into higher-level representations. For instance, arithmetic operations are lifted to the arith dialect, and control flow operations are transformed into the scf (structured control flow) dialect.

Although the IR for the input program is now in MLIR, the SPMD PPM operations are still represented as API function calls without further semantic information, similar to LLVM IR. Therefore as next step, each individual transformer component for the respective PPM converts the API calls to their counterparts in the SPMD IR. For example, function calls like MPI_Put, MPI_Rput, shmem_put, and shmem_put_nbi become a put operation in the spmd dialect with enriched typed operands and attributes like isBlocking differentiating similar operations. The optional extended multi-value analysis pass finalizes the SPMD IR toolchain by adding attributes on multivaluedness, execution kind, and executing ranks before forwarding the IR to a tool or pass, e.g., for data race detection.

The chosen approach of MLIR generation is robust because it relies on mature, non-prototype components—clang and the transformation of LLVM IR to the llvm dialect. The main drawback is the potential loss of (higher-level) information when lowering the input program AST (Abstract Syntax tree) to LLVM IR as part of clang. For example, memory allocations and references appear as untyped, opaque llvm pointers rather than memref values holding rich information on element type, shape, stride, and layout, which would be generally more suitable for the SPMD IR's abstraction level. There is currently no universally applicable method to reintroduce memref types after this transformation. An ideal solution as part of a future workflow would involve the high-level, MLIR-based CLANG IR [23]. It promises improved analysis potential and a suitable level of abstraction for the SPMD IR. However, CLANG IR is still in an early stage.

The presented SPMD IR workflow is also applicable to other programming languages that compile to LLVM IR (e.g., Fortran or Julia). While NCCL support is already provided, it is worth noting that RCCL [3] could also be supported in principle due to their identical API interface. Other PPMs relevant to this work encompass GASPI [11] and UPC++ [51]. The workflow now also supports analyzing GPU kernels (CUDA) and GPU-initiated API calls (NVSHMEM), extending beyond the (host-initiated) NCCL calls supported in previous work [7]. The limitation of inlining from previous work is kept and extended to also inline GPU kernel calls in MLIR to ease the implementation of the prototype. Callees of nvshmemx_collective_launch calls are inlined too. In total, the current prototype of the SPMD IR toolchain, along with its use cases in collectives verification and data race detection, continues to assume that the input IR consists of a single main function. All function calls within it are treated as external.

4 Data Race Detection

A *data race* occurs when two units of execution (e.g., threads or processes) access the same memory location concurrently without proper synchronization, with at least one of them performing a write. For RMA, existing literature [44] distinguishes between local (origin) and remote (target) races. *Local* refers to the side calling the operation, while *remote* denotes the other side of communication. This distinction is crucial because synchronization semantics differ between local and remote completion, and the concept extends further to non-blocking communication in general. Both kinds of data races are classified as undefined behavior in RMA programming models such as MPI and SHMEM. This work focuses on local data races within the context of SPMD PPMs (cf. Fig. 2).

The challenge lies in the fact that side effects, including memory access behavior and completion mechanisms, are hidden behind API calls, which conventional compilers cannot directly analyze or understand. Tools therefore had to integrate this information into their detection algorithms.

4.1 Basic Static Algorithm and Realization for the SPMD IR

This work presents a static local data race detection approach that extends, generalizes, and adapts existing techniques for the SPMD IR, offering significant improvements over PARCOACH(-static) [39]. The general idea of detecting local data races is to iterate over all control-flow paths (but not all combinations) and track memory accesses. Completion operations reset the recorded memory access state (memState) for accesses associated with them, such as those identified by the same request handle or window. For SPMD operations, the local perspective is targeted, e.g., for a get only the local write is tracked, not the remote read. Further, for completion operations such as a flush only the local completion semantics are decisive. To avoid state and path explosion, memStates are propagated along control-flow paths, branching at fork points and merging at join points. If a local memory access occurs on the same buffer after an RMA or non-blocking communication operation has started, and before the underlying operation is guaranteed to be locally completed, and at least one access is a write, a data race is reported.

The SPMD IR verification performs data race detection by carrying over memStates to individual path instances when encountering an operation of the scf (*structured* control flow) dialect and merging the resulting memStates once the operation is processed. At merge points, it aggregates memState information in form of a union and adopts a conservative strategy for diverged synchronization, favoring false positives over false negatives. Specifically, a pending RMA or non-blocking operation that is completed in only one of the path instances will remain pending after a merge point and continues to influence the successor memStates. Unlike PARCOACH, the SPMD IR and its verification process leverage MLIR and specifically choose to use the scf dialect for representing control flow. In contrast to the low-level, block-based control flow of the cf dialect or LLVM IR, this dialect is region-based rather than block-based. It provides a higher-level abstraction of control flow (if, switch, for, and while) that closely resembles high-level programming languages. For example, a loop is represented through a loop operation instead of a cyclic pattern of conditional branches similar to gotos. This representation simplifies implementing algorithms, making it more intuitive, enhances code readability, and may allow for further optimizations [28].

As an example for the data race detection, at an if operation with then and else regions, both regions are processed separately using the memory access information from the state preceding the if. This results in two distinct memStates, which are then merged once both regions have been processed. At a for operation, the verification generates a memState by traversing the loop body twice, accumulating state information. This one is then merged with the initial memState that represents the scenario where the loop is not executed at all. This ensures that data races caused by multiple loop iterations are detected. For instance, in Fig. 4, the control flow is linear up to the if operation at Line 5, which branches into a then region and an (empty) else region. While in the then region a put is performed, which induces a read access on buf, it is not in the else region. When subsequently the differing memStates of both branches are merged, the resulting one conservatively retains the pending read access. Later, at Line 7, a local write to buf is encountered, and a data race is correctly reported. Finally, the fence operation at Line 8 resets all pending memory accesses associated with win, thereby preventing further race reports.

In PARCOACH, which operates on LLVM IR, the data race detection involves tracking LLVM branch instructions, with each basic block potentially having multiple predecessors and successors. Their algorithm maintains a queue of blocks to be processed, where a block is only processed once all its predecessors are processed. For blocks with multiple predecessors, memStates are merged. Successor blocks inherit this aggregated information and eventually lead to a new memState. Loops, represented by cyclic block-successor patterns, are handled by temporarily severing the cycle, processing the "loop body" once and then reinserting the cyclic blocks for a second pass.

While the SPMD IR verification supports local data race detection also for GPU kernels and PPMs, the data race detection is limited to kernels and operations on a single stream. Data races among multiple streams is explicitly not supported. Moreover, remote data races are neither covered by the SPMD IR verification nor existing static tools such as PARCOACH. Supporting remote races would require tracking back the remotely accessed memory regions (which is comparatively easier in SHMEM, as it does not rely on windows) and understanding completion and synchronization on and among remote processes. While global completion calls (e.g., MPI_Win_fence or shmem_barrier_all) can be statically analyzed more easily, operations such as locks, flushes, and context-based variants in SHMEM present significant challenges. These difficulties are further compounded by dynamic control flow (e.g., branching) and the lack of runtime information such as precise data access bounds. As a result, static tools would struggle to generate reliable reports and especially to avoid false negatives.

4.2 Generalization and Extensions

The SPMD IR verification involves several key benefits compared to the basic PARCOACH approach. First, it incorporates utilizing the results of the extended MV-analysis introduced in previous work [7] into the data race detection, enabling it to accurately distinguish local accesses among different processes. In contrast, PARCOACH does not differentiate between executing ranks for operations like MPI_Put or local store instructions, assuming either all processes execute these operations or a dynamically unknown subset. SPMD IR verification, however, distinguishes static from dynamic cases by leveraging executing rank information where feasible at compile-time, reducing possibly false positives.

The second enhancement is conducting the race detection in a unified compiler pass for both RMA and non-blocking communication in general, including their different completion semantics. Unlike PARCOACH, SPMD IR provides detection across communication features, capturing race conditions caused by a mix of RMA and non-RMA. Separate routines could miss such intertwined errors.

The third extension is a generalized approach that leverages traits, attributes, and memory side effects defined within the SPMD dialect in MLIR, e.g., for a get operation, a write on the origin buffer and the traits RMA and Communication are specified. This replaces the need to explicitly encode API calls and their memory effects directly in a detection tool. It decouples the data race detection algorithm from specific PPMs. This design significantly improves extensibility and reusability. Still, a transformation pass from the concrete PPM to the spmd dialect is required. For instance, if a new PPM emerges or MPI introduces another API call, it is sufficient to either transform it into existing operations or define a new operation using the established traits and attributes. The data race detection algorithm will continue to function seamlessly without any modification.

5 Evaluation

This section evaluates the SPMD IR and its extension using the use case of data race detection. The key idea is that the utility and correctness of an IR cannot be reliably approved through manual inspection alone, as such analysis is inherently subjective. To ensure a more objective assessment, these properties together with the IR itself are validated through their successful application to the use case.

5.1 Setup

The detection capabilities of the SPMD IR are evaluated against three established tools: PARCOACH [2,39] (static and dynamic), RMAsanitizer [44,46] (dynamic), and MUST [14,29] (dynamic). The evaluation consists of three parts. The first part employs the generic, state-of-the-art MPI correctness benchmark suite, MBB [16,17], which offers a broad set of test cases for multiple error types across various communication features. It is utilized to assess the coverage of SPMD IR over MPI and its ability to detect basic data races for RMA and non-RMA (P2P, COLL, partitioned, and persistent) communication. This suite is generated at level 3.2, which is the level with the largest test base and the most combinations of MPI calls, and is filtered to include only local data race cases, resulting in 1276 test cases. Each test case is small in size, containing either a single basic error or none.

The second part emphasizes the unique focus of this work: RMA data race detection and support for multiple PPMs. Since MBB is MPI-only with limited coverage of data race patterns, the second part uses RMARaceBench [41,42]. It contains local and remote hand-written RMA data race test cases for MPI, SHMEM, and GASPI, in total 64 local data race cases for MPI and SHMEM. This work extends the suite with 47 new test cases emphasizing the strengths and weaknesses of static and dynamic tools, and 15 cases addressing RMA combined with non-RMA. Additionally, a three-fold port to NVSHMEM is provided, i.e., host-, GPU-, and hybrid-initiated versions, to cover the different call initiation possibilities, resulting in 139 new test cases. Six PPM mixing (MPI+SHMEM) cases are added as well. Altogether these are additions not covered yet by MBB or RMARaceBench.

The final part applies the static tools to three proxy apps: Stencil (PRK) [12], MiniWeather [31], and TeaLeaf [22]. Although proxy apps often lack complex or multi-facetted SPMD PPM usage, they can check the robustness of toolchains due to their size and multi-module structure, closer to real-world applications. Additionally, the evaluation assesses performance overhead by the transformation to and verification of the SPMD IR and contrasts it to PARCOACH-static. All proxy apps are implemented using MPI and C/C++. Although the Stencil comes with a SHMEM port, it uses deprecated calls and relies on concurrent non-atomic writing and reading on remote memory locations which is undefined behavior according to the recent OpenSHMEM standard. Therefore, this work provides an updated SHMEM port. While Stencil involves RMA, MiniWeather and TeaLeaf utilizes non-blocking P2P communication.

The evaluation uses version 2.4.2 of PARCOACH [15], version 1.11 of MUST [29], and version 1.10 of RMAsanitizer [46]. The SPMD IR toolchain uses a patched LLVM 20, including CLANG and MLIR. For MPI, MPICH 4.0.2 and for SHMEM, Sandia OpenSHMEM 1.5.2 is utilized. Since NVSHMEM headers contain inlined implementations that interfere with the transformation to the SPMD IR, a simplified, header-only version, mimicking v3.2, was created. All SPMD IR project sources, the patched LLVM project, utilized benchmarks and proxy apps, individual results, and an Apptainer environment are available for reproducibility.[1]

5.2 Classification Quality Results

The upper part of Table 2 presents the classification quality results for the evaluated tools on MBB, organized by the type of communication feature used in each test case. The 14 test cases involving partitioned and persistent communication are categorized under P2P. For the 1197 RMA test cases, both SPMD IR verification and RMAsanitizer correctly handle all cases with an accuracy of 100%. In contrast, PARCOACH(-static and -dynamic) exhibits false positives (FPs) and false negatives (FNs), with precision values of 25% and 59% and recall values of 16% and 14%. In the COLL category, the SPMD IR verification and MUST classify all 47 cases correctly. For P2P, MUST has three FNs out of 32 cases, resulting in 9% lower accuracy compared to the SPMD IR verification. These FNs occur due to only partial support for partitioned communication by MUST.

The lower part of Table 2 summarizes the classification quality results for RMARaceBench, divided by PPM usage. NVSHMEM is uniquely supported by the SPMD IR verification, leading to results further categorized by the type of API call initiation (Host-, GPU-, and Hybrid-initiated). For the 73 MPI cases, PARCOACH reports FPs and FNs, with accuracies of 60% and 67% respectively and a recall value of 45% for PARCOACH-dynamic. While the SPMD IR verification has 90% accuracy, RMAsanitizer has the highest accuracy with 97%. RMASanitizer has two FNs for dynamic cases involving not observable data races at runtime.

The five FPs by the SPMD IR verification stem from cases that involve recursion, pointer arithmetic, and necessary analysis for loop and communicated data bounds. A false race is reported when a data access is aliased to the same allocated memory region as a pending RMA or non-blocking access, even though the accesses refer to distinct subregions. Cases where the pointer arithmetic or access pattern is available at compile-time, the FPs are avoidable in principle. False positives in cases involving dynamic access patterns are generally unavoidable for a static tool unless the analysis is augmented with runtime information.

The two FNs by the SPMD IR verification stem from windows embedded within arrays, which prevented the prototype implementation from correctly associating the conflicting data accesses with their corresponding RMA operations. This limitation arises because pending RMA operations are tracked using the window as an identifier. While one of the cases is inherently challenging to classify due to the dynamically determined index of the window array, the other

---

[1] https://github.com/RWTH-HPC/SPMD-IR-EuroMPI25-Artifact.

Table 2. Classification quality results on MBB and RMARaceBench, MBB separated by communication type and RMARaceBench by programming model.

MBB	TP	TN	FP	FN	TO	P [%]	R [%]	A [%]
RMA								
PARCOACH-static	48	744	144	261	0	25	16	66
PARCOACH-dynamic	42	859	29	267	0	59	14	75
RMASanitizer	309	888	0	0	0	100	100	100
SPMD IR	309	888	0	0	0	100	100	100
COLL								
MUST	7	40	0	0	0	100	100	100
SPMD IR	7	40	0	0	0	100	100	100
P2P								
MUST	10	19	0	3	0	100	77	91
SPMD IR	13	19	0	0	0	100	100	100
RMARaceBench	TP	TN	FP	FN	TO	P [%]	R [%]	A [%]
MPI								
PARCOACH-static	26	18	13	16	0	67	62	60
PARCOACH-dynamic	19	30	1	23	0	95	45	67
RMASanitizer	40	31	0	2	0	100	95	97
SPMD IR	40	26	5	2	0	89	95	90
SHMEM								
RMASanitizer	26	21	0	6	0	100	81	89
SPMD IR	32	15	6	0	0	84	100	89
MPI+SHMEM								
RMASanitizer	3	3	0	0	0	100	100	100
SPMD IR	3	3	0	0	0	100	100	100
NVSHMEM (SPMD IR)								
Host-initiated	26	15	6	0	0	81	100	87
GPU-initiated	26	15	6	0	0	81	100	87
Hybrid-initiated	25	15	5	0	0	83	100	89

TP: True Positive, FP: False Positive, TN: True Negative, FN: False Negative, TO: Timeout
P: Precision, R: Recall, A: Accuracy; $P = \frac{TP}{TP+FP}$, $R = \frac{TP}{TP+FN}$, $A = \frac{TP+TN}{TP+TN+FP+FN}$

could be resolved with improved static analysis. These cases are all newly added to the suite for demonstrating the current limitations of the SPMD IR verification and static approaches in general.

The 13 FPs and 16 FNs reported by PARCOACH-static involve cases that require an MV-analysis, understanding synchronization and completion with locks, flushes, or requests, support for atomic RMA calls like `MPI_Get_accumulate`, proper analysis of cases with deep call nests, multiple window usage, and non-blocking collective or P2P communication, and additionally include the static cases also challenging the SPMD IR verification. The same unsupported features, e.g., multiple windows or locking, as by PARCOACH-static lead to mostly FNs for PARCOACH-dynamic, with better coverage of the static cases, and additional FNs for the not observable race including dynamic cases.

It is noteworthy that one major reason for the slightly higher accuracy by RMAsanitizer is the composition of RMARaceBench, which includes 32 static but only 8 dynamic MPI cases—primarily designed to highlight the limitations of the SPMD IR verification and static analysis tools in general. A similar trend holds for the ports to other programming models.

For the 53 SHMEM cases, RMAsanitizer and the SPMD IR verification achieve 89% accuracy. Compared to the MPI results, the two window array including FNs are not present (not portable to SHMEM) and one new FP is added that occurs due to improper support for P2P signaling (leads to an FN for RMAsanitizer). RMAsanitizer produces additional three FNs in the category of RMA combined with non-RMA, because it does not correctly interpret the local buffer accesses of the SHMEM collectives.

Both tools correctly classify all six PPM mixing test cases. SPMD IR verification is the only tool supporting and correctly classifying NVSHMEM cases (in all three versions). The FPs are consistent with the FPs observed within the SHMEM cases. Two cases could not be ported to hybrid-initiated NVSHMEM, as they require expressing a recursive access pattern (one FP less).

In summary, the SPMD IR verification detects local data races as reliable as the special-purpose tools RMAsanitizer for RMA and MUST for P2P and COLL. Additionally, it finds errors in RMA and non-RMA mixing scenarios (which lead to three FNs for RMAsanitizer), while also supporting NVSHMEM that involves GPU kernels and GPU-initiated API calls. In contrast, the SPMD IR verification does this at compile-time and also clearly outperforms its static counterpart PARCOACH in both accuracy and PPM support (limited to MPI).

5.3 Proxy App Assessment

As PARCOACH-static only supports local race detection in MPI RMA, it is not applicable to MiniWeather and TeaLeaf, as they involve non-blocking P2P communication. SPMD IR verification correctly does not report an error for MiniWeather. The SPMD IR verification reports the same two FPs for the Stencil codes as PARCOACH-static does for the MPI version. The FPs arise because Stencil uses a single memory allocation for the Halo exchange, accessed via two pointers with different offsets. Having concurrent access through both pointers involving one write, the analysis reports a potential conflict. In fact, both false positives can be eliminated using a static approach, as the necessary information is available at compile time. However, this requires the static analysis to perform advanced reasoning about loop structures and the bounds of communicated data.

The same category of limitations—namely the inability to accurately interpret array accesses involving both indexing and pointer arithmetic, as well as the inability to distinguish between accesses in different loop iterations—results in 50 FPs for TeaLeaf. One cause specific to TeaLeaf is the simplified alias analysis in the data race detection: TeaLeaf mainly uses an array of one large struct object that embeds multiple fields and data arrays. The alias analysis assumes potential overlap, leading conservatively to false data race reports for any field

Table 3. Performance overhead breakdown for the SPMD IR toolchain and its data race detection, along with compilation time, code size, and file count of each proxy app.

	Stencil	MiniWeather	TeaLeaf	
Code Size (KLOC)	0.9	0.6	3.1	
File Count	11	1	53	
Compilation Time (s)	0.04	0.59	8.28	
Phase		Overhead (s)		Share (%)
LLVM IR → MLIR	0.08	0.23	0.47	42/7/0
MLIR → SPMD IR	0.07	0.34	1.68	37/10/0
MV-Analysis (optional)	0.02	2.85	979.54	11/83/99
Data Race Analysis	0.01	0.03	0.01	5/1/1
Total Overhead (s)	**0.19**	**3.45**	**990.55**	

access within this array of structs while non-blocking communication calls are still incomplete. 30 out of the 50 FPs can be attributed to this cause and could be avoided through more advanced alias analysis. These scenarios, both for cases with and without the information available at compile-time, leading to FPs in Stencil and TeaLeaf are also demonstrated in new test cases of RMARaceBench, as discussed in the previous section.

Table 3 gives an overview on the size of each project together with a breakdown of the performance overhead introduced by the SPMD IR toolchain and its data race detection. An indicator of the overall compilation time is also provided, based on the time required to obtain LLVM IR out of the source codes. PARCOACH-static needs 0.07 s for its data race analysis directly on LLVM IR for Stencil as opposed to 0.01 s by the SPMD IR verification. For Stencil and the SPMD IR verification, the overhead is dominated by the IR transformation phases, in total 79 %, but is in acceptable range compared to general compilation time. For MiniWeather and TeaLeaf, the MV-analysis dominates the overhead, contributing 83 % and 99 % respectively, and constitutes a significant amplification of the general compilation time in absolute terms. The MV-analysis is an optional pass, not included by PARCOACH-static, and not necessary for data race detection, but can in principle reduce the number of FPs, as reflected in two additions to RMARaceBench.

The reason for the observed bottleneck in the MV-analysis is that the inlining leads to a single very large function. This in turn results in significantly expensive local alias analysis by MLIR. Unlike the MV-analysis, the transformations into the SPMD IR and also the data race detection pass rely only on a simplified alias analysis and thereby avoid the overhead caused by inlining. Future work shall address this by incorporating an inter-procedural analysis, replacing the inlining together with substituting simplified alias analysis by a full-fledged one. This should eventually solve the overhead issue, enable support for recursive functions, and through a proper alias analysis enhance static analysis capabilities for covering observed FPs.

6 Related Work

Expressing parallelism in IRs is an active area of research. Examples include UPIR [52], a broad consortium of IR constructs spanning different parallelism patterns and principles with the purpose of unification, LLVM PIR, a parallel extension to LLVM IR demonstrated for SHMEM, and TAPIR [40], which embeds recursive fork-join parallelism into LLVM IR. The general aim is to enable the compiler to recognize and leverage the parallelism present in the program. Several comprehensive surveys have examined various approaches to encoding parallelism in IRs [4,47,48,53]. Susungi and Tadonki [48] conclude that most parallel IRs primarily target shared-memory models, with comparatively few approaches addressing distributed-memory, host-accelerator, or PGAS paradigms.

Upstream MLIR has a basic `mpi` dialect [26], which was not available when the SPMD IR was introduced. Compared to the `mpi` dialect, the `spmd` dialect not only covers a much larger portion of the MPI standard but also provides the necessary transformations. In future work, the MPI dialect could serve as an intermediate step in-between the transformation of API calls to the `spmd` dialect or during lowering. One reason the SPMD IR is realized as a separate dialect rather than an extension of the `mpi` dialect, despite their overlap, is that `spmd` unifies multiple PPMs and adds features beyond the MPI standard, which would break MPI compliance.

Similar to this work, Jammer et al. [18] identified performance potential in making semantic information from the MPI standard, such as memory side effects of API calls, explicitly available to the compiler. They developed an LLVM pass that enriches LLVM IR with additional attributes, enabling existing optimization passes to exploit this information. The semantic data already embedded in the SPMD IR can likewise be leveraged during its lowering to LLVM IR, enabling similar optimizations without compromising the abstraction and benefits of a unifying IR. While memory-side effects are already reflected in the SPMD IR, the rest of Jammer et al.'s proposals could be integrated in future work.

PARCOACH consists of two independent analysis tools, namely PARCOACH-static [39] that statically detects local data races, as detailed in Sect. 4, and PARCOACH-dynamic [2] that detects both local and remote data races at runtime of the application, respectively in MPI RMA. PARCOACH-dynamic instruments load and store accesses at compile-time and additionally intercepts relevant MPI RMA calls during execution. It stores the accessed memory intervals in binary search trees and checks for overlapping, conflicting accesses for detecting races.

MUST [14] is another dynamic correctness checking tool for MPI programs. It intercepts MPI calls at runtime and can check for typical MPI programming mistakes such as argument errors, data type mismatches, and deadlocks. Combined with the data race detector ThreadSanitizer [45], MUST can also detect local data races in (non-blocking) point-to-point and collective communication.

RMAsanitizer [44] is an extension of MUST for RMA programs. It detects RMA local and remote data races in MPI, SHMEM, and GASPI. RMAsanitizer intercepts all relevant RMA calls and maps these concrete PPM calls to abstract primitives in a generic data race detection model.

7 Conclusion

This work introduces a comprehensive extension of the SPMD IR to support RMA communication and completion operations. It provides an MLIR-based prototype and workflow compatible with C/C++ for MPI, SHMEM, NCCL, and NVSHMEM. In order to broaden the assessment of the SPMD IR beyond previous work [7] that focused on collectives verification, local data race detection was selected as a key use case. The new detection based on the SPMD IR toolchain is compared against three established tools: PARCOACH [2,39], RMAsanitizer [43,44], and MUST [14]. For evaluation, this work utilizes specialized micro-benchmark suites: RMARaceBench [42], with codes in multiple parallel programming models (PPMs), and MBB [17], the largest MPI correctness micro-benchmark suite. Notably, this work contributed extensions and ports for NVSHMEM within RMARaceBench.

The evaluation demonstrated that the SPMD IR approach achieves as high detection accuracy as the established dynamic tool RMAsanitizer (MUST), clearly outperforming the only other static tool PARCOACH-static. Compared to PARCOACH-static, the SPMD IR offers broader support for PPMs, including hybrid cases, and consolidates RMA and non-RMA local data race detection into a single compiler pass that operates independently of API calls. It embeds the semantic information into the IR itself, enhancing reusability and extensibility. This approach supports both host-initiated code and GPU kernels. Assessments based on MBB approved that the necessary transformations and the SPMD IR itself cover significant portions of the MPI standard.

Moreover, an application study was conducted using the proxy apps Stencil [12], MiniWeather [31], and TeaLeaf [22], covering non-blocking point-to-point communication and RMA in both MPI and SHMEM. This study complements previous work [7] by successfully applying proxy apps to the SPMD IR for the first time. All in all, the evaluation confirmed both the feasibility of transformations and applicability of the SPMD IR, including the newly introduced RMA extensions. It demonstrated the toolchain's robustness and scalability, even for larger, multi-module codebases. However, the assessment revealed two limitations to be addressed in future work. First, the static analysis for loop and communicated data bounds requires improvement. Second, inlining function calls causes a performance bottleneck in alias analysis, impacting the optional multi-value analysis. Additionally, in future work the static approach of the SPMD IR shall be coupled with the dynamic approach of RMAsanitizer (MUST) to reduce false positives on one end and false negatives on the other, and secondly to improve the overall performance overhead, especially by the dynamic tool.

Acknowledgments. This work has received funding from the Federal Ministry of Research, Technology, and Space (BMFTR), the state of North Rhine-Westphalia as part of the NHR Program, and the European HPC Joint Undertaking (JU) under Grant Agreement No. 101143931. The JU receives support from the European Union's Horizon Europe research and innovation program as well as Spain, Germany, France, Portugal, and the Czech Republic.

References

1. Aiken, A., Gay, D.: Barrier inference. In: Proceedings of the 25th ACM SIGPLAN-SIGACT Symposium on Principles of Programming Languages, POPL 1998, pp. 342–354. Association for Computing Machinery, New York (1998). https://doi.org/10.1145/268946.268974
2. Aitkaci, T.C., Sergent, M., Saillard, E., Barthou, D., Papauré, G.: Dynamic data race detection for MPI-RMA programs. In: EuroMPI 2021 - European MPI Users's Group Meeting, Munich, Germany (2021). https://hal.science/hal-03374614
3. AMD: ROCm Communication Collectives Library (RCCL) Documentation, Version 2.22.3 (2025). https://rocm.docs.amd.com/projects/rccl/en/docs-6.4.1/. Accessed 11 June 2025
4. Belwal, M., TSB, S.: Intermediate representation for heterogeneous multi-core: a survey. In: 2015 International Conference on VLSI Systems, Architecture, Technology and Applications (VLSI-SATA), pp. 1–6 (2015). https://doi.org/10.1109/VLSI-SATA.2015.7050496
5. Brown, N., Bareford, M., Weiland, M.: Leveraging MPI RMA to optimize halo-swapping communications in MONC on Cray machines. Concurr. Comput. Pract. Exp. **31**(16) (2019). https://doi.org/10.1002/cpe.5008
6. Brown, N., Jamieson, M., Lydike, A., Bauer, E., Grosser, T.: Fortran performance optimisation and auto-parallelisation by leveraging MLIR-based domain specific abstractions in Flang. In: Proceedings of the SC 2023 Workshops of the International Conference on High Performance Computing, Network, Storage, and Analysis, SC-W 2023, pp. 904–913. Association for Computing Machinery, New York (2023). https://doi.org/10.1145/3624062.3624167
7. Burak, S., Ivanov, I.R., Domke, J., Müller, M.: SPMD IR: unifying SPMD and multi-value IR showcased for static verification of collectives. In: Recent Advances in the Message Passing Interface: 31st European MPI Users' Group Meeting, EuroMPI 2024, Perth, WA, Australia, 25–27 September 2024, Proceedings, pp. 3–20. Springer, Heidelberg (2024). https://doi.org/10.1007/978-3-031-73370-3_1
8. DeepEP Developers: DeepEP - Git Repository. https://github.com/deepseek-ai/DeepEP. Accessed 02 June 2025
9. DeepSeek-AI, Liu, A., Feng, B., Xue, B., et al.: DeepSeek-V3 Technical Report (2025). https://arxiv.org/abs/2412.19437
10. Dinan, J., Balaji, P., Buntinas, D., Goodell, D., Gropp, W., Thakur, R.: An implementation and evaluation of the MPI 3.0 one-sided communication interface. Concurr. Comput. Pract. Exp. **28**(17), 4385–4404 (2016). https://doi.org/10.1002/cpe.3758
11. GASPI Forum: GASPI: Global Address Space Programming Interface, Version 17.1 (2017). https://raw.githubusercontent.com/GASPI-Forum/GASPI-Forum.github.io/master/standards/GASPI-17.1.pdf. Accessed 02 June 2025
12. Hammond, J.: Parallel Research Kerneles (PRK) - Git Repository. https://github.com/jeffhammond/PRK. Accessed 02 June 2025

13. Hammond, J., Dalcin, L., Schnetter, E., PéRache, M., et al.: MPI application binary interface standardization. In: Proceedings of the 30th European MPI Users' Group Meeting, EuroMPI 2023. Association for Computing Machinery, New York (2023). https://doi.org/10.1145/3615318.3615319
14. Hilbrich, T., Schulz, M., Supinski, B.R., Müller, M.S.: MUST: a scalable approach to runtime error detection in MPI programs. In: Müller, M.S., Resch, M.M., Schulz, A., Nagel, W.E. (eds.) Tools for High Performance Computing 2009, pp. 53–66. Springer, Heidelberg (2010). https://doi.org/10.1007/978-3-642-11261-4_5
15. INRIA Researchers: PARCOACH - Git Repository. https://gitlab.inria.fr/parcoach/parcoach. Accessed 02 June 2025
16. Jammer, T., et al.: MPI-BugBench - Git Repository. https://git-ce.rwth-aachen.de/hpc-public/mpi-bugbench. Accessed 28 May 2025
17. Jammer, T., et al.: MPI-BugBench: a framework for assessing MPI correctness tools. In: Blaas-Schenner, C., Niethammer, C., Haas, T. (eds.) Recent Advances in the Message Passing Interface, pp. 121–137. Springer, Cham (2025). https://doi.org/10.1007/978-3-031-73370-3_8
18. Jammer, T., Schmidt, A., Bischof, C.: Annotation of compiler attributes for MPI functions. In: Recent Advances in the Message Passing Interface: 31st European MPI Users' Group Meeting, EuroMPI 2024, Perth, WA, Australia, 25–27 September 2024, Proceedings, pp. 21–35. Springer, Heidelberg (2024). https://doi.org/10.1007/978-3-031-73370-3_2
19. Lattner, C., Adve, V.: LLVM: a compilation framework for lifelong program analysis & transformation. In: International Symposium on Code Generation and Optimization, CGO 2004, pp. 75–86 (2004). https://doi.org/10.1109/CGO.2004.1281665
20. Lattner, C., et al.: MLIR: scaling compiler infrastructure for domain specific computation. In: 2021 IEEE/ACM International Symposium on Code Generation and Optimization (CGO), pp. 2–14 (2021). https://doi.org/10.1109/CGO51591.2021.9370308
21. Lazzaro, A., VandeVondele, J., Hutter, J., Schütt, O.: Increasing the efficiency of sparse matrix-matrix multiplication with a 2.5D algorithm and one-sided MPI. In: Proceedings of the Platform for Advanced Scientific Computing Conference, PASC 2017. Association for Computing Machinery, New York (2017). https://doi.org/10.1145/3093172.3093228
22. Lin, T., et al.: TeaLeaf Proxy App - Git Repository. https://github.com/UoB-HPC/TeaLeaf. Accessed 02 June 2025
23. LLVM Community: Project Website of CLANG IR (2024). https://llvm.github.io/clangir/. Accessed 02 June 2025
24. LLVM Community: Project Website of FLANG (2025). https://flang.llvm.org/. Accessed 02 June 2025
25. Message Passing Interface Forum: MPI: A Message-Passing Interface Standard, Version 5.0 (2025). https://www.mpi-forum.org/docs/mpi-5.0/mpi50-report.pdf. Accessed 06 June 2025
26. MLIR Community: Project Website of Upstream MLIR on the MPI Dialect (2024). https://mlir.llvm.org/docs/Dialects/MPI/. Accessed 02 June 2025
27. Moses, W.S., Chelini, L., Zhao, R., Zinenko, O.: Polygeist: raising C to polyhedral MLIR. In: 2021 30th International Conference on Parallel Architectures and Compilation Techniques (PACT), pp. 45–59 (2021). https://doi.org/10.1109/PACT52795.2021.00011

28. Moses, W.S., Ivanov, I.R., Domke, J., Endo, T., Doerfert, J., Zinenko, O.: High-performance GPU-to-CPU transpilation and optimization via high-level parallel constructs. In: Proceedings of the 28th ACM SIGPLAN Annual Symposium on Principles and Practice of Parallel Programming, PPoPP 2023, pp. 119–134. Association for Computing Machinery, New York (2023). https://doi.org/10.1145/3572848.3577475
29. MUST Developers: MUST - Project Website. https://itc.rwth-aachen.de/must. Accessed 05 June 2025
30. Mutlu, E., et al.: COMET: a domain-specific compilation of high-performance computational chemistry. In: Chapman, B., Moreira, J. (eds.) Languages and Compilers for Parallel Computing, pp. 87–103. Springer, Cham (2022). https://doi.org/10.1007/978-3-030-95953-1_7
31. Norman, M., Larkin, J., Lyngaas, I.: MiniWeather Proxy App - Git Repository. https://github.com/mrnorman/miniWeather. Accessed 02 June 2025
32. NVIDIA: NVIDIA OpenSHMEM Library (NVSHMEM) Documentation, Version 2.8.0 (2023). https://docs.nvidia.com/nvshmem/archives/nvshmem-280/api/index.html. Accessed 02 June 2025
33. NVIDIA: CUDA Toolkit Documentation, Version 12.9 (2024). https://docs.nvidia.com/cuda/archive/12.9.0/. Accessed 02 June 2025
34. NVIDIA: NVIDIA Collective Communications Library (NCCL) Documentation, Version 2.26.5 (2025). https://docs.nvidia.com/deeplearning/nccl/archives/nccl_2265/user-guide/docs/index.html. Accessed 02 June 2025
35. OpenSHMEM Team: OpenSHMEM Application Programming Interface Specification, Version 1.6 (2024). http://openshmem.org/site/sites/default/site_files/OpenSHMEM-1.6.pdf. Accessed 02 June 2025
36. Perplexity Developers: Perplexity MoE Kernels - Git Repository. https://github.com/ppl-ai/pplx-kernels. Accessed 02 June 2025
37. Potluri, S., Lai, P., Tomko, K., Sur, S., et al.: Quantifying performance benefits of overlap using MPI-2 in a seismic modeling application. In: Proceedings of the 24th ACM International Conference on Supercomputing, ICS 2010, pp. 17–25. Association for Computing Machinery, New York (2010). https://doi.org/10.1145/1810085.1810092
38. Potluri, S., et al.: Exploring OpenSHMEM model to program GPU-based extreme-scale systems. In: Gorentla Venkata, M., Shamis, P., Imam, N., Lopez, M.G. (eds.) OpenSHMEM 2014. LNCS, vol. 9397, pp. 18–35. Springer, Cham (2015). https://doi.org/10.1007/978-3-319-26428-8_2
39. Saillard, E., Sergent, M., Ait Kaci, C.T., Barthou, D.: Static local concurrency errors detection in MPI-RMA programs. In: 2022 IEEE/ACM Sixth International Workshop on Software Correctness for HPC Applications (Correctness), pp. 18–26 (2022). https://doi.org/10.1109/Correctness56720.2022.00008
40. Schardl, T.B., Moses, W.S., Leiserson, C.E.: Tapir: embedding recursive fork-join parallelism into LLVM's intermediate representation. ACM Trans. Parallel Comput. 6(4) (2019). https://doi.org/10.1145/3365655
41. Schwitanski, S., Jenke, J., Klotz, S., Müller, M.S.: RMARaceBench - Git Repository. https://github.com/RWTH-HPC/RMARaceBench. Accessed 05 June 2025
42. Schwitanski, S., Jenke, J., Klotz, S., Müller, M.S.: RMARaceBench: a microbenchmark suite to evaluate race detection tools for RMA programs. In: Proceedings of the SC 2023 Workshops of the International Conference on High Performance Computing, Network, Storage, and Analysis, SC-W 2023, pp. 205–214. Association for Computing Machinery, New York (2023). https://doi.org/10.1145/3624062.3624087

43. Schwitanski, S., Jenke, J., Tomski, F., Terboven, C., Müller, M.S.: On-the-fly data race detection for mpi rma programs with MUST. In: 2022 IEEE/ACM Sixth International Workshop on Software Correctness for HPC Applications (Correctness), pp. 27–36. IEEE, Dallas, TX, USA (2022). https://doi.org/10.1109/Correctness56720.2022.00009
44. Schwitanski, S., Oraji, Y.M., Pätzold, C., Jenke, J., Tomski, F., Müller, M.S.: RMASanitizer: generalized runtime detection of data races in remote memory access applications. In: Proceedings of the 53rd International Conference on Parallel Processing, ICPP 2024, pp. 833–844. Association for Computing Machinery, New York (2024). https://doi.org/10.1145/3673038.3673109
45. Serebryany, K., Potapenko, A., Iskhodzhanov, T., Vyukov, D.: Dynamic race detection with LLVM compiler. In: Khurshid, S., Sen, K. (eds.) RV 2011. LNCS, vol. 7186, pp. 110–114. Springer, Heidelberg (2012). https://doi.org/10.1007/978-3-642-29860-8_9
46. Simon Schwitanski: RMASanitizer - Git Repository. https://github.com/RWTH-HPC/rmasanitizer-artifact. Accessed 02 June 2025
47. Spanier, A., Mahoney, W.: Static vulnerability analysis using intermediate representations: a literature review. European Conference on Cyber Warfare and Security **22**, 458–465 (2023). https://doi.org/10.34190/eccws.22.1.1154
48. Susungi, A., Tadonki, C.: Intermediate representations for explicitly parallel programs. ACM Comput. Surv. **54**(5) (2021). https://doi.org/10.1145/3452299
49. Tian, R., Guo, L., Li, J., Ren, B., Kestor, G.: A high performance sparse tensor algebra compiler in MLIR. In: 2021 IEEE/ACM 7th Workshop on the LLVM Compiler Infrastructure in HPC (LLVM-HPC), pp. 27–38 (2021). https://doi.org/10.1109/LLVMHPC54804.2021.00009
50. Tiotto, E., et al.: Experiences building an MLIR-based SYCL compiler. In: 2024 IEEE/ACM International Symposium on Code Generation and Optimization (CGO), pp. 399–410 (2024). https://doi.org/10.1109/CGO57630.2024.10444866
51. UPC++ Specification Working Group: UPC++ Specification, Version 1.0 (2023). https://bitbucket.org/berkeleylab/upcxx/downloads/upcxx-spec-2023.9.0.pdf. Accessed 02 June 2025
52. Wang, A., Yi, X., Yan, Y.: UPIR: toward the design of unified parallel intermediate representation for parallel programming models. In: Proceedings of the International Conference on Parallel Architectures and Compilation Techniques, PACT 2022, pp. 530–531. Association for Computing Machinery, New York (2023). https://doi.org/10.1145/3559009.3569646
53. Zhang, B., Chen, W., Chiu, H.C., Zhang, C.: Unveiling the Power of Intermediate Representations for Static Analysis: A Survey (2024). https://arxiv.org/abs/2405.12841

Concepts for Designing Modern C++ Interfaces for MPI

C. Nicole Avans[1], Alfredo A. Correa[2], Sayan Ghosh[3],
Matthias Schimek[4], Joseph Schuchart[5], Anthony Skjellum[1],
Evan D. Suggs[1], and Tim Niklas Uhl[4](✉)

[1] Tennessee Technological University, Cookeville, TN, USA
{cnavans42,askjellum,esuggs}@tntech.edu
[2] Lawrence Livermore National Laboratory, Livermore, CA, USA
correaa@llnl.gov
[3] Pacific Northwest National Laboratory, Richland, WA, USA
sg0@pnnl.gov
[4] Karlsruhe Institute of Technology, Karlsruhe, Germany
{schimek,uhl}@kit.edu
[5] Stony Brook University, Stony Brook, NY, USA
joseph.schuchart@stonybrook.edu

Abstract. Since the C++ bindings were deleted in 2008, the Message Passing Interface (MPI) community has recently revived efforts in building high-level modern C++ interfaces. Such interfaces are either built to serve specific scientific application needs (with limited coverage to the underlying MPI functionality), or as an exercise in general-purpose programming model building, with the hope that bespoke interfaces can be broadly adopted to construct a variety of distributed-memory scientific applications. However, with the advent of modern C++-based heterogeneous programming models, GPUs and widespread Machine Learning (ML) usage in contemporary scientific computing, the role of prospective community-standardized high-level C++ interfaces to MPI is evolving. The success of such an interface clearly will depend on providing robust abstractions and features adhering to the generic programming principles that underpin the C++ programming language, without compromising on either performance or portability, the core principles upon which MPI was founded. However, there is a tension between idiomatic C++ handling of types and lifetimes and MPI's loose interpretation of object lifetimes/ownership and insistence on maintaining global states.

Instead of proposing "yet another" high-level C++ interface to MPI, overlooking or providing partial solutions to work around the key issues concerning the dissonance between MPI semantics and idiomatic C++, this paper focuses on the three fundamental aspects of a high-level interface: type system, object lifetimes, and communication buffers, while also identifying inconsistencies in the MPI specification. Presumptive solutions can be unrefined, and we hope the broader MPI and C++ communities will engage with us in productive exchange of ideas and concerns.

Keywords: Message Passing Interface · C++ · Concept-based Interface

1 Introduction

Many modern C++ projects rely on MPI extensively, but MPI cannot natively handle most C++ data structures or constructs [19]. We plan to derive a basic C++ interface that takes into account new features and capabilities of C++ without compromising either performance or portability. This paper seeks to derive key concepts and design considerations to promote the creation of a full modern MPI C++ interface, while highlighting issues complicating this endeavor.

C++ bindings were included in the MPI standard, but were deprecated by MPI 2.2 [17]. These bindings have been entirely removed in version 3.0 (2012), since they only added minimal functionality over the C bindings while adding significant maintenance complexity to the MPI specification [16]. C++ has changed significantly since the deprecation of C++ bindings in 2009, requiring a new look at its capabilities and the feasibility of a MPI C++ interface.

There are no guidelines now for developing efficient modern C++ interfaces over MPI (it is impossible to successfully enforce recipes such as C++ Core Guidelines [26] without standardizing the behavior of underlying MPI objects, which is usually left up to concrete implementations). Here, we expand on some general considerations for designing C++ interfaces over MPI in good faith, without imposing ad hoc rules that might limit productivity, performance, and/or portability.

Build on Existing Ideas. We consider, re-evaluate, formalize and extend upon ideas presented in existing language bindings (Sect. 2).

Derive a C++ Representation of MPI's Object Model. We discuss how to bridge the gap between MPI objects and C++, particularly how to handle their life cycle and formalize mutability in terms of constness (Sect. 3.1).

Enabling Type Safety in MPI. The MPI C API currently does not utilize type information provided by the language. In Sect. 3.2, we categorize C++ types and how these different classes can support type safe compatibility with MPI.

Contiguous Ranges as First Class Communication Buffers. Section 3.3 describes rules defined through C++-20 concepts, which specify which kind of C++ containers are directly supported by MPI for communication operations. This enables direct support for many STL containers and provides a powerful interface to derive more complex abstractions. We also describe how to handle data ownership, which is necessary to conform to the best practices of resource management in modern C++ (namely, RAII) in Sect. 3.4.

Idiomatic Error Handling. We describe how C++ can enhance MPI error handling via compile-time checking and exceptions in Sect. 3.5.

These are the major aspects and principles to which a future C++ MPI interface should adhere. Rather than proposing a complete standardized interface, which risks repeating the shortcomings of the removed bindings, our primary goal is to define *semantic guidelines* and *core conceptual interfaces* that align idiomatic C++ with MPI. These concepts could serve as the foundation for a MPI standard side document. Standardizing concepts rather than concrete APIs offers the advantage of long-term maintainability and adaptability as both MPI and the C++ language evolve. A C++ interface could introduce additional quality-of-life features to enhance productivity and provide safer abstraction, but these often introduce overheads that conflict with MPI's performance-portability while increasing the complexity of a specification. Still, we outline major ideas and provide suggestions on how they could be aligned to our previously introduced design considerations. Particularly, we focus on serialization of more complex data types (Sect. 4.1), first steps towards automatic life cycle handling of more complex MPI data types with direct mappings to C++ (Sect. 4.2) and how to increase MPI programmer's productivity by a sane set of defaults (Sect. 4.3).

In Sect. 5, we conclude our discussion with suggestions on how the MPI standard could support language interface designers (not limited to C++) by carefully extending the MPI specification.

2 Existing C++ Interfaces over MPI

Since the removal of the "official" C++ MPI interface, a large number of third-party library interfaces have emerged, joined by efforts to bridge the gap between MPI implementations, C++, and high-level performance portability frameworks (e.g., Kokkos). We will briefly outline notable works and their distinctive features in the following, as they serve as inspirations and proofs of concept for the technical discussion in the rest of this paper.

The `mpl` library [3] is a C++-17 based, header-only library meant to provide an easy to use MPI interface for C++ developers after the deprecation and removal of the C++ API in MPI 3.0. Recent work [10] have extracted communication-specific interfaces from the main `mpl` codebase (reducing about 4K LoC in main `mpl`), and consider it as a prototypical modern C++ interface for studying MPI-specific language bindings. To support bulk communication, `mpl` uses built-in `mpl::layout` class to manage derived data types.

Boost.MPI [13] offers a near one-to-one mapping of MPI-1 via free functions using communicators. Dynamic types are handled as skeletons containing address info, which must be updated if data is relocated (e.g., invalidated iterators).

B-MPI3 [7] wraps MPI-3 with a C++ interface based on communicators and member functions, emphasizing const-correctness and iterator-based ranges. It uses compile-time strategies to select communication methods: contiguous ranges use direct C-MPI calls; non-contiguous ones are copied; unsupported types are serialized via Boost.Serialization.

RWTH-MPI [9] is a C++ interface for MPI that supports contiguous STL containers as send/receive buffers and offers overloaded MPI procedures with automatic parameter inference. For custom types, it can auto-generate MPI data types using the PFR library [20]. Dynamic-size types are unsupported. While it covers MPI 4.0, its bindings largely mirror the C interface with limited added abstraction or safety.

KaMPIng [27] uses modern C++ features like move semantics to enhance safety, enabling return-by-value and memory-safe non-blocking communication. It constructs MPI data types automatically for STL and custom types when possible and supports compile-time C++ to MPI type mapping. Its named parameter interface with compile-time defaults facilitates both high-level prototyping and low-level control, keeping the full MPI interface accessible.

The Enhanced Message Passing Interface (EMPI) [4] is based on modern C++, which is built on top of a customized version of Open MPI, eliding runtime checking overheads to directly map EMPI objects to low-level MPI objects within the Open MPI implementation. To enable RAII, EMPI proposes a *program context* that wraps the MPI environment, and specializes MPI group from the context for abstracting communication and synchronization.

Kokkos Comm [2] utilizes modern C++ language features to provide more intuitive support of inter-node communication of Kokkos Views. Templates provide the needed flexibility to adapt to diverse data layouts and memory spaces.

MPI Advance [5] provides lightweight libraries that complement available system MPI installations to leverage tuned performance while also implementing support for the newest features from the MPI standard (e.g., partitioned communication) and additional capabilities and optimizations beyond the current scope of the standard.

3 High-Level Design Considerations

Existing work on designing C++ interfaces to MPI has brought up a huge amount of interesting design concepts and ideas, but most of the time they are hidden behind the details of the actual implementation. In this section, we will take a step back and clearly define the underlying semantic concepts of modern and idiomatic C++ MPI interface and how MPI's design can be made "compatible" with the C++ language. These concepts can then be used by implementers to design a concrete interface.

We start by defining how MPI objects map to C++ (Sect. 3.1). Then we focus on how to model the actual data involved in communication, in terms of types (Sect. 3.2) and the actual memory involved (Sect. 3.3). We then discuss how combining C++'s ownership model and MPI to obtain additional memory safety (Sect. 3.4) and how to handle errors in an idiomatic way (Sect. 3.5).

3.1 Mapping the MPI Object Model to C++

MPI introduces a range of *MPI objects*, such as communicators, data types, and requests, which are represented in the C API using *opaque handles*. While this is the only viable approach in C, it hides key semantic properties of these objects, including ownership, lifetime, and identity. In contrast, C++ offers native language features that allow these properties to be expressed explicitly and safely.

For more than a decade, C++ MPI library designers have advocated for representing MPI objects as first-class C++ objects that act as proxies for the implementation-defined objects behind the handles [23].

It is worth noting that most MPI procedures operating on these objects can be expressed either as member functions or as free functions. Both choices are equally valid, and this decision is largely independent of the conceptual model discussed here. In this work, we present communication operations as member functions, without advocating for one approach over the other.

Modern C++ idioms—particularly RAII (Resource Acquisition Is Initialization) [25, 16.5][26, E.6] and move semantics—naturally support resource management: MPI objects can be constructed via `MPI_*_create` in class constructors and released via `MPI_*_free` in destructors, with ownership safely transferable through move operations. However, the original MPI design deviates from this model because of its reliance on global state and implicitly managed global objects—an approach discouraged by the C++ Core Guidelines [26, I.3,I.22]. For example, global communicators such as `MPI_COMM_WORLD` are automatically initialized via `MPI_Init` and cannot be explicitly created or freed. Further, MPI prohibits reinitialization after `MPI_Finalize`, limiting modular or library-based usage patterns.

Sessions, Groups, and Communicators. MPI 4.0 addressed some of these limitations by introducing the *Session Model*, an alternative to the traditional World Model for process management. Although originally designed to support better isolation in multi-threaded and multi-component environments, the session model aligns well with modern C++ object-oriented design. In this model, no global communicators are predefined; instead, communicators must be explicitly created from process sets via user code. This makes ownership explicit and fully under user control, enabling clean integration with RAII-based designs as shown in Fig. 1. For example, communicators and groups are constructed and destroyed as part of their enclosing scope.

```
mpi::session session{};
mpi::group group = session.group_from_pset("mpi://WORLD");
mpi::communicator comm{group}; // create communicator from group
comm.send(...);
```

Fig. 1. Example of the proposed object model using the MPI Session Model

const-Correctness of MPI Objects. The concept of constness is important for both the compiler and, more crucially, libraries, as it indicates variable mutability and restricts modifications in certain contexts. This applies straightforwardly to the data being communicated: For instance, a receiving buffer cannot be `const`, which already enhances the program's safety, which we discuss in detail in Sect. 3.3. In a less obvious way, constness can also be applied to library objects of a MPI C++ interface, such as communicators, data types, and requests and procedure calls on them, making it even more important to discuss here.

When creating a C++ wrapper for MPI or any C interface that does not account for constness, adding the keyword `const` requires a good grasp of the interface semantics and precise knowledge of the implementation (internal mutation). Without explicit guarantees from the MPI standard specification, it is difficult to gather sufficient information to determine whether a particular operation can be marked as `const`.

We want to illustrate this for MPI communicators. Most procedure calls leave a communicator in the same state as before, which would *naively* allow them to be specified as `const`. Conversely, one could argue that posting a message is not the same as not having posted it; in the former case, the message can be received on the other side, while in the latter, a receive operation may hang. We think this is a strong argument to mark communication calls as non-const. But this can still be challenged for procedures that send and receive in a single call (such as `send_recv` or collectives).[1]

To resolve these cases, we invoke a modern interpretation (post C++11): Since the communicator is likely undergoing internal mutation during any non-trivial operation, it is reasonable to conclude that most communication procedures should be marked as non-`const` at the communicator level.

```
class mpi::communicator {
  communicator(communicator const& other) = delete;   // no copy-constructor
  ...
  auto duplicate() /*non-const*/ -> communicator;
  ...
  auto send(/*const data*/ ...) /*non-const*/;
  auto receive(/*mutable data*/ ...) /*non-const*/;
  auto broadcast(/*mutable data*/ ...) /*non-const*/;
  ...
  auto size() const;   /*most likely can be marked const in a reasonable implementation*/
};
```

Fig. 2. Interpretation of const-ness in a MPI C++ interface

If we adhere to the conclusion that communication procedures should not be marked `const`, an important and somewhat unexpected result follows: a communicator class should *not* have a duplicate mechanism that is const on the original communicator. Incidentally, there will be no canonical copy constructor (taking original communicator as a constant reference). This is consistent, since even communicators duplicated from each other cannot receive or complete operations initiated in another communicator. Thus, two communicators are never copies of each other; they are at most alternative virtual fabrics for subsequent communication. Figure 2 summarizes our discussions about the communicator class which also align with the interpretation of the B.MPI3 [7] interface.

For other parts of the library, the situation might be simpler. For example, most datatype manipulation is likely to take advantage of `const`, since datatype manipulation usually generates new types instances from other types instances.

---

[1] Note that this is a fundamental problem, not exclusive to const-qualified member functions; if the procedures are free functions the questions will still stand regarding the constness of the communicator argument parameter.

In summary, a key problem is that the MPI standard says little about the mutation of MPI "objects" (communicator, data types or request objects), which is further complicated by the existence of a global mutable state at the level of the environment. In most cases, the internal mutation seems only to be implied by common knowledge, which makes the decision on the correct usage of const-ness in a C++ interface difficult.

Design and conventions on this issue, have important ripple effect in the design of C++ MPI programs, specifically C++ classes that contain communicators and other MPI objects, which is common in programs written at a high level of abstraction [1,11]. Classes that use their own internal communicator even for non-mutating operations would require mutation of the communicator, internally at least (i.e., `mutable` attribute, and possibly synchronization).

3.2 Modeling and Mapping Types

Applications using MPI use a variety of data types that need to be communicated. The MPI standard distinguishes between *basic datatypes* and arbitrarily complex *derived datatypes*, which can be recursively constructed from other data types using type constructors (`MPI_Type_create_*`). C's lack of type introspection features forces users to always pass the type explicitly to a communication call, which is both tedious and error-prone, since type definitions need to be kept in sync with the actual data layout. Fortunately, for many C++ types, there is a one-to-one mapping to MPI data types. C++ defines a set of *fundamental types*: `void`, `std::nullptr_t`, *integral types* (including integers, character types and `bool`) and *floating-point types*. For integral and floating-point types, there exist matching predefined *basic data types* in MPI.

Using template-metaprogramming, a C++ MPI interface can therefore deduce an MPI type directly from a data buffer (as defined in Sect. 3.3), in case its underlying `value_type` is fundamental. This approach is implemented by all major MPI C++ bindings [3,7,13,27]. More complex types require explicit creation and a subsequent commit step, and have to be freed before MPI is finalized. To enable proper cleanup we again use RAII and represent data types as `mpi::datatype` objects, which support move construction and assignment and free the data type when the destructor is called.

To prevent users from using uncommitted data types in communication, we propose to encode the commit information as part of the type, similar to the approach of *rsmpi* [24]. The function `mpi::commit` takes an rvalue `mpi::datatype` object, and converts it to a `mpi::committed_datatype` as shown in Fig. 3. Accordingly, communication calls only accept data type objects of this type.

In addition to fundamental C++ types with direct mappings to predefined MPI basic types, there exists a broader class of C++ types that can be safely mapped to MPI data types. These are precisely the types classified *trivially copyable* by the C++ standard. A type is trivially copyable if its binary representation can be safely copied byte-by-byte (e.g., via `memcpy`), without violating language rules and invoking undefined behavior. More concretely, an object of such type can be copied to an array of `char`, `unsigned char`, or `std::byte`, and then back

```
struct MyType {
  int a;
  std::array<int, 3> b;
  double c;
  char d;
};
mpi::datatype type = mpi::datatype::for<MyType>();
mpi::committed_datatype struct_type = mpi::commit(std::move(type));
```

Fig. 3. Example for constructing a type for a C++ type and committing it

into another object of the same type, which will hold the same value as the original. This property is essential for MPI communication: when transmitting data across processes, the memory content of a variable must be sent as a sequence of raw bytes over the network and reconstructed correctly on the receiving end. If the type is not trivially copyable, this round-trip may not preserve the original value or may result in undefined behavior. Thus, restricting to trivially copyable types ensures that the MPI type correctly matches the actual in-memory layout and semantics of the transmitted data.

These types can be safely supported by automatically constructing the corresponding MPI datatype using a compile-time reflection mechanism to call the correct MPI type constructors. This ensures that the C++ type is compatible with MPI's type system and enables safe type handling, even on heterogeneous systems. Although C++ currently lacks native language support for such reflection, concrete proposals are in place to introduce compile-time type reflection in C++26 [22]. In the meantime, third-party libraries such as Boost.PFR [20] can be used to implement this feature, although they have some limitations, for example for types using inheritance or private members.

Beyond fundamental and trivially copyable types, there remains a broad class of other (potentially user-defined) C++ types that do not have a direct or automatically derivable mapping to an MPI data type. For these types, the correspondence between memory layout and type semantics cannot be safely inferred by the prospective C++ MPI interface. Consequently, it becomes the user's responsibility to explicitly define how the type is laid out in memory and how that layout corresponds to an appropriate MPI datatype. While the handling of fundamental and trivially copyable types can be automated to reduce programming errors and ease MPI development, a prerequisite for such automation is a clear conceptual model of the data involved in communication. The core abstraction in this model is the *data buffer*, which we introduce in the following Sect. 3.3.

3.3 Modeling Memory Involved in MPI Communication

We now explore how a C++ MPI interface can offer idiomatic abstractions for the data sent or received in MPI communication operations. In MPI, this data is described in terms of a pointer to a memory region, an (MPI) datatype, the number of elements to be sent, and (for some collective operations) their displacements. While this number of parameters makes MPI flexible, it also leads to verbose function calls. Further, the flexibility of MPI is only required in a few use cases and results in unnecessarily complicated code in other cases [27].

Particularly when using standard library containers such as `std::vector<T>` with the MPI C API, users have to access underlying raw pointers and sizes of the containers and pass them to MPI individually, while the actual vector object already comprises the whole send data context. This is both non-ergonomic to use and conflicts with the C++ Core Guidelines [26, I.13]. Most existing MPI C++ libraries therefore introduce support for a subset of standard library containers [3,7,9,13,27] as their core abstraction feature. However, this has certain shortcomings. First, this is often defined ad-hoc only including a fixed set of containers [9,13]. Second, design decisions within the approaches of supporting (standard library) containers introduce hidden, additional overheads through memory allocations or additional MPI calls [3,13,27]. For example, in an `MPI_Recv` call, Boost.MPI resizes the container into which it receives the data to match the size of the incoming message. If the user does not want this, they must instead pass raw pointers again. The KaMPIng library internally invokes `MPI_Probe` when the user issues a receive operation without a `count` argument. Such unexpected overheads are not desired from the perspective of a standardized C++ interface.

Therefore, in the following, instead of reiterating the specific approaches of existing MPI wrappers and defining how a particular container is "fitted" to support MPI, we will define a small set of underlying rules and categories for memory involved in communication in terms of C++ *concepts*. Concepts are a (modern) C++ language feature for specifying constraints on (custom) types. C++ provides easy-to-use mechanisms to check that types satisfy a given concept at compile time. This gives us well-defined semantics on which kind of containers can be used directly with MPI, deducing size and type information safely from C++, without imposing any additional overhead. Additionally, C++ objects not satisfying required concepts result in easy-to-understand error messages, as opposed to previous often very verbose and complicated error messages caused by template metaprogramming errors [8].

For each send or receive buffer involved in a communication call, MPI's C API expects a pointer to a contiguous memory location, a count argument and an MPI data type. C++ already provides type information, and automatically matching types is crucial for type safety. A high-level standardizable C++ interface, can use type introspection to provide such type safety, which we detail in Sect. 3.2. For now, let us assume that we can always deduce an MPI data type from a provided container. We call this basic building block of MPI communication (memory location, count and type) a *data buffer*. In the following, we describe a minimal interface of data buffer objects in terms of C++ concepts.

A data buffer object has to satisfy the concept `std::range`; that is, it must expose an iterator to the beginning (and to the end) of its underlying storage. Additionally, data buffers must satisfy the following (built-in) concepts:

- `std::ranges::contiguous_range`, that is, its underlying memory has to be contiguous in memory. This captures MPI's requirement that data which is communicated must reside in *sequential storage*[2].
- `std::ranges::sized_range`, that is, a data buffer exposes a `size()` function returning the number of its elements.
- Typed, that is, either the data buffer exposes a constant reference to a committed MPI data type or the data buffer's `value_type` is a fundamental type (for which a direct mapping to predefined MPI data types exists and can directly be used if not overwritten by the user).

```
namespace mpi {
    // Concept ensuring that t exposes MPI data type information
    template <typename T>
    concept Typed = requires(T t) {
        { mpi::datatype(t) } -> std::same_as<committed_datatype const&>;
    };

    template <typename T>
    concept DataBuffer =
        std::ranges::contiguous_range<T> &&
        std::ranges::sized_range<T> &&
        (std::is_fundamental_v<typename T::value_type> || Typed<T>);

    // Concept for data buffers storing send data
    template <typename T>
    concept SendDataBuffer =
        DataBuffer<T> &&
        std::ranges::input_range<T>;

    // Concept for data buffers encapsulating data to be received
    template <typename T>
    concept RecvDataBuffer =
        DataBuffer<T> &&
        std::ranges::output_range<T, typename T::value_type>;
}
```

Fig. 4. Concept definition for a data buffer

An example of how these constraints can be expressed in plain C++ is given in Fig. 4, which defines the concept `mpi::DataBuffer` in terms of the three concepts described above. A convenient property of this data buffer definition is that many C++ standard library containers like `std::vector` or `std::array` storing fundamental C++ types such as `char`, `int`, `double`, ... already satisfy the `mpi::DataBuffer` concept. This also holds for lightweight, non-owning views such as `std::span`. Hence, they can be directly used in an MPI C++ interface adhering to these principles.

For more complex cases, for example, to communicate a container of a `trivially_copyable` custom C++ datatype, we first have to construct and commit such a datatype (see Sect. 3.2) and then pass it to the data buffer.

---

[2] An exception to this requirement is the usage of `MPI_BOTTOM` which relies on absolute memory addresses to describe data and should be treated separately.

For communicating data using complex derived datatypes without a one-to-one mapping to the underlying C++ type, we not only have to construct and commit an MPI datatype but also pass the number of corresponding elements to the data buffer. For these more complex cases, there is no direct C++ standard library support but an MPI C++ interface could easily provide a lightweight *adapter* with multiple constructors not only accepting a contiguous `std::range`, but also a count and a `mpi::committed_datatype` parameter.

This also makes this interface extensible to support more complex containers from third-party libraries like `Kokkos::View` or `thrust::device_vector`, backed by memory located on accelerators such as GPUs. Therefore the data buffer concept naturally extends to the notion of *memory allocation kinds* [18], providing direct support for accelerator-aware MPI on C++ containers backed memory located on GPUs or other accelerators.

Figure 5 illustrates exemplary communication calls showcasing the different cases discussed above. Note that we do not suggest a concrete API or function signatures but rather want to show the underlying concept of using data buffers as an abstract description for communication data.

Orthogonal to the `mpi::DataBuffer` concept presented so far, we additionally have to model that data buffers describing send data have to be *readable* and data buffers for receive data have to be *writable*. This can be expressed using the (built-in) concepts, `std::ranges::in/output_range` (see Fig. 4).

To conclude, in many (simple) cases, this approach leads to clean and less convoluted code with direct C++ standard library integration. For more complex cases, we end up with the same number of parameters as in the C API, as we need to leverage its full flexibility. However, in all scenarios, we gain clear semantics directly documented *in* source code by using C++ concepts.

```
std::vector<int> v = ...
comm.send(v, /*additional parameters*/);

std::vector<MyType> v = ... // static custom type defined in Fig. 3
mpi::datatype type = mpi::datatype::for<MyType>();
mpi::committed_datatype type_c = mpi::commit(std::move(type));
comm.send(mpi::buffer_adapter(v, type_c), /*additional parameters */);

std::vector<char> v = ...
int count = ...
mpi::datatype complex_type = ... // complex derived type manually defined by user
mpi::committed_datatype complex_type_c = mpi::commit(std::move(complex_type));
comm.send(mpi::buffer_adapter(v, complex_type_c, count), /*additional parameters */);

int local_count = ...;
comm.reduce(mpi::single_adapter(local_count), ...); // support for non-range single arguments
```

Fig. 5. Exemplary communication calls using the data buffer concept when MPI procedures are implemented as member functions.

Extending the Data Buffer Concept. In collective communication calls with varying counts (such as `MPI_Alltoallv`), MPI requires not just a single *count* parameter but a separate count for each MPI process (aka rank). Additionally, displacements can be specified for each rank. To reflect these semantic changes, we have to extend the `mpi::DataBuffer` concept as previously defined (Fig. 4) and define *irregular* `mpi::DataBuffers`. These buffers are still based on the concept `std::ranges::contiguous` and have to expose MPI datatype information. Additionally, they also have to expose `size_v()` and `displacements()` functions, which return the respective counts and displacement data. For brevity, we refrain from providing an example definition of this additional concept. Again, simple lightweight adapters can be provided for standard library and similar custom containers. Similarly, scalar arguments (such as a single `int` or `bool` in a reduction) can be easily supported via lightweight adapters, which implicitly return `size` 1 and implement the data buffer concept (Fig. 5).

3.4 Ownership and Non-blocking Communication

Using the data buffer concept instead of raw pointers already offers benefits such as an ergonomic interaction with standard library containers, improved type safety and the potential to prevent out-of-bounds accesses. Another important advantage of this object-oriented data handling is that it allows us to model a proper concept of ownership. In C++, if an object *owns* a resource—such as heap-allocated memory—the object is responsible for releasing this resource when it goes out of scope. This is usually achieved by placing the clean-up code in the object's destructor and the key idea behind the RAII idiom. A data buffer owning its underlying memory is therefore responsible for freeing this memory once it goes out of scope, thus preventing memory leaks. This plays well with C++'s move semantics. During move-construction or move-assignment, ownership of the underlying resource is transferred from the source to the destination object. Using this mechanism it is for example possible to move a (receive) data buffer to an MPI call as shown in Fig. 6. Then the MPI call receives data into the provided buffer, which it now owns. Once the communication is completed, it returns the updated receive buffer by value resulting in a clean and idiomatic pass through of the underlying memory resource. This data flow allows us to avoid the use of *out* parameters that are discouraged in C++ [26, F.20].

In terms of library interface design, this "pass through" of data can be achieved by considering the *value category* of data buffers passed to communication calls. We propose that a C++ interface should explicitly distinguish between arguments passed as r- or l-values: If a data buffer is an *r-value*, the data buffer is moved to the MPI operation, and returned to the caller as a return value of the function call. If a data buffer is an *l-value*, it is passed by reference to the operation, ownership is not transferred, and it is not returned. For an example see Fig. 6.

Further, (moving) ownership is particularly useful for enhancing the safety of non-blocking communication. In MPI, a call to a non-blocking communication operation *initiates* the operation but does not *complete* it. Instead, it returns a request handle, which the user can test for completion via `MPI_Test` or wait (blocking) on via `MPI_Wait`. This return of control between initiation and completion of the underlying call introduces a potential source of programming errors since MPI semantics require that any buffer involved in a non-blocking operation remain unmodified by the user until the operation has completed.

A robust solution to this problem is to transfer ownership of data buffers involved in non-blocking communication calls to the C++ interface, which forward it to request object as show in Fig. 6. The request object is conceptually similar to `std::future`[3]: Users can only access the data upon completing the request via `wait` or `test`, which move the data back to the caller, either directly by value in the former case, or encapsulated in `std::optional` in the latter. This way, invalid accesses to data involved in non-blocking communication can be prevented entirely through library semantics. This idea was first introduced and implemented in the MPI wrapper KaMPIng [27].

```
std::vector<int> recv_buf = {...};
recv_buf = comm.recv(std::move(recv_buf), ...); // ownership transferred to call
                                                 // and back to caller
comm.recv(recv_buf, ...); // buffer only captured by reference, and nothing returned

// Non-blocking communication with ownership transfer
mpi::request<std::vector<int>> req = comm.irecv(std::move(recv_buf), ...);
recv_buf = req.wait(...);
std::optional<std::vector<int>> result = req.test(...);
```

Fig. 6. Transferring ownership through C++'s move semantics

3.5 Error Handling

MPI notifies users of errors by returning error codes from almost every function defined by the MPI standard. Although this is the most common way to handle errors in C, this does not fit well with modern C++. Most current MPI C++ interfaces either ignore errors completely or encapsulate the returned error code in an exception and throw it. This has a shortcoming: MPI makes no distinction between failures, which may be recoverable, such as insufficient buffer space or node failures (when using a ULFM-enabled MPI implementation [6]) and usage errors, such as providing invalid parameters, which cannot be resolved. The strategy of converting all returned errors to exceptions is opposed to the C++ Core Guidelines [26] which give the following suggestions on error handling: (E.2) "Throw an exception to signal that a function can't perform its assigned task," and (P.5) "Prefer compile-time checking to run-time checking." Guided by this, we propose the following strategy (implemented by KaMPIng [27] and B.MPI3 [7]):

---

[3] Using `std::future` to provide a safe interface for non-blocking communicating is not possible, as they are tied to asynchronous progress happening in the background, which the MPI standard does not guarantee.

First, usage errors, such as invalid parameter combinations or invalid types, are handled at compile time via `static_assert`. Since C++ template meta-programming is notorious for complex, hard-to-read compiler errors, we try to ensure that compile-time assertions fail early and provide helpful human-readable error messages. Looking ahead, C++-26's enhancements to `static_assert` will enable us to supply constant-expression diagnostic messages, potentially leveraging `std::format`, so that compile-time checks can convey rich contextual information.

For invariants that can only be verified during execution, we use a layered assertion system: We verify invariants ranging from lightweight checks to assertions involving additional communication. These can be disabled level-by-level at compile-time, encouraging developers to use exhaustive checking while writing and testing code, yet permitting a lean, high-performance configuration for production builds. By integrating error-handling controls directly into the C++ interface—rather than relying on rebuilding the MPI library itself in a "debug" mode—we provide an ergonomic, flexible framework. If an assertion is enabled and fails, we call `MPI_Abort` because execution can not safely continue.

Errors that may be recoverable are signaled to the user. This can either by done by throwing an exception, or by returning `std::expected` from MPI procedures. C++-23's `std::expected<T, E>` offers a lightweight, value-based alternative to exceptions, by encapsulating either a valid `T` or an error `E` in one object. Using `std::expected` makes error handling explicit, avoids hidden blocking operations inside distant `catch` handlers, and allows for easy error chaining and propagation. Together with the return-by-value-based design proposed in Sect. 3.4, this extends the concept of error codes in MPI's C interface, by only providing access to the return value of a procedure in case of success.

4 Considerations Beyond a Preliminary C++ Interface

In the following, we discuss additional features which improve the usability of preliminary C++ MPI language bindings. These features are perhaps beyond the scope of initial standardization, since they introduce additional overhead on top of the current MPI specification, such as allocation or communication under the hood. Nevertheless, they make working with MPI from C++ easier and often safer. In the following, we discuss how to easily communicate data not directly compatible with MPI (Sect. 4.1), how to improve the handling of type lifetimes (Sect. 4.2) and to improve programmer productivity and reduce boilerplate code by offering sane defaults to programmers (Sect. 4.3).

4.1 Serialization

The data buffer concept defined in Sect. 3.3 provides a type-safe and easy-to-use way to use standard C++ containers and user-defined types with a regular memory layout and a direct mapping to an MPI data type in MPI communication. Commonly used complex C++ types, such as `std::list`, `std::unordered_map`, or polymorphic class hierarchies, do not provide contiguous storage or a well-defined memory representation. These are *dynamic types*: their size or layout may vary at runtime, they may require logic to (re)construct from memory (on both ends of the communication) and may involve intermediate allocations associated with data copies. While such types cannot be communicated directly using the MPI type system, a user-defined *data buffer* encapsulating packed data data can be used. However, constructing this is cumbersome and error-prone.

Instead, we propose a general serialization mechanism: The solution is to serialize complex types into a contiguous byte buffer (e.g., a `std::vector<char>`), which are directly transmittable via MPI. The deserialization step on the receiving side reconstructs the original object from this representation.

Importantly, serialization libraries such as Boost.Serialization [21] or Cereal [12] let users define what data members of a type should be serialized; that is, what constitutes the object's logical state. The concrete binary layout or packing is handled automatically by the library and is treated as an implementation detail[4]. This cleanly separates the intent of serialization from its mechanics, which is especially useful for complex types. Constructing such a serialized buffer may itself involve MPI communication, for example to exchange message sizes ahead of receiving the actual payload. While this is beyond the scope of the MPI standard, it can be built naturally on top of the previously defined data buffer concept. A user-defined type wrapping the serialization logic and exposing the required interface (contiguous, sized, and typed buffer) integrates seamlessly with the rest of the system.

In summary, even though dynamic types require custom logic and cannot be described via static type traits, the buffer abstraction is general enough to accommodate them. Serialization turns arbitrary C++ objects into something communicable without burdening the MPI interface with additional complexity.

4.2 Safer Usage of Complex Types

The type classification and data buffer concept introduced in Sects. 3.2 and 3.3 provide all necessary building blocks to work with complex types. Even if a type is not *directly* supported by MPI, for the large class of trivially copyable types, there still exists a type-safe, direct type mapping. This allows the user to semi-automatically construct a type, and pass it alongside a container to the communication call as a data buffer, as shown in Fig. 5.

But this has shortcomings: Committing an MPI data type is not free, since implementations may optimize the internal representation of a type when it is committed. So in a C++ interface, it is the user's responsibility to commit the type and free it when it is no longer needed (by destructing the type object using the RAII pattern). This introduces additional problems, since now the user has to keep the type around all the time, and the type correspondence between the container and the data type object is lost. To improve usability here, we suggest

---
[4] Implementations may even avoid byte packing and communicate in chunks.

the idea of a *type pool* that allows to store committed data types and to perform a lookup based on type information.

Users then just construct a data buffer from a container of a trivially copyable type and a reference to the type pool and pass it to the communication call. The communication call can then perform a runtime lookup based on `std::type_info::hash_code` of the containers value type to obtain the MPI data type used in communication.

There is one caveat to this approach: The lifetime of types in MPI is currently not clearly defined. In the session model, the lifetime of types is allowed to span across multiple sessions which suggests that the MPI type system exists orthogonally to MPI initialization. But it also mandates that types may only be created once a session or the world model is initialized, yet users are encouraged to commit types separately for each session.

This inconsistency appears to be unintentional but has not been resolved since sessions were introduced[5]. Fixing this will enable language bindings to MPI, not only limited to C++, to handle types more easily. For example, when type lifetime is tied to sessions, a C++ implementation can associate a session-local type pool with each session object, which can be queried for types without providing a pool explicitly. Types can then be freed automatically when the session is finalized.

4.3 Improving MPI Productivity with Sensible Defaults

Many libraries improve usability features beyond a high-level standardized interface: automatically resizing receive containers, computing missing counts or displacements in collectives with varying counts, or even performing additional communication to determine missing arguments. For example, Boost.MPI [13] and RWTH-MPI [9] offer various overloads for communication calls with default arguments, preventing users from writing a lot of boilerplate code.

KaMPIng [27] goes even further: It chooses an alternative approach inspired by *named parameters*, where parameters passed to a function can be named at the caller site and passed in arbitrary order (as seen in languages like Python). This allows to check for the presence of each parameter and to compute default values only if the respective parameter is omitted, without resorting to many overloads exploring the complete combinatorial explosion of parameters. To avoid run-time overhead, they rely on template meta-programming to only generate the code paths required for computing missing parameters at compile time.

While this is well beyond the scope of a low-level interface due to additionally introduced allocations or communications, concrete implementations building on this interface could introduce such improvements to make writing MPI code easier, less error-prone and more productive, by handling resources on behalf of the user.

---

[5] https://github.com/mpi-forum/mpi-issues/issues/733.

5 Conclusions

Standardizing a modern C++ interface is an ambitious—and perhaps impractical—undertaking. Instead, we advocated here for the creation of language support guideline documents, similar in spirit to what this work aims to contribute.

While many desire a truly modern C++ interface for MPI, this paper has laid out the conceptual and technical challenges that need to be addressed before such an interface can be standardized. Our goal was to clarify these challenges and provide a foundation of design principles that could guide future development and community discussion. To this end, we covered high-level considerations: a C++ representation of the MPI object model (Sect. 3.1), data representation (Sect. 3.3) and ownership (Sect. 3.4), modeling and mapping types (Sect. 3.2), and idiomatic error handling (Sect. 3.5). We also discussed ideas beyond these core concepts, including serialization (Sect. 4.1) and usability improvements (Sects. 4.2 and 4.3).

Based on these considerations, we identified specific aspects where the MPI standard requires clarification—most notably the lifecycle of user-defined data types, which remains under-specified in the context of sessions and makes automated resource management more difficult.

We also support ongoing efforts to improve attribute support across the standard, particularly for sessions and requests, as this is essential for associating higher-level interface constructs with the lifetime of MPI objects (see Issue #664).

Finally, while callback support already exists in the standard, not all callbacks currently support user-defined state. Enabling this consistently would improve the design and usability of language bindings (see Issue #839).

We hope that our discussion can serve as a blueprint for other MPI language communities. A prime example for language support is Vapaa [14], a standalone implementation of MPI's Fortran interface built on the C API, which strongly influenced the addition of an MPI Application Binary Interface in the MPI 5.0 standard [15]. Also, many of the mentioned concepts can be applied to or were inspired from the Rust MPI bindings `rsmpi` [24], since modern C++ and Rust share many conceptual similarities. For other languages, it might be helpful to derive their own, independent set of guidelines. This will enable MPI continue to evolve together with popular languages that define the future of high-performance computing.

Acknowledgements. PSAAP Funding in part is acknowledged from these NSF Grants OAC-2514054, CNS-2450093, CCF-2405142, and CCF-2412182 and the U.S. Department of Energy's National Nuclear Security Administration (NNSA) under the Predictive Science Academic Alliance Program (PSAAP-III), Award DE-NA0003966. AAC work performed under the auspices of the US Department of Energy by Lawrence Livermore National Laboratory under contract DE-AC52-07NA27344, and supported by the Center for Non-Perturbative Studies of Functional Materials Under Non-Equilibrium Conditions (NPNEQ) funded by the Computational Materials Sciences

Program of the US Department of Energy, Office of Science, Basic Energy Sciences, Materials Sciences and Engineering Division. This work was also performed under the auspices of the US Department of Energy's Pacific Northwest National Laboratory, operated by Battelle Memorial Institute under contract DE-AC05-76RL01830. Any opinions, findings, and conclusions or recommendations expressed in this material are those of the authors and do not necessarily reflect the views of the National Science Foundation, or the U.S. Department of Energy's National Nuclear Security Administration.

This project has received funding from the European Research Council (ERC) under the European Union's Horizon 2020 research and innovation program (grant agreement No. 882500).

References

1. Andrade, X., et al.: Inq, a modern GPU-accelerated computational framework for (time-dependent) density functional theory. J. Chem. Theory Comput. **17**(12), 7447–7467 (2021). https://doi.org/10.1021/acs.jctc.1c00562
2. Avans, C.N., Ciesko, J., Pearson, C., Suggs, E.D., Olivier, S.L., Skjellum, A.: Performance Insights into Supporting Kokkos Views in the Kokkos Comm MPI Library. In: 2024 IEEE International Conference on Cluster Computing Workshops (CLUSTER Workshops), pp. 186–187 (2024). https://doi.org/10.1109/CLUSTERWorkshops61563.2024.00051, https://github.com/kokkos/kokkos-comm
3. Bauke, H.: MPL - a message passing library (2015). https://github.com/rabauke/mpl
4. Beni, M.S., Crisci, L., Cosenza, B.: EMPI: enhanced message passing interface in modern C++. In: 2023 IEEE/ACM 23rd International Symposium on Cluster, Cloud and Internet Computing (CCGrid), pp. 141–153 (2023). https://doi.org/10.1109/CCGrid57682.2023.00023
5. Bienz, A., Schafer, D., Skjellum, A.: MPI advance : open-source message passing optimizations (2023). https://arxiv.org/abs/2309.07337
6. Bland, W., Bouteiller, A., Herault, T., Bosilca, G., Dongarra, J.: Post-failure recovery of MPI communication capability: design and rationale. Int. J. High Perform. Comput. Appl. **27**(3), 244–254 (2013). https://doi.org/10.1177/1094342013488238
7. Correa, A.A.: B-MPI3 (2018). https://github.com/LLNL/b-mpi3
8. cppreference.com: Constraints - cppreference.com (2025). https://en.cppreference.com/w/cpp/language/constraints.html. Accessed 03 Apr 2025
9. Demiralp, A.C., Martin, P., Sakic, N., Krüger, M., Gerrits, T.: A C++20 interface for MPI 4.0. CoRR **abs/2306.11840** (2023)
10. Ghosh, S., Alsobrooks, C., Rüfenacht, M., Skjellum, A., Bangalore, P.V., Lumsdaine, A.: Towards modern C++ language support for MPI. In: 2021 Workshop on Exascale MPI (ExaMPI), pp. 27–35. IEEE (2021)
11. Godoy, W.F., et al.: Software stewardship and advancement of a high-performance computing scientific application: Qmcpack. Futur. Gener. Comput. Syst. **163**, 107502 (2025). https://doi.org/10.1016/j.future.2024.107502
12. Grant, W.S., Voorhies, R.: cereal – a C++11 library for serialization (2017). http://uscilab.github.io/cereal/
13. Gregor, D., Troyer, M.: Boost.MPI (2005–2007). https://www.boost.org/doc/libs/1_84_0/doc/html/mpi.html. version 1.84

14. Hammond, J.: Vapaa: a standalone implementation of the MPI fortran 2018 module (2023). https://github.com/jeffhammond/vapaa
15. Hammond, J., et al.: MPI application binary interface standardization. In: Proceedings of the 30th European MPI Users' Group Meeting. EUROMPI 2023, pp. 1–12. ACM (2023). https://doi.org/10.1145/3615318.3615319
16. Message Passing Interface Forum: MPI: a message-passing interface standard (2009). https://www.mpi-forum.org/docs/mpi-2.2/mpi22-report.pdf
17. Message Passing Interface Forum: MPI: A message-passing interface standard, version 2.2. Specification, MPI Forum (2009). http://www.mpi-forum.org/docs/mpi-2.2/mpi22-report.pdf
18. Message Passing Interface Forum: Memory allocation kinds: A MPI side document (2024). https://www.mpi-forum.org/docs/sidedocs/mem-alloc10.pdf
19. Message Passing Interface Forum: MPI: A Message-Passing Interface Standard Version 5.0 (2025). https://www.mpi-forum.org/docs/mpi-5.0/mpi50-report.pdf
20. Polukhin, A.: Boost.pfr (2016). https://www.boost.org/doc/libs/1_84_0/doc/html/boost_pfr.html
21. Ramey, R.: Boost.Serialization (2002–2009). https://www.boost.org/doc/libs/1_86_0/libs/serialization/doc/. version 1.86
22. Revzin, B., et al.: Reflection for C++26. Proposal P2996R5 P2996R5, ISO/IEC JTC1/SC22/WG21 (2024). https://www.open-std.org/jtc1/sc22/wg21/docs/papers/2024/p2996r5.html
23. Skjellum, A., et al.: Object-oriented analysis and design of the message passing interface. Concurrency Comput. Pract. Experience **13**(4), 245–292 (2001). https://doi.org/10.1002/cpe.556, https://onlinelibrary.wiley.com/doi/abs/10.1002/cpe.556
24. Steinbusch, B., Gaspar, A., Brown, J.: rsmpi - MPI bindings for rust (2015). https://github.com/rsmpi/rsmpi
25. Stroustrup, B.: The Design and Evolution of C++. Addison-Wesley (1994)
26. Stroustrup, B., Sutter, H., et al.: C++ core guidelines (2024). https://isocpp.github.io/CppCoreGuidelines/CppCoreGuidelines.html
27. Uhl, T.N., et al.: Kamping: flexible and (near) zero-overhead C++ bindings for MPI. In: Proceedings of the International Conference for High Performance Computing, Networking, Storage, and Analysis, SC 2024, Atlanta, GA, USA, November 17-22, 2024, p. 44. IEEE (2024). https://doi.org/10.1109/SC41406.2024.00050, https://dl.acm.org/doi/10.1109/SC41406.2024.00050

Open Access This chapter is licensed under the terms of the Creative Commons Attribution 4.0 International License (http://creativecommons.org/licenses/by/4.0/), which permits use, sharing, adaptation, distribution and reproduction in any medium or format, as long as you give appropriate credit to the original author(s) and the source, provide a link to the Creative Commons license and indicate if changes were made.

The images or other third party material in this chapter are included in the chapter's Creative Commons license, unless indicated otherwise in a credit line to the material. If material is not included in the chapter's Creative Commons license and your intended use is not permitted by statutory regulation or exceeds the permitted use, you will need to obtain permission directly from the copyright holder.

Author Index

A
Avans, C. Nicole   165

B
Bischof, Christian   54
Brabec, Matyáš   36
Bridges, Patrick   106
Burak, Semih   143

C
Correa, Alfredo A.   165

D
Domke, Jens   143

G
Ghosh, Sayan   165
Guo, Yanfei   18, 122

H
Hück, Alexander   54

J
Jantz, Michael   1
Jenke, Joachim   54, 73, 89

K
Klepl, Jiří   36
Kreutzer, Sebastian   54
Kruliš, Martin   36

L
Li, Yicheng   1

M
Moraru, Maxim   106
Müller, Matthias   143

O
Optenhöfel, Alexander   73
Oraji, Yussur Mustafa   54

P
Pritchard, Howard   106

R
Raffenetti, Kenneth   18

S
Schafer, Derek   106
Schimek, Matthias   165
Schuchart, Joseph   73, 89, 165
Schwitanski, Simon   54, 89, 143
Shipman, Galen   106
Skjellum, Anthony   165
Snir, Marc   122
Suggs, Evan D.   165

T
Thakur, Rajeev   18
Thärigen, Ben   73
Tomski, Felix   143

U
Uhl, Tim Niklas   165

W
Wilkins, Michael   18

Y
Yan, Jiakun   122

Z
Zhou, Hui   18

MIX
Papier aus verantwortungsvollen Quellen
Paper from responsible sources
FSC® C105338

If you have any concerns about our products,
you can contact us on
ProductSafety@springernature.com

In case Publisher is established outside the EU,
the EU authorized representative is:
**Springer Nature Customer Service Center GmbH
Europaplatz 3, 69115 Heidelberg, Germany**

Printed by Libri Plureos GmbH
in Hamburg, Germany